T0278249

BACK TO
BHARAT

Celebrating 35 Years of
Penguin Random House India

ADVANCE PRAISE FOR THE BOOK

'I have been pleading for a new variety of business, a business that doesn't seek any personal return from the business but is dedicated to solving a human problem in a sustainable way. It covers all its costs and creates a surplus, which is ploughed back into business. I call them social businesses, defined as non-dividend companies that solve human problems. Naga's book is a good personal account of one's journey in striving to build a world of three zeros: net zero carbon emission, zero wealth concentration and zero unemployment'—Professor Muhammad Yunus, 2006 Nobel Peace Prize laureate

'The work contains extensive references to the start-ups that Naga has observed, analysed, interacted with and invested in, which make the book a good study of the entrepreneurial sector'—Kris Gopalakrishnan, co-founder, Infosys

'*Back to Bharat* brings us face to face with important parameters that are often ignored when we are measuring GDP and progress. Naga asks tough questions based on the new criteria that have been developed to evaluate the sustainability of economic activity'—Professor Rishikesha T. Krishnan, director, Indian Institute of Management Bangalore, and author of *From Jugaad to Systematic Innovation: The Challenge for India*

'To quote from *Back to Bharat*: "Even as late as the year 1700, it is estimated that India was the largest economy globally, comprising over 20 per cent of the world's Gross Domestic Product (GDP)" . . . "On the one hand, we were building walls to hide the poverty reflected in our slums from the eyes of the then US President Donald Trump during his visit in February 2020. On the other hand, from the second day of the lockdown, we had poor migrants who were working in our cities walking back to their villages in a 'human tragedy' witnessed by the whole world." These issues present a conundrum to many educated young Indians today and the book wonders: "If the 'old economy' of ancient India spelt prosperity, inclusiveness and sustainability, then what prevents us from drawing lessons from our past to build a more robust present?" The book is an attempt to "bridge the 'old economy' of a prosperous and mighty ancient India with the resurgence and empowering of a new and happy India that is sustainable and inclusive . . . The spirit of enterprise can be seen in the humblest of Indians, in what is called the 'unorganized sector' of our economy, as much as in the best-known Indian brands." Fascinating.

Worth reading. The book will be a step towards India finding an answer to the questions that puzzle many'—Ashok Jhunjhunwala, institute professor, IIT Madras, and president and board member, IIT Madras Research Park, IIT Madras Incubation Cell and Rural Technology and Business Incubator

'If only we knew what we know, could ascribe value to what ought to be valued and rewarded the real risk-takers in our economy, India would be in a far better place than it is in now. Naga offers us pathways for precisely this transformative journey that our country needs'—Mukund Rajan, author of *Outlast: How ESG Can Benefit Your Business*, chairperson, ECube Investment Advisors, former member of the Tata Global Sustainability Council, and former chief ethics officer and brand custodian, Tata Group

'*Back to Bharat* is an inspiring reminder that change is possible—and that this is a moment to be part of the change. For it will take all of us'— Jacqueline Novogratz, CEO, Acumen, and author of *Manifesto for a Moral Revolution* and *The Blue Sweater*

BACK TO
BHARAT

In Search of
a Sustainable Future

NAGARAJA
PRAKASAM

PENGUIN
BUSINESS

An imprint of Penguin Random House

PENGUIN BUSINESS

USA | Canada | UK | Ireland | Australia
New Zealand | India | South Africa | China | Singapore

Penguin Business is part of the Penguin Random House group of companies
whose addresses can be found at global.penguinrandomhouse.com

Published by Penguin Random House India Pvt. Ltd
4th Floor, Capital Tower 1, MG Road,
Gurugram 122 002, Haryana, India

First published in Penguin Business by Penguin Random House India 2023

ISBN 9780670097166

Typeset in Sabon by MAP Systems, Bengaluru, India
Printed at Replika Press Pvt. Ltd, India

www.penguin.co.in

To my beloved wife, Abirami Nagaraja, who pushed me every time and provided me with needed criticism. Only with her support was I able to embark on this uncharted path, leaving a cushy life to make this book happen. I lost her to cancer recently, which emphasizes more on the need to relook at sustainable living!

To Chinnaswamy, my maternal grandfather, an uneducated migrant farmer and businessman with whom I spent most of my first fourteen years. He passed away within twenty-four days of my leaving for a boarding school, in ninth grade. He made a great impact on me in terms of empathy, resilience and business acumen!

Contents

x Contents

Part II: Individual Social Responsibility:
What Can I Do?

Introduction

'Paravaiyaikkandaan vimaanam padaiththaan
paayum meengalil padaginaikkandaan
edhiroli kaettaan vaanoli padaiththhaan
edhanaikkandaan panamdhanai padaiththhaan'

(Seeing birds, he invented the airplane
Among rising and diving fish he imagined ships
Hearing an echo, he brought about the radio
What did he see that he invented money?)

'Manidan Maarivittaan'—
song heard travelling at night through Tamil Nadu
Poet: Kaviarasar Kannadasan; Film: *Paava Mannippu* (1961)

The Problem of the Present through the Prism of the Past

I grew up in twentieth-century India and turned fifty in 2021. All through my life, I was struck by the contrast presented by the reality that surrounded us and the stories of our golden past. As a schoolboy, I was introduced to the only small government library in the small town of Manamadurai near Madurai, Tamil Nadu, while studying in Class V. I recall the thrill of walking alone to that library to pick up a book and I still remember the first one I picked up—about sea cows (manatees) and the oceanic kingdom. My whole family was into reading various genres of books from that library.

Over the years, I was drawn to historical novels, mostly by the authors Bhashyam Iyengar (popularly known as Sandilyan) and Ramaswamy Krishnamurthy (popularly, Kalki). They wrote about kings who had ruled Tamil Nadu, directed the creation of architectural marvels and encouraged maritime expeditions to far-off countries. Stories about those kings and their visible legacy left a profound impact on me about our glorious past.

That influence is with me even today. Wherever I travel, I study the history of that place and visit many of the sites I read about. This led me to discover more about our golden past, across the country. There are many wonders across India that I have had the privilege to visit.

All these achievements suggest periods when our people were prosperous and happy. In my imagination, our ancestors' creativity was unleashed by a freedom from anxiety about mere survival. It was based on economic strength, not deprivation. Even as late as the year 1700, it is estimated that India was the largest economy globally, comprising over 20 per cent of the world's Gross Domestic Product (GDP). Even today, India's entitlement continues as we are one of the world's leading economies.

2022 was special for India. It marked the seventy-fifth year of Independence. India became the world's fifth-largest economy, measured in current dollars. In March 2023, India's nominal GDP was approximately US$3.4 trillion. In real terms, the economy is expected to grow at 7 per cent in March 2023, followed by an 8.7 per cent growth in the previous financial year.[1] After the deadly 'second wave,' of Covid-19, growth in FY22 was nearer to the range of 7.5 to

12.5 per cent—still putting India among the fastest-growing economies in the world.[2]

Notwithstanding our economic standing in the world, India ranks poorly in several key indicators such as the Global Hunger Index, which put India at 94 among 107 countries in 2020.[3] Likewise, while the government claims that only about 28,000 households across two states—Chhattisgarh and Jharkhand—are not electrified, most households in the country do not have all-day access to electricity.

According to the World Inequality Database (WID), the difference between the top 10 per cent's income and the bottom 50 per cent's is 24.5 percentage points, that is, the top 1 or 10 per cent of the population, on average, have higher incomes.[4] Further, by the end of the second wave of Covid-19, ten million or one crore people lost their jobs. Besides, 97 per cent of households' incomes have declined since the beginning of the pandemic in 2020.[5]

Today, in the twenty-first century, the lessons of being colonized are well behind us and we face the challenges of climate change and growing inequality along with the rest of the world. As an informed investor in social enterprise, it is natural for me to now wonder: How can we bring back India's contribution to the world economy and raise it again to 25 per cent of the world's GDP? How can we forge ahead in a more planet-friendly and inclusive way so that there is widespread happiness?

I was searching for a thread to connect the glorious India of the past to the India of the present. I have immense faith in our ability to be creative, industrious and happy. Have these qualities deserted us? In the years I have spent as a professional and later as an investor, I have seen our people's ingenuity and drive in action. People respond to challenges and work under extremely limiting circumstances to produce great results across all sectors and regions of this vast country. Clearly, we needed to introspect on the models and yardsticks that we have come to accept as the definition of development.

If the 'old economy' of ancient India spelt prosperity, inclusiveness and sustainability in environmental terms, then what prevents us from drawing lessons from our past to build a more robust present? If the 'developed world' has produced enormous corporations and immense wealth but its visibly destructive side effects have increased inequality and environmental destruction, then are we bound to follow the same practices and model?

The Eternal Nature of Enterprise

I have explored many ideas around these questions in my articles and blog posts over the last few years. The pandemic reinforced my belief that we have reached a critical period in our history, when we can bridge the gap between our glorious past and our threatened present by making important decisions and changing our perspective on many ideas around development.

Our development model came into question when we witnessed 'Bharat saying bye to India' when an estimated 100 million predominantly daily wage migrants, without job security, were among the worst affected by tough lockdown restrictions between March and early June 2020, as they were forced to return to their villages.[6] The pandemic made our problems more visible and widened every small crack in the system for everyone to see. On the one hand, we were building walls to hide the poverty reflected in our slums from the eyes of then-US President Donald Trump during his visit in February 2020. On the other hand, from the second day of the lockdown, we had poor migrants who were working in our cities walking back to their villages in a 'human tragedy' witnessed by the whole world.

In April–May 2021, when the pandemic's second wave hit our cities and towns, the vast gap between our rich and poor showed up even more starkly, besides raising other questions about our lack of investment in medical infrastructure. The discovery of a vaccine in record time gave humans a false hope of winning over nature, but the second wave also underlined—in India and elsewhere in the world—the need to pay heed to our own survival. Nature has her own way of humbling humans, which can be seen as a huge opportunity for us to reimagine a new world while we are listening with humility.

However, in spite of the disaster that seems to have hit us harder than the rest of the world, I have seen that our compatriots react well during crises. Some of the thoughts I articulated in my *Forbes* article in 2016, 'Needed: Entrepreneurial Models That Work for "Bharat"', began taking wing through government initiatives such as the Social Stock Exchange. Also, in the past few years, some of my investments towards sustainable and inclusive India— in the areas of waste management, farm-to-home, organic farming, sustainable fashion (Go Swadeshi), waste to energy, electric vehicle (EV) vending and Environment, Social and Governance (ESG) norms—have been implemented through agricultural reforms, EV policy, priority sector lending for BioCNG, Swachh Bharat Abhiyan, Vocal for Local, self-reliant India, mandated by SEBI ESG reporting for corporate entities, among other initiatives.

I believe I have zeroed in on the thread that can bridge the 'old economy' of a prosperous and mighty ancient

India with the resurgence and empowering of a new and happy India that is sustainable and inclusive. For me, this means entrepreneurially building the nation. The spirit of enterprise can be seen in the humblest of Indians, in what is called the 'unorganized sector' of our economy, as much as in the best-known Indian brands. Since my school days, the attitude of Indians towards entrepreneurship has also changed for the better. As a society, we have grown more respectful of enterprises and entrepreneurs, from previously looking down upon business people and encouraging children to take up government jobs for their security, tenure and retirement benefits. Business was seen as risky and businessmen were widely regarded as people who earned their wealth through unethical means. Today, entrepreneurship is being celebrated.

Should We Play Follow-the-Leader, or Catch-Me-if-You-Can?

I have always been interested in exploring how we can leapfrog rather than simply play catch-up with other nations. Today, our start-up policy is going in the right direction with over 93,435 start-ups registered with Startup India.[7] With this, India became the world's third-largest start-up ecosystem. I've invested in about twenty-nine start-ups and serve on many of their boards. I've spoken about entrepreneurship to—and motivated—students in over 110 colleges and have been invited to the launch of start-up policies in states like Assam and Rajasthan. I'm a member of the NITI Aayog consultation group on science, technology and innovation. I've also participated in numerous government round tables on entrepreneurship, evaluated thousands of start-ups for the

National Entrepreneurship Award (NEA) instituted by the Government of India, Elevate of the Government of Karnataka, the Kerala Startup Mission, StartupTN and at various start-up programmes across the country. For about ten years, as the first resident mentor, I mentored students, women entrepreneurs, social businesses and non-profits at the N.S. Raghavan Centre for Entrepreneurial Learning (NSRCEL), a twenty-year-old initiative of the Indian Institute of Management Bangalore (IIMB). As a member of the investment and incubation committee of the Indian Institute of Technology (IIT) Madras incubator, I have seen faculty members turning into entrepreneurs. I co-founded Nativelead Foundation to promote entrepreneurship in the Tier 2 and Tier 4 towns of Tamil Nadu, encouraging entrepreneurs with ideas, irrespective of their educational background. We focused on Enable, Nurture, Incubate and Invest, with successful local entrepreneurs anchoring the programme as chapter chairs, mentors and investors, which brought in the concept of locals solving local problems. As part of the Indian Angel Network (IAN), India's oldest angel investor group, I witnessed fellow angels invest in over 160 start-ups. Some of India's policies are beneficial and should help India move up from being ranked 130 in terms of ease of doing business. But this appears to be a move to catch up rather than being a pioneer. India has an opportunity to build a nation that can be a model for the rest of the world.

One way to achieve this would be to look in directions beyond the highly developed nations of the capitalist West for inspiration. We can, instead, learn from the mistakes of the developed world, as exemplified by some African nations. In a 2015 report, the Global Entrepreneurship Monitor (GEM) ranked Angola as the most entrepreneurial

nation in the world. According to GEM, nearly 50 per cent
of the adult population of Angola is 'starting or running a
new business', with about 83 per cent of Angolans professing
entrepreneurial intentions. There is a vast, untapped
reservoir of enterprise waiting to transform India as well.

Our policies in India can be framed in such a way that
entrepreneurs build the country cautiously, with long-term
goals in mind. Such goals need to be assessed against the
global challenges of climate change and social inequality,
and how best we could address them for our country. In the
past decade, I have attempted to apply these parameters to
my own investment in such start-ups. The results of these
initiatives are shared in the chapters ahead.

Another way forward is to evaluate our own strengths
differently and preserve them for well-being and prosperity.
A simple example can be seen in how we look at the
environmental cost of the economic activities we undertake.
Elon Musk's Tesla, a leading electric vehicle manufacturer
in the US, makes billions of dollars each year by selling the
regulatory carbon credits the company gets for free to other
car manufacturers that don't meet emission standards. But
have we ever measured or appreciated the carbon credits
that must be accruing to our textile sector by the handloom
weavers across our country? The richness of our country is
reflected in how our manufacturing practices in the traditional
sectors still prevent large-scale environmental destruction.

It is time to ascribe value in modern and scientific
terms to much that we have considered 'old' or 'traditional'
or 'tribal'. We should consider many of the economic
activities of our ancestors and even of many backward
pockets of our population, in terms of their contribution
towards building a more sustainable future. Compare, for
instance, the carbon footprint of a farmer living in a village

of thatched-roof houses whose family weaves textiles to someone living in Bengaluru, New York or London. Obviously, he is more considerate about the future than his counterparts elsewhere, but we call him poor instead of celebrating his simplicity and providing him carbon credits. We have become focused on encouraging carbon fixers, without appreciating or rewarding the carbon preventers. While India's GDP, totalling \$3.6 trillion,[8] is one-eighth that of the US whose GDP is \$25 trillion (IMF 2022), per capita carbon emission in the US is 6.9 times more than that in India. If carbon is the new gold, then who is rich? India's per capita greenhouse gases (GHG) emissions, at 2.7 tonnes of CO_2, are significantly lower than the global average (6.6 tonnes), the US's (18.4 tonnes), or China's (8.2 tonnes), a fact we need to recognize urgently.

CSR and Our Combat for the Future

The destructive effects of climate change and the suffering caused by growing inequality have emerged as the two biggest threats to our survival and happiness on this planet. I believe the problem of climate change can be partially addressed by harnessing the potential of Corporate Social Responsibility (CSR).

In India, CSR aims at ensuring that businesses 'endeavour to become responsible actors in society'. Originally framed as National Voluntary Guidelines in 2009, CSR became enshrined in law in 2014. At present, the law requires companies with either 'a net worth of rupees five hundred crore or more', or a 'turnover of rupees one thousand crore or more', or a 'net profit of rupees five crore or more' during any financial year to constitute a CSR committee. This committee must ensure a CSR spending of 'at least two per cent of the average net profits of the company made during the three immediately preceding financial years', in every financial year. But a CSR spending of 2 per cent of a company's net profit is akin to a dip in the holy Ganga. What about corporate responsibility for the remaining 98 per cent of profit? Can start-ups help in this respect?

One of my investments, Solaron, analysed and rated publicly listed companies worldwide, including the top 100 Indian firms listed on the BSE and NSE for their adoption of ESG principles. Solaron's ESG rating would affect the company's portfolio in the stock market, thus spurring them to adopt ESG principles and improve their rating. However, instead of a company needing a watchdog for its compliance with ESG norms after having grown in size, can we not build our companies with ESG principles embedded in their DNA? Doing so would create sustainable corporations and eliminate the need for rating agencies that monitor the company's ESG norms adoption.

What if we build start-ups measured on people, planet and profit? The government can help by making suitable changes in company law modelled around B-Corp certification practised in the US. A policy that gives sops to entrepreneurs (who start this kind of ventures), investors (who come forward to invest in these companies) and consumers (who are buying these companies' products) will incentivize such initiatives and help them build the ventures of the future.

Individual citizens also need to have a vision of their Individual Social Responsibility (ISR) in terms of thinking about roti (food), *kapda* (clothes) and *makaan* (shelter)—what we eat, what we wear, where we live—and looking at their sustainability. If disruptive ideas and innovation are required for this, we need to welcome them. Customers have the power to bring about big change through their choices of

The Solaron Story

Vipul Arora and his wife, Sonali, co-founded Solaron Sustainability Services in 2007 in India and began deploying their framework for rating companies' adoption of ESG principles. Based on 400–500 data points, Solaron's proprietary framework involved a total corporate assessment to arrive at a rating for the company, with a value between AAA (the highest) and CCC. After eight years of struggle in India, Vipul and Sonali relocated Solaron successfully to the UK, and the firm was ultimately acquired by Sustainalytics (now a Morningstar company) in 2018.

The journey of contributing to a sustainable future began much earlier for Vipul who, as an engineering student, read an inspiring article by sustainable development expert Dr Stuart L. Hart, 'Beyond Greening: Strategies for a Sustainable World'. Dr Hart would later become an adviser to Solaron. During Vipul's fellowship years at Stanford University, he envisioned an online marketplace akin to eBay or Amazon.com but offering sustainability-rated or ESG-rated products and services. But in the early 2000s, even Silicon Valley did not take sustainability seriously—and Al Gore was yet to win the Nobel Prize.

In such a milieu, finding partners to either fund the venture or even help develop the ESG ratings was a considerable task. Meeting (the ESG ratings pioneer) Innovest and partnering with ESG World proved the crucial breakthrough for Vipul, who also learnt that rating companies (for adopting ESG principles) was more realistic than rating products.

This partnership directly led to launching Solaron as a back-office research firm based in Bengaluru, providing ESG ratings for firms globally. Solaron also partnered with the CII-ITC Centre of Excellence for Sustainable Development to develop ESG ratings specific to Indian companies.

For the past thirty to forty years, investors have relied on ratings agencies' reports on the performance and value creation of companies, as part of investing responsibly. ESG ratings add a further dimension to companies' value creation. But the challenge of developing ESG ratings for Indian companies, according to Vipul, was twofold: first, getting investors and promoters to understand the need for assessing a company's adoption of ESG principles; and second, getting sufficient, accurate data for the companies under assessment. Solaron researchers, for instance, would need to download data from the company's website or look for other sources.

Working in Europe, in contrast, was smooth sailing, with the idea of developing ESG ratings gaining rapid traction. This led the Solaron founders to wonder if they should have moved earlier. In the three years before Solaron's acquisition by Sustainalytics, they developed ESG ratings for as many as twenty clients. Today, companies seeking to improve their valuation can request Sustainalytics to gauge their ESG compliance and get a ratings report to take to potential investors. Vipul, now an independent consultant, has moved on to helping individuals, companies and investors adopt Real ESG in creating win-win-win solutions that work for all stakeholders.

buying, using and disposing of products sustainably, which can affect 70 per cent of the greenhouse gas footprint.[9] Without contributions from every individual, the goalposts will keep shifting, just like the Millennium Development Goals (MDG) set to be achieved by 2000 by the United Nations. These have now been named the Sustainability Development Goals (SDGs) and need to be achieved by 2030. Since we have already crossed 2022, I doubt if we are in any way closer to achieving the 17 SDGs by 2030!

Development, when it exists alongside inequality, does not deliver the happiness or satisfaction that we deserve. In 2023, 1 per cent of the world's population holds 50 per cent of the wealth.[10] We have reached here by thinking that big is best! Taking a cue from capitalistic thinking, we are building companies today that are growth-hungry. During the recession of 2008, companies in the US used the slogan 'Too Big to Fail' to get government support. The bigger companies accumulate wealth for a few top management people and investors. As can be seen increasingly, once people have disposable wealth, they begin to engage in philanthropic activities. So why is there such a rush to grow big and then try figuring out how to spend that money? This appears to have been the practice right from the days of the Nobel Prize; where first, money was earned creating dynamite, but the money so earned was then spent on the Nobel Prize for peace and other fields.

One of the reasons for this 'go big thesis' is the current equity model of investments. I call this a Ponzi scheme wherein the buck is being passed from seed, angel, venture capital (VC), private equity (PE) and finally an initial public offering (IPO). So, it finally lands up at the common man's doorstep. To attract the next round of investors, the venture needs to keep growing. Ventures are thus always working towards what the next investor wants—rather than what the customer wants! Investors are always looking for trending sectors. They have no incentive to take risks because there is not enough risk capital. Many want to ride on the road but few want to lay the road. Once the Internet was invented, companies were formed to ride on it, but someone had to create the Internet first. Risk capital is only available with the government but not in the market. So, countries cannot depend on the market alone to solve their problems.

To address social inequality, we need a different road map, an investment model that turns away from the obsession with going 'big'. To me, the way forward would be to:

- Create investment models that disrupt the idea of 'passing the buck'.
- Create platforms to raise capital ranging from Rs 50 lakh to Rs 100 crore and allow more investors, similar to the IPO market, to spread out the risk across many people.
- Facilitate all three forms of funding, whether debt, equity or grant, through this platform.
- Allow secondary capital for people who want to exit.
- Invite researchers to come up with different models that can then be tested. The government can list out the top five issues that need to be resolved and reach out to entrepreneurs for solutions.
- Support initial requirements and match them with investors.

In my quest for a resurgent India driven by its entrepreneurial strength, I have explored how many of these ideas have been practised and manifested results. I hope you find ideas and inspiration in the stories that lie ahead in this book.

Part I

One

Beginning the Darshan

'While we cannot live without history, we need not live within it either.'

—Amartya Sen

It began with the Portuguese arriving during the reign of the Mughals followed by the British and the other European powers. India, known across the globe as an abundant superpower, was vandalized and exploited, its people impoverished, its riches stolen and left with a destroyed social fabric, a ruined economy, an electoral democracy and confused modernity. In writing this book, I hope to look to an era when India was idyllic, when the people's happiness quotient was high. I strongly believe that India can and should be revived to look like this bygone era. I want India to become again what it once was. This is not because I am someone who likes to live in the past; rather I want us to live in the present but look towards the past as a source of valuable lessons for the future.

India's GDP was 20 per cent of the world's GDP when the British arrived on Indian shores and dropped down to slightly below 4 per cent when they left.[1] The British, many people felt, had ruled India to help the British prosper or, in other words, for the benefit of Britain! A look into the Indian textile weaver community is proof enough of how the British plundered India. Even a brief preamble would lead us to look at the Indian handloom weavers who were famed across the world during a wondrous era. The weavers used to weave a fine fabric called 'muslin' which was as 'light as woven air'. The British destroyed their looms and imposed tariffs and duties on the cloth, and started taking raw materials to ship back to Britain. This left the weavers impoverished and from being world-famous exporters, they were reduced to being importers. Finished Indian textile goods, which accounted for 25 per cent of the world's textiles in the seventeenth century, plummeted to less than 2 per cent in 1947[2]—the Indian weavers paid with their blood, sweat and tears for this oppression!

Yet, as modern citizens of India, it is possible for us to make the decisions and further the practices and policies that will take us to a sustainable future. There is no time like the present to begin this process. And there is no other place we need to go to find inspiration—just look at our forefathers, our present toilers and strugglers and tribal communities. We can build a country with a high happiness quotient if we take the right paths to progress.

Decoding the Drought with P. Sainath

I returned to live and work in India after years spent pursuing educational and professional goals in the US. Several people, associations and ideas shaped my thinking over these years, making it possible for me to come back home. In my thirst to learn and understand more about India, I read a lot of books.

One of the bibles for all Association for India's Development (AID) volunteers is *Everybody Loves a Good Drought* by P. Sainath. This book, based on Sainath's research on poverty in the rural districts of India, revealed a lot to me about how various government projects either work or do not work at the ground level and if, in reality, they actually deliver any of their promised results. Sainath's stories or case studies cover details of projects as well as the lives of villagers living in the places affected by poverty. He supplements his assertions with telling figures. The book won him the Ramon Magsaysay Award.

'How agonized we are by how people die. How unconcerned we are by how they live.'

—P. Sainath

The book was published in 1996; I read it in 1999. In 2019, at the IIMB Sahay event for social enterprises, I received the same book as a memento. Twenty years later and it has remained just as relevant now as it was then. Sadly, the problems that Sainath wrote about are still present. However, he continues to make these problems visible to the next generation as well.

Another influential discourse in my field is Mahasweta Devi's work on the Sabars, the Adivasis who live mainly in Odisha and West Bengal. Categorized as a 'criminal tribe' during the British Raj in 1871, the Sabars still suffer from social stigma and ostracism. Writers like Mahasweta Devi remind us of the wisdom and value that such communities represent, for a sustainable future. Instead of remaining impoverished and marginalized citizens of modern India, tribal communities need to be recognized and rewarded.

Bapu Kuti and the Icons for a Better India

There is no dearth of inspiration if one searches for people and personalities who have applied their knowledge and efforts to make a meaningful impact on Indian society. In her book *Bapu Kuti: Journeys in Rediscovery of Gandhi,*[3] Rajni Bakshi explores the lives and thoughts of twelve people who looked for pragmatic-yet-humane ways of socio-political change by walking away from stable professions and incomes. These were the people whose work showed how it was possible to approach problems from the viewpoint of inclusion and the greater good.

Aruna Roy, conferred with the Ramon Magsaysay Award, has been at the forefront of several campaigns for the rights of the poor and the marginalized. These include, most prominently, the Right to Information, the Right to Work (NREGA) and the Right to Food Security. T. Karunakaran, a proponent of decentralized development called the Rural Economic Zone, was vice-chancellor of two Gandhian rural universities. Ravinder Sharma, whom many knew simply as 'Guruji', was an Indian artist, craftsman, storyteller, historian, educationist, sociologist and economist in the native Indian context. As founder of Adilabad's Kala Ashram, for almost four decades, he played a crucial role in the preservation of India's ancient rural and tribal art forms.

C.V. Seshadri, who founded the Shri A.M.M. Murugappa Chettiar Research Centre to take scientific developments to rural communities, was another inspiration. Padma Vibhushan Baba Amte, known as the modern Gandhi of India, was a social worker who worked to rehabilitate leprosy patients. Vinoo Kaley is dear to bamboo artisans across India, who called him Guruji. He is fondly remembered as 'Bamboo Man' by those who knew him.

Another striking story is that of Uzramma Bilgrami of Dastkar Andhra, who worked with local weavers to help build their livelihood into a stable and sustaining one by developing their skills and trade. The evolution of the cotton textile industry in India and its shift towards centralized mass production spelt doom for the decentralized spinning and weaving industry that comprised village craftsmen. The cotton that farmers sold to traders would be in large ginning factories before being sent to distant spinning mills. This same cotton, which once grew in the weaver's backyard, would be sold to them as expensive yarn.

Can this chain be reworked? This question became the next focus of the Dastkar group.

At the first Congress of Traditional Sciences and Technologies of India held at IIT Mumbai in December 1993, Dastkar Andhra (along with friends like Kannan Lakshminarayan and Vinoo Kaley) presented a paper titled 'Weaving a Vision' that addressed core issues of production, supply and marketing chain.

I attended many Dastkar Andhra events and exhibitions as well since I was curious about Kannan Lakshminarayan's 'weaving vision'. I was glad to observe his innovation, Microspin, in Chennai in 2014, having read a book on the subject in 2000. Microspin is working to locate the entire cotton value chain—production, carding, ginning and yarn-spinning—in one village, making the farmer and the village on the whole, more self-reliant. When I visited their factory, I saw that the machine converting raw cotton into yarn fitted into one room. A process that was once reliant on transportation of the material could now be carried out in a single room. The fabric made by this machine is marketed by Dastkar Andhra as Malkha cotton, whose handspun feel I cherish and proudly wear now.

The book also spoke highly of C.K. 'Bablu' Ganguly of the Timbaktu Collective, who set out to re-establish the links between agriculture and forestry relying on nature's own healing capacities, and J.C. Kumarappa, an Indian economist and a close associate of Mahatma Gandhi, a pioneer of rural economic development theories who is credited for developing 'Gandhian economics'.

Each of the personalities profiled in *Bapu Kuti* made a significant impact on me in terms of how each one addressed vital economic and social questions in their own way.

I decided to start visiting the sites of some of the groups featured in the book and met Bablu Ganguly in Anantapur, Andhra Pradesh, where the Centre for Collective Development (CCD) organizes its Annual Farmer Maha Sabha. I've been to three of these Maha Sabhas and every time I visit Anantapur, I find ways to visit Timbaktu as well. The first time, I met Mary Vattamattam in her lovely house with a thatched roof made of elephant grass. She was sharing how this couple started the journey at Timbaktu. In fact, they were able to plant and nurture trees across thousands of acres in India's second-most arid region. They also encouraged villagers to grow millets that require less water and now, the Timbaktu brand of millet has become popular and is sold through Lumiere Organics (one of my portfolio organizations in Bengaluru).

I visited Baba Amte's Anandwan near Nagpur, Maharashtra, and stayed there to see how the third generation has taken forward the vision of making India's villages (home to people once seen as a burden by our society) smart. Dr Vikas Amte, Baba's son, proudly talks about their contributions to the country's GDP today. Anandwan is a great example of a self-sustaining village of 2300 people, boasting one of the largest solar concentrators in India that provides steam for central cooking. All the clothing required for the hospital and the village is manufactured locally, as are the organically grown vegetables.

I also visited Sewagram in Maharashtra, where Mahatma Gandhi's ashram—his residence from 1936 until his death in 1948—is located. Bapu Kuti is the name of Gandhi's residence at the ashram from which the book takes not only its name but also inspiration through the stories of the wonderful people who often met there. I visited the ashram with a few entrepreneurship students from Lemon Ideas at Nagpur to demonstrate to them the meaning of a social business. My next visit to Sewagram was when I went to speak on 'Building Sustainable India—Rural Entrepreneurship Is the Way' at a Skill Training for Advanced Rural Societies (STARS) Forum Conference in December 2018. The theme of the conference was 'Make in Rural India' and focused on rural enterprises and entrepreneurship. The conference was held at the Centre of Science for Villages—an experiment based on Gandhi's self-sustaining village—at Wardha and various organizations working on a Gandhian philosophy also attended the conference and shared their experiences.

Turn of the Millennium

The year 1999 turned out to be the most significant in my life.

Until then, I was the product of a typical middle-class mindset that focuses on studying-working-settling down in life. Education was clearly seen as a path to prosperity.

I was studying as hard as possible because, as my father said, 'Education is wealth'. I completed my studies in India, worked for a while, and then went to the US, where I worked while completing my post-graduation. Once I was done, I felt a newfound joy at feeling 'settled' and began enjoying life after many years in a competitive rat race.

All that changed in 1999 when I visited the Diwali Mela organized in San Diego. I was roaming around the mela when I happened to stop by a stall named Association for India's Development (AID). A person there asked me to put a pin on the place I'm from, on a map of India. When I put the pin on Madurai, the person at the stall started talking about various projects undertaken by NGOs in Tamil Nadu.

I was pleasantly surprised by the depth of knowledge the volunteer had about the problems in India. It showed me how, sitting in the US, a group of volunteers were trying to address problems back home, instead of merely enjoying their life. They invited me to their Community Service Hour (CSH), usually held at one of the volunteers' homes, or at the UCSD campus where they studied. That was around the time that a bad cyclone had wreaked havoc across Odisha, so I joined a discussion on how to support the relief work.

From the day that I attended my first CSH meeting till I left the US in 2006, I went on to serve as the president of AID for the San Diego and Atlanta chapters and spent most of my weekends at the CSH. We reviewed projects received from Indian NGOs and organized fundraising events featuring music, dance and cricket. We sold soft drinks and hot dogs at baseball games to raise funds for AID. We supported hundreds of projects and, through every project, we gained a more comprehensive understanding of India's issues, including the issues relating to poverty, caste, agriculture, health and even education.

AID on the big screen: *Swades*

The movie *Swades*, released in 2004, was inspired by the story of Aravinda Pillalamarri and Ravi Kuchimanchi, the 'NRI couple' who returned to India and developed a pedal power generator to bring light to off-the-grid, remote village schools. Ashutosh Gowariker, the director and producer of *Swades*, spent considerable time with Aravinda and Ravi, both dedicated to the AID volunteers.

He also reportedly visited Bilgaon, an Adivasi village in the Narmada valley, which was the site of the Narmada Bachao Andolan (NBA). The people of Bilgaon, to make their village energy self-sufficient, are credited with 200 person-days of *shramdaan* (community service). This was depicted in Gowariker's film. We even screened the film in the USA for fundraising.

The film was distributed worldwide by UTV. Some years later, when I met Zarina Screwvala of UTV in her office in 2013, we enthusiastically talked about the movie. That is when I learnt about her spending time with the Swades Foundation, the NGO (whose name is inspired by the film) that is working full-time towards rural empowerment in Raigad and Ratnagiri districts of Maharashtra, with the goal to touch a million lives.

Dialogue: A Vehicle for Action

Even when I was a member and later an office-bearer for AID, I looked forward to the intense intellectual discussions on various issues with our volunteer friends and social stalwarts who happened to be visiting from India. It was in those years that I met and interacted with Mother Teresa

Award for Social Justice recipient Medha Patkar, Ramon Magsaysay Awardee Aruna Roy, and Padma Shri Abhay and Rani Bang from the Society for Education, Action and Research in Community Health (SEARCH), a non-profit organization involved in rural health service. They revolutionized healthcare for the poorest people in India and are overseeing a programme in one of the most poverty-stricken areas in the world to substantially reduce infant mortality rates. At annual AID conferences, volunteers from every chapter met for intense discussions with social activists from India which took place over a couple of days.

At one such conference, we conducted a 'No Dowry' campaign where the AID volunteers took an oath that they won't accept dowry and we exhibited amazing pictures taken by P. Sainath that well explained the extant reality as seen through his lens. Even today, Sainath continues that effort through the People's Archive of Rural India (PARI). His commitment to the cause has not slowed down a bit in over three decades! In 2019, I invited him to IIMB to talk about PARI, which did an amazing job of bringing out the reality across the country even during the pandemic.

Every single AID discussion and debate gave me a valuable opportunity to clarify and further crystallize my thoughts. When I met people who had shown the vision, commitment and drive to overcome seemingly insurmountable barriers, it further strengthened my own intent. I was preparing in earnest to move back to Bharat.

Engaging with Bharat: First Steps on the Path of Action

Before I returned to India, I would ensure as an AID volunteer that I understood the work being done on various projects, through field visits. This helped me gauge the project's progress first-hand.

During my visit to India in 2005, my wife, Abirami, as the project's coordinator and I visited a project by Elango Rangaswamy. Elango was the first elected panchayat president of Kuthambakkam village, which is an hour's drive away from Chennai. He has transformed the village into a model village by bringing in economic opportunities and propagating the twin housing model whereby families from different castes live side by side. Through this, he has helped the village overcome caste barriers and segregated housing. Most importantly, he showed how the Indian administrative structure comprising the Union, states and panchayats requires overhaul and uplift.

Even today the Union and state governments are more active while the panchayats seem to be figuring out their power and significance. Elango taught me how he was able to use the resources available to a panchayat president to transform the village. He has also started teaching the presidents of other panchayats what he learnt through his experience. It is no wonder that, in 2013, he was recognized as the *Week* magazine's Man of the Year.[4]

The next project we visited was by Vellore Srinivasan, whose house we stayed in one night, trekking up the Vellore hills in the early morning to see how he was greening the hills. I saw first-hand how a young person, who simply observed that the deforestation around Vellore was causing the temperature to go up, decided to make a change, built up a Green Force comprising youth and other locals, and started creating bunds and planting trees. He took us to see the waste management work he had undertaken in Vellore town as well. For me, these visits affirmed that going beyond Microsoft Word documents and PowerPoint slides and interacting with others can teach us a lot. There, the seed for Bharat Darshan was planted in my mind.

Acumen: Beginning My Journey as an Investor in Social Business

In 2006, while working in Atlanta for CDC Software, I received an offer to return to India to run our India operations. I came back for a three-year assignment but never went back, as I enjoyed growing the software company in South and Southeast Asia and grew to be the president of the organization. In 2012, the company was sold.

That is when I decided that I did not want more running around. Instead, I retired at forty-one with whatever I had—although my wife debates this and is looking for a new word to describe my state given the time I'm spending on various initiatives. I was keen to give back to society and since I had really enjoyed volunteering for AID, I looked up my AID friends. Some of them were in politics, some were running NGOs—all actively participating in civil society. However, I had experienced both sides of the coin at that point. My long stint in the corporate world—growing from system engineer to president in sixteen years—had taught me how, with a vision and motive, we could build a successful company. However, in AID, I had also seen how we were able to raise more money and support more projects one year and the very next year have far fewer funds.

However, for a business, growth is possible if the product–market fit is done right. This is when I developed a vision of solving problems through businesses by marrying the efficiency of a corporate organization with the heart of a non-profit. I initially thought that this was my realization, but my friend Sadeesh Raghavan pointed out that Acumen, a $100-million impact fund started by

Jacqueline Novogratz, had been working on similar lines for some time. After retiring from Accenture, Sadeesh had been helping Acumen as a partner. I also became a partner and adviser to Acumen.

Acumen began life with the idea of Aid vs Market, which its founder Novogratz has explained in her book, *The Blue Sweater*. The book has become a bible for anyone wanting to understand social business; I myself must have given away around twenty copies of this book to people as a gift. Acumen provides grant, debt and equity support to social businesses. I was amazed about the clarity of their work and started visiting Acumen projects, in the process revisiting India through a fresh Bharat Darshan, by seeing amazing entrepreneurs in action.

Pine Needle Power

Rajnish Jain's Avani was converting Himalayan pine needles into energy using producer gas technology in Kumaon, Uttarakhand. In August 2012, from the last railhead at Kathgodam, we reached Rajnish's beautiful five-acre space after a six-hour drive.

When I mentioned our picture-perfect scenic drive featuring pine trees all the way to Rajnish, he remarked that that was the problem he was trying to solve. The introduction of pine trees in the region during British times almost wiped out the rest of the bio-ecology. The needles shed by the pine trees cover the ground completely and do not allow anything else to grow.

He showed how, by removing the pine needles in his small plot every season, he brought back trees like the Himalayan oak, cypress, etc.

The collected pine needles were converted to producer gas, which powered the turbine generating electricity for his residence. The char by-product, which still has some calorific value, is used as cooking briquette by the locals, thus reducing the need to cut forest wood for fuel. The locals are also employed in collecting the pine needles, thus providing them a livelihood.

Although Avani began as a chapter of the Barefoot College, training the local community to use solar systems, they observed that the proliferation of the pine trees was a local problem and set out to solve the same via evolving the idea of generating bio-energy. They also realized that there were rich local weaving cultures and traditions of using natural materials, including the use of a soap nut-based washing solution. That is when I came to know that we can 'grow soap' on trees! Soap nuts or soapberries are the fruits of a tree naturally found in India containing the cleaning agent saponin and are useful not only for washing clothes but also preventing skin ailments. The Avani team also developed a UNESCO-certified shawl by using a mix of silk and wool that can be worn in either summer or winter.

When I visited Avani, Gyanesh Pandey of Husk Power Systems (HPS, another Acumen Portfolio) was also there providing Avani with the technical knowledge of using pine needles to generate electricity as they had by using HPS and rice husk.

After hearing his inspiring story, I also met with Ratnesh Yadav (the co-founder of HPS) when I was in Patna for a conference in October 2012 and saw Husk Power Plants in Bihar's East Champaran and Vaishali districts. I observed how an entire village was powered by husk, with some small cottage industries also run using that power source.

Toilet Titan

On 16 June 2012, I was invited to attend the annual general meeting (AGM) of an Acumen investee company, Gramalaya Urban and Rural Development Initiatives and Network (GUARDIAN), which is the world's first micro-finance institution (MFI) enabling the installation of water supply and sanitation systems in households through micro lending. I enthusiastically caught a bus to their location in Tiruchirappalli (close to my hometown) and reached there wearing a dhoti. An Acumen representative arriving in such attire definitely surprised people; the photo that Acumen had shared with them had been of me when I still was in my corporate job, clad in a formal suit. It was enlightening to hear what that humble team of people, under the guidance of S. Damodaran, have done with regard to sanitation since 1987. After the AGM, they took me to Musiri, the resource centre of their parent non-profit, Gramalaya.

Nalini, despite little formal education, has been working as a researcher for the past fifteen years at Gramalaya's Centre of Technology and Training. She explained that the ventilation pipes connected to the leach-pit toilets kill the anaerobic bacteria needed to convert faeces into compost, which necessitated the use of a drainage truck to empty the septic tank once it is full. I was most fascinated to learn about their eco-friendly toilet design, one of which consisted of an airtight model with double pits. The toilet can be connected to the second pit once the first pit is full, allowing anaerobic bacteria to grow in the first pit naturally over a period of about six months. By the time the second pit is full, the first pit can be emptied and the compost generated can be used in the fields. Speaking to Nalini helped me realize how often we overcomplicate things by not letting nature take its course.

The centre serves as a one-stop knowledge base for the design and construction of different models of toilets for visitors, who include masons, villagers from nearby communities, NGO representatives and government officials. The models on display varied based on afford-ability, availability of space and water, geographical conditions, cultural habits and access to skilled manpower. In addition to waterless toilets, the centre also showcased zero-budget toilets built using locally available materials such as banana leaves, bamboo sticks and gunny bags.

By empowering individuals to construct their own low-cost, location-specific and culturally familiar toilets—backed by GUARDIAN's loans when needed—Gramalaya provides rural low-income households with the choice and means to improve their lives, resulting in better health outcomes and increased productivity. Other Indians can find the inspiration to solve the country's sanitation crisis in individuals like Nalini who are effectively bringing accessible and affordable solutions to the last mile. The next day I went to visit the Great Living Chola Temples.

I was greatly impressed by the work that they were doing and when Acumen requested me to join the board of GUARDIAN, I immediately agreed.

During my six years as a GUARDIAN director, I always looked forward to the quarterly meetings, for which I would usually catch a train from Bengaluru to Trichy. Wherever possible, I prefer trains and have clocked over 1,00,000 train kilometres, as trains necessitate the lowest carbon footprint along with the most comfort. Train journeys also help us understand Bharat better as we see many people sleeping at the stations in the odd hours of the night, as well as people running to get into the unreserved compartments.

The train arrived at Tiruchirappalli Junction early in the day. After a few hours of rest, I continued my journey to visit a village where GUARDIAN had provided loans to build toilets. I inaugurated newly built toilets and saw the happy faces of people who, for the first time, could access their own toilet. In nearly twenty-four visits, I saw thousands of toilets and heard various stories in each village. Members of Gramalaya would first visit the village and spend time creating awareness of the need for toilets through various programmes, including street plays. Then, they identified a local volunteer who could continue spreading the message and build self-help groups (SHGs).

Once the SHGs had highlighted the demand for toilets, GUARDIAN provided the necessary loans through them. However, when I asked an elderly woman her opinion of the toilet in the house, she called it a waste of money. I have even seen new houses built without registering the need for a toilet. After GUARDIAN's intervention, they are now building toilets. I have also seen people spending more money—over and above the loan provided by GUARDIAN—and building good quality concrete structures using expensive tiles. When I asked one such person why they had spent money on a toilet than on other things like their children's education, they answered that they had a thatched roof house and the toilet was their sole 'pukka' structure. They added that when they built a new house later, they wouldn't demolish the toilet.

As Damodaran is also a history buff who grew up in the Chola country, every visit included discussions over lunch after our meeting. Through these interactions, he would ensure that I visited many of the historic places nearby, taking me to Sittanavasal and many other cave temples in interior villages.

Now, with the Government of India running the Swachh Bharat Mission and building toilets across the country, Damodaran's work is complete. He is currently focusing on menstrual hygiene. This is a great learning, where a social business fills in the gap created by a lack of governmental service delivery. The government may not be able to innovate but, once social entrepreneurs innovate and scale up, the government can pick up from them and adapt the model across the country. Thus, Damodaran was feted by the vice president of India as a 'Toilet Titan'— thirty years after he started Gramalaya. In January 2022, I was delighted to see Damodaran felicitated with India's fourth-highest civilian award, the Padma Shri.

McDonald's and an Eye Hospital

I also learnt about the Aravind Eye Hospital model in Madurai. It was chastening to know that growing up in Madurai, I had never understood the significance of the model. However, through Acumen, I understood how the Aravind Eye Hospital does 60 per cent of their eye surgeries for free and are still profitable. When I visited Aravind in October 2012, Deepa showed me around this great example of a social business.

Started in 1976 by Dr Govindappa Venkataswamy (Dr V) at the age of fifty-eight, the hospital had treated thirty-two million people by the time I visited. To bring in service efficiently, Dr V emulated the McDonald's model. The entire system is built efficiently so that the most expensive resource—the doctor—is used most efficiently. In the operation theatre, there are two tables; once the doctor finishes surgery for one person, he turns to the next table and starts the surgery, while the first person is being moved. Aravind, therefore, performs five times the number of surgeries performed in the country. This efficiency brought down the cost; so by providing 60 per cent of its surgery for free, Aravind Hospital still does well.

Another great learning that I emphasize with every social business even today is that there should be no double standards for the poor. The poor pay more for everything and still get sub-substandard service. From HPS, I learnt that people spend Rs 500 a month to buy kerosene for lamps that provide little brightness. On the other hand, my electricity bill, despite all my different appliances, used to be around Rs 2500 per month.

Arvind handles this principle beautifully: the same doctors serve for paying and free patients, and no questions are asked for providing free service. I was told that Dr Abdul Kalam, who later became the President of India, once walked into the free section and got his eyes tested. Deepa handed me the book *Infinite Vision* written about Aravind Hospital, which is a must-read for all social entrepreneurs.

Social Entrepreneurs of Acumen

Acumen held its portfolio CEO summit at Aravind in May 2013, which gave me a chance to visit the hospital again. It was like having knowledge served to me on a platter since I was able to meet fifteen wonderful social entrepreneurs solving very important problems. I met Rajiv Vasudevan of AyurVaid, who brings science and processes into the traditional Ayurveda system and calls it precision Ayurveda. He holds the honour of leading India's first Ayurveda hospital accredited by the National Accreditation Board for Hospitals & Healthcare Providers (NABH), Quality Council of India.

Since meeting him, we have switched over to Ayurveda wherever possible as there are AyurVaid hospitals in Bengaluru. The youngest entrepreneur of all was Sweta Mangal, who co-founded Ziqitza Healthcare Limited (ZHL) providing affordable ambulance services, which can be booked through the unique number 1298. She shared some stories of reacting quickly to needs, such as in November 2008, when ZHL was the first ambulance service to arrive at the Taj and Trident Hotels during the Mumbai terrorist attacks. ZHL was also the first to reach the scene of the July 2011 bomb blasts in Mumbai at Zaveri Bazaar, Opera House and Dadar, saving eleven lives.

I saw how Water Health International (WHI) was providing clean drinking water in rural areas; Lifespring was providing maternal and paediatric care to low-income families; Satyan Mishra of Drishtee was enabling community access to critical services and products, market linkages or channel support and providing capital and capacity building support to rural micro-entrepreneurs. During that visit, we even had time to go to Aravind's world-class Aurolab that produces the world's cheapest lens!

* * *

After understanding the Acumen model, I spearheaded this thought process within the Indian Angel Network (IAN). While earlier I had invested only in technology start-ups (Druva, Orangescape, Gamiana, Unbxd) as an angel investor, I now launched IAN Impact to focus on investing in social business. Since then, my focus has been on social business.

Believing in the need to understand things first-hand, I continued on my Bharat Darshan, travelling extensively in rural areas across twenty-eight Indian states and union territories. Through these travels over the years, Kerala— God's own country—has grown dear to me.

Kappad, 12 km from Kozhikode, is a quiet place that witnessed a historical event that changed the history of India forever. It is the place where Vasco da Gama landed in 1498. I had mixed feelings when I was visiting there on the way back from Areacode (yes, that is how Ariakode is also spelt), an hour away from Kozhikode, with entrepreneur Shamil. The beach at Kappad has been nicely developed and there is a marble stone near a house there with the inscription 'Vasco-da-Gama landed here Kappakadavu in the year 1498'. I wondered what these shores must have been like over 500 years ago when the Portuguese explorer Vasco da Gama landed here with four small ships and 170 men.[5]

The Malabar Coast will be remembered not merely for the landing of Vasco da Gama but for the advent of colonialism in India as well. Having started out from Europe, Vasco da Gama's voyage had sailed into the pages of Indian history. I stood on the sands of time at Kappad, reflecting on India's past glory. It is here, by the shores of the Arabian Sea that the seeds of writing a book on 'Bharat' sprouted in my mind.

Two

What We Grow: Clues to a Better Tomorrow

'There are two major challenges before Indian agriculture today: ecological and economical. The conservation of our basic agricultural assets, such as land, water and biodiversity, is a major challenge. How to make agriculture sustainable is the challenge.'

—M.S. Swaminathan

Any human being's survival is directly tied to what we eat and how. Production and distribution of agricultural produce is an important aspect of a country's economic growth. What lessons can we draw from our lost past for the way forward?

Famine, Abundance and Healthy Practices

Famines used to occur frequently in India until the 1960s and their impact was devastating. In the nineteenth century, famines were believed to be triggered by harvest failure. However, one of the most severe famines of the twentieth century, the Bengal Famine of 1943, was triggered by the diversion of food exclusively for the soldiers fighting in World War II. Famine-like conditions recurred again in

1966 and 1972, but the extent of damage and the death toll due to starvation was limited and not so drastic on both occasions. Why did these famines develop? Why and how did the frequency of their occurrences fall in later years?

Back in 1965,[1] India had to feed 480 million people but was already importing food grains. Resource economist Lester Brown had travelled to India at the behest of the US Agency for International Development and made the dire prediction that India was staring a famine in the face. The data available to Brown suggested that India's food grain output would fall well short of the government-projected demand of ninety-five million tonnes—by ten million tonnes at a minimum. In reality, the output would be even less, with the total deficit hitting eighteen million tonnes. Many then felt that the blame was on the Indian bureaucracy, their procrastination and their inability to take speedy action.

But this impending famine was no surprise, as American economists had been warning about it since 1959, based on their studies of India's birth rate and crop growth rate. In response to the 1965 food grain crisis, the government of the day began promoting awareness among people as part of a campaign requesting them not to waste food. At the same time, attempts were made to increase grain output and farmers were asked to grow more than one crop in a year. People were also encouraged to grow food in their backyards, thus creating kitchen gardens. Another popular initiative was the 'miss a meal' campaign, which pushed the idea of a 'dinnerless day' advertised in newspapers across the nation. However, the following year, 1966, India's food crisis got even worse, requiring the US to export as much as 20,000 tonnes of food grains every day. The experience of 1965–66 put India firmly on the path toward the Green

Revolution and achieving some level of self-sufficiency in producing food grains.

At this stage, it is good to understand what exactly a famine is. 'Famine' has become a politically loaded word and it is therefore important to understand its causes and conditions. Traditionally, famines are thought to be caused by the reduction in food output or a population outgrowing its regional carrying capacity of food. In this perception, the operative cause of famine is an imbalance of population with respect to food supply (and could be solved by population control methods). Famine could also come from the problem of food distribution and poverty, as observed by economist Amartya Sen. In his book *Poverty and Famine,* Sen mentions that he was able to influence the way international organizations and governments dealt with food crises. He showed that famine was not just a consequence of nature, but also an avoidable economic and political catastrophe. He also argues that the apathy and inaction of the government, compounded by market failure, caused the Bengal famine of 1943.

Until famine hit India, the agrarian community was comfortable growing and eating their food. There was no such thing as waste from food and no segregation of waste as is the practice now. In villages, a huge pit would be dug and waste was dumped there to compost and later use as manure. I remember my grandfather, who was a farmer, had a huge pit in front of his house, where the whole street would dump their waste. Once in three months, he would take that compost to the fields and the concept of waste was barely evident. Today, waste and garbage is piled up on every street corner in the country, and this has reached uncontrollable volumes.

Over time, the Green Revolution slowly crept into India and agriculture was transformed into a non-sustainable, industrialized system by adopting modern methods and technologies. India, in its quest to become a developed nation, was concentrating on boosting the industrial sector and agriculture took a backseat. Farmers' agricultural practices were changed through the introduction of high-yielding varieties of seeds to increase food production volumes. This contributed to a massive systemic problem in the country that gradually began to affect people's health, small farmers' sustainability, soil erosion and earth degradation.

The Green Revolution started in the early 1960s to help India overcome poor agricultural productivity. With these initiatives, food grain production initially increased, especially in Punjab, Haryana and Uttar Pradesh. With this, India reached a position where there was no worry about producing food, although this came at a cost. To increase production, seeds had to be genetically modified and artificial chemicals and pesticides were used. When fertilizers were excessively used, the spillover would seep into and contaminate the groundwater, which affected the food grains and the vegetables. The same water containing the fertilizer or pesticide spillover was also used to feed cattle, which sometimes also grazed in the fields. Consequently, the milk from these cows was contaminated, as was the meat from poultry and sheep which were subsequently consumed by people.

For instance, the pesticide nitrate is present in groundwater in quantities well beyond safe limits, rendering the water unpotable. Excessive concentrations of nitrate-nitrogen or nitrite-nitrogen in drinking water can be hazardous to health. Several cases of cancer and other diseases have been linked to the overutilization of pesticides on food grains. In Kerala, Endosulfan—another pesticide— is sprayed widely in cashew plantations by farmers who need to cover their faces with masks to protect them from inhaling these chemicals. One can imagine the potency of the pesticides.

One can also ask why pesticides are used at all, knowing the dangers associated. A new age economy wherein life seems to depend on being the quickest to market and selling enough quantities that can be stored for a long time places a premium on using fertilizers and pesticides as they increase the yield manifold and increase the produce's shelf life. However, we need to ask once again—at what cost? And who must be blamed for this state of affairs?

The farmer looks at his benefit and uses pesticides. The consumer would like food produce without pesticides as it would prevent diseases but at the same time would not like the produce to be expensive, which is bound to happen as food grain production would become more expensive without using pesticides. The government encourages farmers to use pesticides under pressure from the large pesticide lobby in India. Each one looks at their own individual benefit, resulting in a collective disaster for everyone concerned.

This is where individual social responsibility (ISR) comes in. As an individual consumer, you should encourage farmers to go organic and avoid using fertilizers and pesticides. Later on in this book, we will examine the healthy choices that consumers have now and meet the organic farming entrepreneurs who are putting these ideas into practice, whom I have supported.

An older generation would say, 'Leave it to the farmers'; they are aware of many age-old traditions of cultivating. Farmers know that, after spraying pesticides on plantations, it takes three days for the spray to evaporate and the produce grown subsequently is safe for human consumption. In the quest to go to market with speed, this knowledge is not heeded and some people literally end up eating the pesticide as the crop is planted while the spray still lingers on. The farmers are also reluctant to go organic as there is a belief that the produce quantity will be lower besides which many consumers are unwilling to pay the premium necessitated by this type of farming. The farmers somehow need to pass on this knowledge to the consumers.

Although more consumers are now becoming aware of the dangers of using pesticides and have begun encouraging organic farming by purchasing produce solely from organic producers, they still comprise a small percentage of the population. The only encouraging aspect is that a movement has started and, hopefully, its momentum will increase and benefit future generations.

Only a couple of generations back, people would buy enough to last for a few days. Now with the world moving at a rapid pace and people having no time for anything apart from the pursuit of money, they buy enough to last a month to avoid repeat visits to the market. However, to increase the shelf life of rice, for example, its husk is polished to remove the nutrient coat that is meant to guard against pest attacks.

Even in our dietary habits, we have changed much over a few generations. An old custom involved soaking leftover rice in a clay pot in water overnight. By the following morning, the fermented rice-water mix, which is extremely beneficial to health, would be eaten as the first meal of the day. Many modern-day children would not even have heard of such a practice, let alone follow it. But many older customs are fading, so much so that many good things are being forgotten. With the invention of refrigerators, leftover food is stored for several days and eaten to avoid spending more time cooking fresh food. This can cause several health problems which most people don't realize. The frequency of visiting the doctor has increased as a result. Just think, if consumers partake of pesticide-infected food or eat stale food, would that not result in a health calamity?

Fortunately, there are ways to overcome this problem and organic farming is one of them. The other option is to eat food with a shorter shelf life and buy from markets closer to where you live. Eat local produce instead of imported foods, which take less time to reach the consumer. Consume cooked food immediately and cook just enough to last that meal. Encourage consuming seasonal food so that no processing is needed to increase the shelf life of the food. The greater the number of people who produce organic food, the lower the price and the more the healthy eaters. This is seemingly too much of an effort but living a sustainable life is also a luxury. We need to decide what kind of luxury are we aspiring for: a large house, a big car or a sustainable life? If growing organic produce is made a priority, it will bring back the old economy anew.

Consider the US as a parallel, where people live in what is called a microwave economy. They buy packaged food that can be heated in a microwave and eaten. No wonder illnesses are on the rise. Another example I can give you is that of fertilizers and pesticides that have contaminated the Mississippi River which flows into the Gulf of Mexico, resulting in fish dying. We need to avoid falling into such traps and instead find ways to build businesses that link farmers to local people. The goal is to increase the incomes of small farmers and enhance their positive, sustainable impact on the local environment, while also making healthful organic food more easily available to city dwellers.

What can bring us some hope and heart is that although pesticides are used all over the world, India uses the least quantity of fertilizers compared to the rest of the world, including China, for which we should be thankful. Comparing a tomato or an onion either grown in India or sold in the Indian market with one grown and marketed in the US will drive home the point about boosting and increasing volumes for better profit. And the beauty of India is that we can learn from the mistakes of the West.

Take the case of Japan where the production of rice is high but they have an ageing population and are in constant fear that there would be no farmers left once the existing ones die of old age. In India, on the other hand, we have a booming youth population who can be induced to take up farming. Many youngsters have left their homes in rural areas to find jobs, but they need to be told about the virtues of living in rural areas and the benefits of farming not just for them but as an extended benefit to the community.

Agriculture: Our Inescapable Foundation

Agriculture plays a crucial role in India's economy and covers 54.6 per cent of the rural household's dependency as their principal means of livelihood. But agriculture's contribution to the country's GDP is hardly 17 per cent. India ranks third in farm and agriculture outputs worldwide.[2] Agricultural clusters, geographic concentrations of interconnected crops, were formed to make Indian agriculture more competitive worldwide, in Assam, Uttar Pradesh, West Bengal, Madhya Pradesh, Karnataka,

Gujarat, Punjab and Haryana. Unfortunately, every agriculture-dependent state in India is struggling today.

West Bengal has plenty of rich natural resources but it is one of India's low-income states where a significant percentage of the population is economically backward. Bihar was once among the most prosperous states of India and served as a base from which three different dynasties established vast ancient empires. But those days are now only a distant memory. In 2012 when I visited Bihar, I absorbed what this region must have meant in the ancient world.

I went to Nalanda, one of the oldest universities in the world, and was awestruck by the UNESCO-certified ruins still majestically relating a 1600-year-long story. Nalanda obtained significant fame, prestige and relevance during ancient times and rose to legendary status due to its contribution to the emergence of India as a great power around the fourth century. I went to Bodh Gaya which gave the world the Buddha and saw the mighty Ganga flowing 5.75 km wide under the Mahatma Gandhi Setu in Patna.

For about a thousand years, from around the middle of the first millennium to around the middle of the second millennium, India enjoyed great prosperity, but then the slide began. The commercial economy had become stagnant from around the close of the fourth century and declined further, more sharply, after the Gupta era, with India almost turning derelict. Taxila, one of India's key trade centres, began to decay slowly sometime in the seventh century. Another major reason for the trade decline was the breakdown of India's trade with Europe following the collapse of the Roman Empire. The transformation of the Indian ethos and society as fatalism and passivity crept in and replaced self-reliance and enterprise was also largely to blame for India's drop. As prosperity declined, so did the culture.

Whatever may be the reasons for the slide, we know where we stand in the twenty-first century. What is important to decide, however, is—where do we go from here?

Hello, Spanish Ganesha?

Reflecting on our country's diminishment has brought me several insights to share with you.

As I thought more about the fact that over 50 per cent of our population is employed in agriculture—and the textile sector is our second-largest employer—I wondered whether we stagnated since we missed the industrial revolution.

There is a luxury mall in Bengaluru wherein expensive products are sold from all over the world, dominated by European apparel, home and travel accessories and other luxury brands and you would hardly see any Indian brands. An Imagine store here sells Apple computer products. Next to it is the showroom of Lladró, a Spanish company that sells porcelain figurines and other home accessories. In the Apple showroom, I saw a computer costing Rs 4 lakh (a new economy product) and in the Lladró store, there was a handmade (old economy) porcelain figurine of Ganesha, the Indian elephant god, also worth Rs 4 lakh. Out of curiosity, I asked the sales executive why this Ganesha figurine cost so much when similar and better-looking figurines may be available at a far lower price in other parts of Bengaluru. He proudly started explaining the European craftsmanship involved in making the Ganesha, with exquisite care for detail and the meticulous finish that characterizes the best Lladró creations. He explained the figurine's intricacies using a magnifying glass and detailed the time spent and the effort taken to make that incredible piece of work. This brought to my mind that both old economy and new economy products can thrive in today's world side by side. What about us, in that case? If we were not good at making computers, having lost out on the industrial revolution, did this also mean we were not good at making handicrafts? Even as the question formed itself in my mind, I knew the answer was a resounding 'no'.

Tracking the Tomato

I next began to look at agriculture through a single, important kitchen staple—the tomato.

The price of tomatoes, be it at a farm or grocery store, seems mysteriously random, almost erratic and all over the place. It is truly puzzling. Where do these numbers come from? Why are the prices so different? And when I buy a kilo, where is most of that money going?

Let's start at the beginning—a farmer oversees several thousand tomato plants on his farm. He probably has his farm financed so he repays that, pays for seeds and the workers needed to maintain and get the crop ready and then harvest it. He has to foot transportation costs in taking the tomatoes to the market and he pays for the boxes the tomatoes travel in. The farmer plants, tends, harvests and then packs the tomatoes. But to ensure that tomatoes bring in a profit, farms must make every acre—and every plant—count. Maintaining the health and quality of the tomatoes entails a higher cost. There are also losses to account for, during travel from the farm to the market, for instance. Against the context of all of these costs, from labour to losses to farm expenses and overheads farmers have no control over the price set by the market and that may or may not leave them anything to take home.

But only around 30 per cent of what we pay for the tomato we eat goes to the farmer. Why?

Farm-to-Home

There is no change in the tomato from the time it is plucked and the time it arrives at our table. So around 70 per cent of the price ends up being spent on the number of hops that tomato makes before it reaches the customer! By making the customer buy directly from the farmer, the intermediaries' hops can be reduced, which is the journey of Farm-to-Home. When a person is connecting the farmer to his customer, they need to be honest enough to pass the benefit of that connection to the farmer, which underpins fair price/fair trade. While such a practice is becoming more accepted in the crafts sector, we are yet to see it take root in agriculture.

Many start-ups that claim to offer Farm-to-Home services are hardly able to procure directly from farmers as that requires setting up procurement centres at the farms' gates so that they can guarantee a Farm-to-Home delivery. Otherwise, what usually happens is that they end up using the word 'farmer-partners' and use the middleman to procure, which increases the number of hops for the tomato and directly impacts the price the farmer gets.

Another issue that arises with many Farm-to-Home entities is that they prefer buying the farmers' grade-A produce, leaving the farmer to figure out a way to sell the grade B/C produce. Invariably, the farmer ends up going to the *mandi* again, where procurers and buyers know that the grade-A produce has gone somewhere else. As a result, farmers end up relying on a middleman to buy and sort their entire produce and send the grade-A product to one buyer and the rest to someone else.

Some start-ups can ensure true Farm-to-Home deliveries by tying up with local NGOs or Farmers Producer Organizations (FPOs). Others can set up direct procurement using the Agripreneur model where a progressive farmer or a local youth provides the service of collecting from local farmers for the start-up. Farm-to-Home does end up reducing the number of hops for the humble tomato, but how much benefit does the farmer get from this reduction?

A Tamil saying goes, 'உழுதவன் கணக்கு பார்த்தால் உழக்கு கூட மிஞ்சாது'—*uzhuthavan kanakku paarthal uzhakku kooda minchadu*—meaning, 'If a ploughing man (farmer) calculates his costs, he won't be able to save even a *uzhakku*, a small device for measuring grains.' This reflects the attitude of people over the years, which needs to change.

When it comes to farming, unlike manufacturing or services, crop prices tend to be dictated by the procurers rather than calculated based on the costs incurred. Farmers have little room to negotiate their profit margin, especially considering the perishable nature of their products, and are often forced to sell to recoup even a part of the costs rather than risk getting no value for their crops. Thus, while a manufacturer may realize profits many times the cost involved, farmers often end up making a loss. Worse, we still can't agree on a precise method for calculating a farmer's cost of production.

According to an *Indian Express* article, 'The Cost+50% Swaminathan Formula Mirage',[3] the Indian government-appointed National Commission on Farmers, headed by Professor M.S. Swaminathan, produced as many as five reports without adequately defining a farmer's 'weighted average cost of production'. The Commission for Agricultural Costs and Prices (CACP) suggested the three formulas that are commonly discussed: A2, A2+FL and C2. A2 costs basically cover all paid-out expenses, both in cash and in kind, incurred by farmers on seeds, fertilizers, chemicals, hired labour, fuel, irrigation, etc. A2+FL cover actual paid-out costs plus an imputed value of unpaid family labour. C2 costs are more comprehensive, accounting for the rentals and interest forgone on owned land and fixed capital assets respectively, on top of A2+FL.

The government is expected to utilize one of these formulas when calculating the minimum support price (MSP) for various crops, which is the lowest price at which the produce can be procured at a mandi. This MSP can be the base for agricultural start-ups when they calculate the farmer's cost of production, to which they can then add a 50 per cent margin to arrive at a Fair Price/Fair Trade. Sadly, when I look into many of the start-ups that claim to offer Farm-to-Home delivery, they seldom know about the farmer's profit and loss (P&L) accounting.

If Farm-to-Home start-ups can work out a cost-plus model in tandem with the farmers and charge their customers accordingly, then farming may become viable and align with Fair Price/Fair Trade principles. Further, if the government can recognize such Fair Price models, customers can buy a more informed product. At present, when a venture claims Fair Price/Fair Trade, Farm-to-Home, etc., there is no way for the customer to verify the same. Here, technological methods like blockchain traceability can also come into play.

If the Farm-to-Home start-ups, with the support of the agripreneur or progressive farmer, can capture information about each farmer reflecting what they sow and what they use to cultivate their crops, with pictures taken at every stage of the growth, this information can help the customer make a more informed decision. Farmers Fresh Zone, one of my investments, is implementing such technology in Kerala. They have the catchy slogan, 'Our Tomatoes Can Talk'. Using the know-your-farmer feature, customers can scan the QR code on the tomato crate in the store and it gives them the details of which farmer grew it and what fertilizer was used.

Making Farmers Deer

Continuing our tomato story, another way to benefit the farmer is by adding value to the tomato. Looking at the processed food industry, the same tomato into which the farmer puts his heart and soul is turned into ketchup or tomato puree priced at probably 100–200 per cent more. And that's only because there is a value added to the tomato!

Of course, there are other production costs and overheads incurred in the processing. Even then, the food processing companies profit while the farmers remain poor. Each time there is value addition, the customer pays a premium when they buy! Even for the tomato that the farmer produces, much of the cost is eaten up by the transportation and the supply chain. I like to compare this to the food chain wherein a deer eats grass and a tiger eats a deer. In agriculture, whoever is selling to the consumer directly comes closest to the tiger—he decides the price and asks the deer, the processing companies, to sell the product at a particular price. The deer in turn eats grass; here the farmer is the grass at the bottom of the food chain. The processing companies want to buy the produce from the farmer at a lower price. So, if you are not close to the customer (top of the chain) you are being squeezed by someone above you all the time.

KisanMitr

In April 2020, at the peak of the Covid-19 pandemic and amid ongoing countrywide lockdowns, Dr Sapna Poti, the director—strategic alliances in the office of the principal scientific adviser (PSA) to the Government of India, called me. She shared her thoughts about how we could help reverse migrants—who had returned to their native towns and villages from the cities they were working in—with the technologies available to India's institutions like the Indian Institutes of Technology (IITs), the Council for Scientific and Industrial Research (CSIR), etc. This, when I was putting out messages saying 'Bharat saying bye to India' after seeing around one crore workers walking back home from various cities.[4]

I also started seeing this as a blessing in disguise because in February 2021, just before the pandemic struck, I travelled around three areas in Karnataka—Yellapur, Siddapur and Shivamogga—to visit Rural Livelihood mission projects and improve their income generation. A major learning from that trip and other travels was that the youth have migrated heavily towards cities across the country for better employment prospects as they felt that whatever their parents were doing only brought them poverty.

Many of these livelihood projects involved women, in particular older women, whose children had moved to some city. They ended up making pickles, kokum products, poppadum, miscellaneous food items and areca nut plates—mostly old economy activities. Two of the better projects I saw were a paper cup-making unit and a woman making Kerala (Malabar) parottas. The livelihood mission was effectively a retirement scheme for these women.

For this reason, when I saw the youth going back to their villages, I felt that they can rebuild rural India. When I returned from the US, I was called 'abroad returned' and seen as an example of reverse brain drain. But we were calling the labourers 'reverse migrants' rather than 'city-returned'. They helped build the cities and understood what was good and not good about the cities. By enabling them further, we could definitely look at rebuilding rural India. I started sharing on social media the various social innovations I had come across in rural areas and how NGOs and skilling organizations could utilize them to enable the city-returned youth. As the list grew in size, Prof. Simy Joy of IIM Kozhikode and I brought out 'Improving Rural Livelihoods: Business Models for Rural India—A Social Enterprises Case Compendium' detailing over twenty-three innovations.

Sapna's call was music to my ears and I agreed with her that it was a great idea. However, I suggested that we build a platform using available technologies that city-returned youth and farmers could use, instead of giving the work to a few organizations. Thus, KisanMitr was born amid the pandemic and today hosts over 1650 technologies from CSIR, IIT, Indian Council of Agricultural Research (ICAR), agricultural universities and start-ups across the country. To disseminate this information, we partnered with the National Association of Software and Service Companies (NASSCOM) and NSRCEL, IIMB, hosting some thirty-two sessions in English thus far. These sessions were also hosted in Hindi by IIM Lucknow; in Tamil by VIT School of Agricultural Innovations and Advanced Learning; in

Telugu by Bhagavatula Charitable Trust (BCT). We also partnered with 675 Krishi Vigyan Kendras (KVKs) across the country to ensure that vernacular sessions could be accessed by farmers without Internet access and who only speak their local language. Doing so would help us bridge the digital divide and expose farmers to the various technologies available that are capable of making them Atmanirbhar (self-reliant).

Atmanirbhar Krishi App

As we started working on the technological platform, we grappled with various ideas before launching the Atmanirbhar Krishi App with the support of Tech Mahindra and Nithya Subramaniam of Meark. By using the app on a GPS-enabled smartphone, farmers can learn about everything above and below the ground on their farm, such as moisture level, weather and rainfall forecast, the water level in canals, dams and the water table and soil health. If the farmer has not undertaken soil testing, then the details for a nearby site will be displayed. The entire project was undertaken by volunteers without anyone incurring any costs, with Indian CST coming forward to build and host the platform. Further, city-returned youth could provide farmers who don't have either a smartphone or Internet access the necessary services, as a micro-entrepreneurship opportunity in exchange for a small fee.

Mobile Jaggery Unit

I'm glad that an organic brand has taken the technology developed at IIT Bombay by Prof. Sanjay Mahajani, which converts sugarcane to jaggery at the farm itself using a unit housed in a tractor and made it a mobile jaggery unit. As

IIT Bombay has this technology, Prof. Sanjay established a start-up with one of his employees and the company bought the machine from this start-up. Thus enabling the invention to become an innovation, as we found a buyer for the technology. The first mobile unit was launched in October 2021 in Mandya, where the local youth were trained to support the farmers and told that the entire jaggery output. From the farm, instead of sugarcane, jaggery would be produced.

I felt good that the idea worked and hope that more people come forward to rebuild rural India using these technologies. KalaMitr would next connect technologies in crafts, enabling farmers growing bananas to sell not only the fruit but also convert the stem to rope or yarn which the farmer's family could weave into a fabric. Using livestock technologies, there are ways to raise cows, goats and poultry and thus multiply the revenue streams available to farmers. Through Himalayan Bazar, we've highlighted all the small farmer-producer companies of the Himalayan states and listed their produce to attract businesses to connect with them.

Making Farmers Tigers

The Farmer Producer Organization (FPO) is a new model that could help farmer collectives own the entire value chain, consumer (tiger), processor (deer) and producer (grass). Thousands of FPOs have been created across the country with this purpose and can be called the next generation of cooperatives.

Going by the International Cooperative Alliance's definition, 'a cooperative is an autonomous association of persons united voluntarily to meet their common economic, social and cultural needs and aspirations through a jointly-owned and democratically-controlled enterprise'. In India, the cooperatives were created way back in 1904 and later amended by The Cooperative Societies Act, 1912, for the promotion of thrift and self-help among agriculturists, artisans and persons of limited means. This 100-year-old act, governed by the Registrar of Cooperative Societies, could not prevent cooperative societies from losing their purpose and the ability to market their products over the years. There are instances of them being used for political purposes as well.

However, in the wake of the Great Recession of 2008, the United Nations General Assembly (UNGA) passed a resolution on 18 December 2009 recognizing that cooperatives are a major factor in economic and social development and that they have contributed to the eradication of poverty. The UNGA also proclaimed the year 2012 as the International Year of the Cooperative. Section 5 of the Resolution also 'encourages Governments to keep under review, as appropriate, the legal and administrative provisions governing the activities of cooperatives in order to enhance the growth and sustainability of cooperatives in a rapidly changing socio-economic environment by, inter alia, providing a level playing field for cooperatives vis-à-vis other business and social enterprises, including appropriate tax incentives and access to financial services and markets'.

Taking this as a cue, the next generation of cooperatives was created across the world. In India, the next generation of cooperatives came in the form of producer companies (PCs) as described in Section 465(1) of the Companies Act, 2013, making them governed by the same law as a private limited company. These companies, with better governance, would be owned by producers, i.e., farmers, weavers, etc. In agriculture, they are commonly known as Farmer Producer Organizations (FPOs) or Farmer Producer Companies (FPCs). My visits to various FPOs taught me that the best-run FPOs are all headed by strong CEOs. Examples of such FPOs include Sahyadri Farms, Nasik, which works with grape farmers and their value chain; Satya Sai Farmer Producer Company supported by an NGO, Centre for Collective Development (CCD) in Anantapur, which grows groundnuts; Araku Coffee grown in Andhra Pradesh's Araku Valley supported by the Naandi Foundation; and Uzhavan in Erode, Tamil Nadu, working with turmeric farmers. FPOs that did not have a CEO with strong business acumen invariably struggled to scale up. We, therefore, need skilling programmes on how to run businesses for FPO CEOs, perhaps offered by business schools, or start programmes to skill the children of farmers to become CEOs of such FPOs.

The Covenant Centre of Development (CCD) a Madurai-based NGO mentioned in C.K. Prahalad's book *Fortune at the Bottom of the Pyramid*, ran a campaign making Farmer's Sons Farmers. As agriculture is not viable any more, many farmers don't want their children to come back to farming. However, as a result of growing unemployment, many farmers' children end up working in the cities for meagre salaries, even with engineering degrees. Instead, they could look at agriculture differently and turn their fathers into tigers. Later on in this book, we will take a look at how Lloyd Edward—a farmer's son from Hunsur, Karnataka—achieved this through the Econut Coconut Farmers Producer Company. We can also look at ways to get non-farmers appointed as CEOs of FPOs.

For a long time, Amul, owned by 36 lakh farmers with over Rs 38,550 crore in revenue in 2019-20, was the best-known model of successful supply chain management.[5] To replicate this, we need many more Verghese Kuriens. Often, in my speeches, I point out how Steve Jobs may not be relevant to India as a motivation, as creating a billion-dollar company in the US may not be such a big deal. However, creating a company worth billions of dollars in the social sector is amazing. Our students and aspiring entrepreneurs should find out more about and celebrate the Amul founder who is a legend.

Operation Flood

I have been a mentor at IIM Ahmedabad's Centre for Innovation, Incubation and Entrepreneurship (CIIE) since 2010 and I frequently visit the city. During one of those visits, in 2013, I also visited the Amul facility in Anand, Gujarat. I was awestruck by the mammoth work that is going on there. It is a world-class processing facility with a structure clearly explaining how money and milk are flowing. I learnt how Amul's ability to make milk powder changed the way of looking at milk—a perishable commodity. If there was one technological breakthrough that revolutionized India's organized dairy industry, it was the making of skim milk powder out of buffalo milk. The man who made this possible was H.M. Dalaya. The Anand Pattern Experiment at Amul, a dairy cooperative, was the engine behind the success of the programme. Not just the technology, but the way in which this experiment addressed socio-economic and socio-political issues such as caste before they could attain success makes for a very absorbing film *Manthan* (Churn), released in 1976. I consider this a must-watch film for social entrepreneurs because it shows how we need to transform the mindsets of people before we can achieve the desired results.

Manthan brings out the powerful role that social boycott plays in reinforcing or rejecting certain practices. I was looking for the definition of social boycott and, while it is mentioned in some legal frameworks, I found the definition only in a social science textbook for Class VIII students enrolled in government schools in Rajasthan. It is a method for marginalizing people by preventing them from either participating freely in society or taking advantage of opportunities usually available to members of society. In the 1976 film, social boycott, jealousy and all the processes faced by a group of scientists and entrepreneurs in a village setting are shown convincingly. I have also witnessed these things first-hand, as late as 2019, with one of the ventures incubated at NSRCEL—Rural Caravan, which works in the Palghar district of Maharashtra.

Today, Amul remains a great example of Tiger-Deer-Grass all together! It is also a model of the need to replicate success and scalability. Amul's success story started the white revolution across the country and today, similar cooperatives exist in nearly every state. Aavin of Tamil Nadu, Sanchi of Madhya Pradesh, Milma of Kerala and Nandini of Karnataka are some examples.

Farming Needs the Subsidy

Given that food is a highly sensitive area, can we afford to make food prices market-driven? With organic produce directly sold to premium customers at a suitable price, both customers and farmers are happy. But how will the poor afford higher food prices? For this reason, food prices across the world are kept within reach of the common man even at the cost of letting farmers suffer. However, this necessitates heavily subsidizing farmers. Even a developed country like the US provided $428 billion for five years from 2019 to 2023 of the 2018 farm bill,[6] starting the subsidy as a way to provide income and price support to US farmers and now includes food stamps for the poor as well. I remember talking to Gordon Shannon from Change Alliance, who opined that, in Ireland, nearly every farmer is like a government employee, since they keep getting some form of cash handout to ensure they continue farming. If all food production is turned market-driven, then we risk civil unrest.

This is the point I argue when people say that 50 per cent of employment is in agriculture, but it contributes only 17 per cent to GDP: if all agricultural production is market-driven, without any price control, the tomato should cost Rs 300/kg, which would automatically and substantially increase agriculture's contribution to India's GDP. The problem is elsewhere, but we blame agriculture for it. What is the solution then? Should we let it become market-driven and should the government then take care of poorer people who cannot afford food with cash transfers?

I have been buying only commercially available LPG at home since I returned to India in 2006 and have not signed up for the subsidized cylinder. But it is tough to convince my mother, who lives in my home town, to buy commercial LPG as she wants to buy a subsidized cylinder from Indane Gas. While the government is subsidizing LPG for the poor, even the rich are buying that same LPG. Although the #GiveItUp campaign saw quite a lot of people opt out of receiving the LPG subsidy, even in an upscale apartment like the one where I live, many people continue buying subsidized LPG. This, for me, emphasizes the need for us to consider our Individual Social Responsibility.

Three

Mainstreaming the Marginalized

*From the scene in Swades (2004) when Mohan visits
Birsa's home . . .*

*Postman: Arré oh, Birsa! Yeh Mohan babu hain,
tumhare sang baat karna chahte hain [Hey Birsa!
This is Mr Mohan—he wants to talk to you].*

*Birsa: Kya hua huzoor, humse kuchh galati ho
gayi kya [What's the matter, sir? Have I done
something wrong]?*

*Mohan: Nahin, nahin. Hum aapse sirf yeh poochne
aaye they ki kya aap apne bacchon ko school bhejna
chahenge [No, I just came to ask you whether you'd
like to send your children to school]?*

*Birsa: Huzoor, jis gaaon mein hum pet bharne
ke vaaste kaam nahin kar sakte hain, wo gaaon
humaare bacchon ko kya padhayegi [Sir, in a
village which can't provide enough work to fill
our stomachs, what will our children learn in such
a village]?*

In the march of development witnessed in our country
since Independence, there have often been pockets of

resistance when the acquisition of land or other natural resources has meant the displacement of communities dependent on those resources. As villages become towns and towns become cities, tribal communities that have existed beyond the conventional boundaries of towns and villages for centuries are at risk of becoming invisible. A question of increasing concern for me for many years is: by thrusting a model of development that does not value or enable the skill sets and knowledge base of the tribals, are we losing out on ways to bring more even, inclusive growth across the country?

Trees and Tribal Communities: Growth for Enduring Prosperity

One significant way by which we can draw upon lessons from our past is by honouring and supporting our tribal communities, who represent the wisdom and traditional practices that have endured across millennia. Outside of Africa, India has the largest tribal population in the world, comprising more than a million people across western, eastern and central India and constituting about 8.9 per cent of the total population in India.[1] The majority of these tribal people live in Jharkhand, Bihar, Odisha, Chhattisgarh, West Bengal and Assam. India's tribal people are known as Adivasis, or the original inhabitants of this land. To understand their living circumstances, I have visited them in Jharkhand at Buntu, at Dantewada and Dhamtari in Chhattisgarh, at Attapadi in Kerala, at Pacha Malai, Karantha Malai and the Kalvarayan Hills in Tamil Nadu, in Maharashtra's Amale, in Odisha, in the East Garo Hills of Meghalaya and at Mao in Manipur.

The Aboriginals

Aboriginal is how the dictionary translates the word *tribal*, which is apt. Visiting the Odisha State Tribal Museum[2]—run by the Scheduled Castes and Scheduled Tribes Research and Training Institute (SCSTRTI)—in Bhubaneshwar in 2014 was an eye-opening experience. The museum is well-managed and has a wealth of information that can change the way we perceive our tribal communities, their dresses and ornaments, musical instruments, textiles, paintings, weapons, craftsmanship in bamboo and sophisticated metal tools. In fact, the level of sophistication on display challenges our notion of the *primitive*, as I observed when I saw a silver wine sipper.

Their dances, festivals, beautiful huts and rich heritage set against the simple life they lead made me wonder where we were running. I learnt that there are sixty-two communities in Odisha designated as Scheduled Tribes, whose speech comprises as many as seventy-four dialects and whose ethos and culture differ markedly from other Indian communities. Occupationally diverse, they may be nomads hunting or gathering food but also farmers growing food crops and fruit.

At the museum, an Adivasi Mela was being held, where I could interact with Birhor, Mankirdia and Koya groups from Karanjia, Mayurbhanj district making siali fibre rope baskets. The basket I bought from them years ago is going strong even today! Other groups were making lac bangles. The Chuktia Bhunjia community[3] from Nuapada (Eastern Ghats region) were making and selling bead necklaces with nice beads of bronze. I bought some beads from them then but later learnt from the immensely informative

Scheduled Castes and Scheduled Tribes Research and Training Institute (SCSTRTI) website how their community was designated by the Indian government as one of the Particularly Vulnerable Tribal Groups (PVTG). The PVTGs[4] are among the most remote and marginalized tribal communities and require special developmental focus. Given their accessibility issues, their survival depends on controlling sparse resources via social domination or on government schemes.

In thinking about how the survival of tribals is connected to our own, it is worth remembering that we all were tribes at a point of evolution. From being hunter-gatherers, and then learning agriculture, we evolved and differentiated ourselves from the animal kingdom. That's the reason I call myself a 'farmer growing start-ups'. Because I want the entrepreneur to be like a farmer—to find fertile ground, sow the idea, nurture it and enjoy the harvest like a visionary instead of trying their luck as hunters and gatherers. Another reason is to change the stigma around farming being an unviable profession. Also, my grandfather was a farmer and six of my investments are in agriculture-related ventures.

One series I really enjoyed watching was *Origins: The Journey of Humankind* by National Geographic. This showed how the invention of fire helped us in cooking meat that was hunted. The cooking softened it, so it reduced the chewing time. With more time in hand, the human race evolved faster compared to our animal friends and started to dominate the world. Today, we study, take a job, get married and settle in life. Once in a while, we pause and take a vacation to unwind, rewind or destress and we do all that by visiting a resort or going into the wilderness, or camping in the woods, calling it a 'digital detox' and other such trendy terms. But the tribals today, living in those wild places, should then be enjoying a resort 365 days. Instead, it is difficult for them to survive without the most basic facilities that we take for granted. As for their traditional lifestyle, connected to the forest and the environment, that is being threatened not only by the shrinking forest cover but also by the faulty judgement of their city-dwelling fellow citizens, who say that their lifestyle is wrong, they should not live in the forest and will spoil it.

A typical upper-middle-class house in a city contains a number of tables, beds and doors, which are all made of wood that was once a tree. So, who would need more wood, the city dwellers or the tribals? What is worse, the wood used by a city dweller is one-way consumption. The tribal lifestyle has always been about regeneration—where they cut trees, they also plant more.

But we say to them, come out of your forests, study, settle down and go back to your forest for a one-week vacation! If living in those forests for 365 days is wrong and invites being labelled as poor or ignorant, how is going to a forest resort for a mere week acceptable as development? Who defines who is rich and who is poor? What is considered valuable changes from time to time. In Europe, tulip flowers were once considered a valuable possession but today, gold is the object of value, which may be replaced tomorrow by something else. If carbon is tomorrow's gold, then the tribal communities are the richest. Why can't we leave these communities with enough resources for them to lead a peaceful life? They have fulfilled their role admirably as guardians of our forests for thousands of years.

Supporting and Showcasing the Amish Way of Life

I visited Amish County[5] when I lived in the US as I had heard quite a lot about their lifestyle. They are primarily agriculturists and lead very self-sustaining lives.

They make their own cloth, build their houses and perform most such tasks by coming together as a community. They don't completely rely on modern technologies as these reduce the time for hard work and also family time. They strongly believe in the value of time spent together. They use electricity and electrical appliances to a much lower extent than elsewhere in the US. Instead, they use oils, natural gas and other resources that they believe the earth has provided.

Their clothes are simple and they are against wearing jewellery, so as to avoid falling into the trap of vanity and to have more humility. This modest and close-to-nature lifestyle of theirs is not kept secret. In fact, they are proud of their values and their produce and they flaunt it in their villages, where you can go to see them and buy their amazing products. Is it possible for us to extend that kind of respect and exclusivity to preserve and honour the lifestyle of India's tribals? Let them live as they have always done. If any of them would like to be part of the fast world, they can study and experience the outside life. However, living in simplicity is always confused with poverty. So, how do we ensure they are not considered poor?

Pride Is the Key

Peggy Dulany Rockefeller, the heiress and philanthropist, has served on many corporate and non-profit boards and is the chair of Synergos, an organization that seeks to address how leadership can help solve complex issues. During her visit to Bengaluru in 2015 in connection with her Global Philanthropists Circle (GPC), she mentioned that the tribals of the Amazon Forest are today saying that they don't want to change their way of life. They are, however, still requesting people to document their lifestyle and share it with the outside world. What they are seeking to establish is pride in being who they are, how they are.

A city dweller who gives up their urban life and corporate career and moves to a village is considered as someone doing a great thing. Then why not evaluate someone living in a forest all their life similarly? Their simplicity makes them different from city dwellers, but how can we preserve and celebrate that? Should we compare a tribal person's carbon footprint with mine or that of someone living in New York or London? Doing so will prove that they are carbon preventers and probably the most sustainable people on the planet.

Amale Tigers

On 15 November 2018, after attending a round table organized by the National Bank for Agriculture and Rural Development (NABARD) on the agricultural start-up ecosystem, Rohit Pillai of Rural Caravan (RC) and Chaitanya Nadkarny of STARS Forum picked me up and we drove toward Amale, a small tribal village in the Palghar district of Maharashtra, located a few hours' drive from Mumbai.

I first met Rohit Pillai at the Tribal Entrepreneurship Summit in Dantewada, Chhattisgarh on 15 November 2017. The trip to Dantewada is a different story that I will describe later in this chapter. After I made my speech at the Dantewada summit, Rohit approached me and told me about his initiative of bringing access to technology especially suited to rural areas. I was really impressed by our short discussion and recommended that he apply for NSRCEL's Social Incubation.

So, exactly one year later, I was with him doing a field visit as his mentor at NSRCEL Social Cohort 2.

The drive of the entrepreneur is often just this: grabbing every opportunity presented and making full use of it. The supposedly short drive of 112 km took much longer as it took us around three hours just to get out of Mumbai and we reached Amale by midnight. On the way, we picked up Manish, another RC co-founder, who brought some nice chivda (a rice flake snack) for the trip since it was just after Diwali, giving me a tasty introduction to the Maharashtrian snack.

The last kilometre to Amale village is not accessible by road, so we had to walk. The villagers came to pick us up while we were parking, as they were waiting to have dinner with us that night. There was no electricity and even the solar microgrid installed by an NGO was not functional at that time. We went to Raju Barat's house, which was built in 2007 under a government programme and had a small solar panel powering 2 CFL lights in the house. After a nice simple dinner, had sitting on the floor, all four of us visitors and the family slept on the same floor—the house had a living area and a kitchen, that's all. When I woke up in the morning, there was already evidence of much action. I came out and saw the nice courtyard. Raju was the proprietor of a tiny shop, in fact, the only shop in the village, in front of his house. The kitchen wall was built of woven bamboo with a covering of mud to hold it together. I walked across to the bank of the stream, where RC had built a modern toilet with running water, pumped by the treadle pump from the stream up to a small overhead tank.

When I got back, breakfast was being prepared— bhakri, made with ragi, jowar and bajra flour. Raju and Rohit took me to their kitchen and showed me their product at work there—a clean cooking stove built by Raju and his team! RC was started by Rohit and a few of his friends from

IIT Bombay who were studying at the Centre for Technology Alternatives for Rural Areas (CTARA). The treadle pump is one such innovation by another team there. RC aimed to make a rural village self-sustaining, without people feeling the need for migration. They identified Amale where, during the monsoon, people are focused on agriculture, but during the summer, they migrate temporarily to Mumbai as they don't have enough money saved up.

RC noted that Amale had a small stream with a beautiful waterfall a few kilometres upstream, so water was not an issue. It is surrounded by an extension of the Western Ghats and Tansa Hills with stunning views on all sides. So, there was the potential to invite tourists for a homestay or bring schoolchildren for a few days of rural immersion. For this reason, they built toilets equipped with an overhead tank and set up small shed for discussions. Next, they developed a technology that could provide them with additional livelihoods and reduce the temporary migration from Amale to Mumbai during the summer. They developed a smokeless cooking stove that could be built using local earth and materials, needing only a smoke pipe for the chimney to be brought from outside. They also designed a simple mould which reduced the skill required to make the stove. Now the villagers just needed to keep the mould and place bricks appropriately, plaster it with earth and place the chimney pipe. Knowing the science of how the flame behaves and using the closed structure technology, a three-burner stove is ready, on which they can use their usual firewood but without the smoke. We sat around on the floor for a nice breakfast with no plates required as the bhakri was kept in one hand and chutney served in its middle. As we were eating, the whole team of stove-makers also began to gather around us for a meeting.

Raju Barat has two children. Aruna had passed the Class 12 examinations with 64 per cent marks and studied *Arthashastra* (economics) at the Ashram Shala residential school run by the state government in Palsunda, about 60 km away. People in Amale usually get their children to study from Class 1 to Class 4 at the village school, Class 5 to Class 10 in residential schools and Classes 11 and 12 at Suryamal, which is a 3-km walk through shortcuts across forests and fields. Only 30 per cent of the girl students study as far as Class 12. They are attracted by the city but don't like it after some time. I spoke to several young girl and boy students in this regard. Mathu told me she didn't want to go to the city. She wanted to learn how to operate computers and help with the RC initiative.

Savarpada, who was twenty-six years old then, said, 'Amale is better, the only problem is after the rains, we have to go out for work. If people here don't need to migrate and have some economic activity, that would be very good.' In his estimation, a job paying Rs 7000 per month was good and Rs 15,000 per month was great. Then, even for emergencies, they need not worry, he felt. Some of the people I spoke to told me how they got employment under the Mahatma Gandhi National Rural Employment Guarantee Act (MNREGA) scheme that provided Rs 200 per day. They were earlier getting this amount in cash. Now, with the shift to digital India, they had to make four trips to the bank.

What about local herbals, I asked them. Hadumodi was used to treat fractures. At Rs 1200 a kg, samta paste provided a good income, but they could only collect half a kg in a day as they had to go to the hills to do so. The village had around twenty pukka houses and fifty mud houses built with a government support of Rs 28,000 per house in 2007.

I noticed that the older generation was used to hard work and agriculture but did not have much outside exposure. The next generation had a little education, did not want to do agriculture and appeared confused. Amale is not well-connected to the outside world, so it still feels like a village from older times. The third generation, still in school or college, wanted education and thought about migrating. Some had degrees but were still not able to clear interviews and therefore unable to find well-paying jobs.

Some of the older people who talked to me recalled the good old days when, after a good rain, they ate tubers from the forest. Tubers grown around running water reduces their bitterness. When the rains began slowing down, they started agriculture but it did not seem as viable as their earlier existence and they felt stuck. Some were trying out other agricultural products apart from paddy, such as cauliflower and jasmine, and were making around Rs 40,000 a month.

Raju used to work for a sand-mining company and he had to dive 60 feet into the Arabian Sea to place the trawlers in the precise spot to collect sand from the ocean bed for the construction industry, making Rs 1200 a day. Divers usually wear all kinds of gear such as wet suits, underwater goggles and oxygen tanks, and even undergo training for SCUBA diving. Raju, however, dives without any such gear and one wrong move could put his life in jeopardy.

The quality of life is better in the village and those who had lived in the city revealed that they were not happy there. If the village got a good mobile network and electricity, they would live here and look for newer opportunities in their own environment.

Now, making cooking stoves has become an additional livelihood. The stove costs around Rs 1000–1500. It consumes 66 per cent less wood, as the earthen coat with local mud reduces heat. The team had built 200 stoves since my visit, in villages within a 40 km radius. It takes three people to make one stove and they can make up to three stoves a day. Until then, five people had been trained. The government provides them with one free LPG gas cylinder and they have to buy cylinders subsequently. Receiving the replacement can take up to a week. As a result, they use LPG only as a backup and prefer cooking with firewood, as food cooked with firewood tastes different and is part of their culture.

I was sad to hear that, a few weeks before my visit, someone in the village had died of a snakebite. At the village entrance, we see the deities meant to protect the villagers. I saw a statue of the tiger, whom they also worship. I asked them, your forefathers lived here with tigers and they knew the forest well and its herbal remedies for many ailments. Now, is the current generation feeling ashamed of all that, losing precious information, so that they couldn't even handle a snakebite? I told Mathu that she needed to document what the elders in the village knew and store it on a computer! We need to bring back their pride in their own knowledge systems.

After the breakfast discussion, we went to a nearby village from where the team had received an order to make the smokeless stove. That customer looked relatively well-off and the team made the stove pretty quickly using the mould and available local earth. They were very happy with the extra income making smokeless stoves, which reduced their need to migrate.

We had lunch at Raju's house and then looked around Amale, where I saw a family threshing their newly harvested paddy. The husband, wife and children were all working to collect and bag the grains. A few kilometres away, we reached the top of a beautiful waterfall at a height of about 50 feet. We walked down and I enjoyed a nice bath at the falls. I saw pictures of young children diving from the top into the pool that was created by the falls. These children would definitely win diving competitions, alongside someone learning similar techniques with a coach in the city. On the way back as well, I saw around five or six children on top of a huge tree, enjoying their beautiful village. But soon, they would be fed with thoughts that would make them consider all the beauty of the village irrelevant. 'We are poor and must join the rat race with people in the cities to get ourselves a better life,' they may begin to think.

Such perceptions can only be changed if the value of the knowledge, skills and the environment that they have always known as their own is recognized and upheld. They can then continue to enjoy what they have. If we calculate their carbon footprint based on their simple houses and needs and their life without electricity, they would emerge richer than many so-called rich people. After these rich life lessons in Amale, we drove to Nashik and caught a train back to Mumbai, with Rohit ensuring that I was loaded with chivda in Nashik!

Dantewada Adventure

On 4 November 2017, I received an email from Saurabh Kumar, IAS, the collector and district magistrate of Dakshin Bastar Dantewada, Chhattisgarh, stating, 'The tribal regions in India are bestowed with the wealth of natural resources like forest and minerals and traditional knowledge that the tribal communities possess about the natural eco-system, medicinal plants, forest produce, handicrafts and agriculture. Ironically these regions are also one of the most underdeveloped and face problems of great scale such as poverty, malnutrition, low literacy and poor health. These mammoth problems can only be solved when inspired individuals challenge the status quo with their entrepreneurial zeal and spirit of innovation and develop solutions building on the core strengths of the tribal regions.'

Saurabh invited me to speak at India's first Tribal Entrepreneurship Summit on 14 November 2017 at Dantewada, Chhattisgarh. This summit was organized by NITI Aayog as part of the 8th Global Entrepreneurship Summit being held in India for the first time through the joint efforts of the governments of India and the US. They sought the participation of tribal entrepreneurs from various sectors across the country.

I was really cheered to know about this initiative by the government and wholeheartedly accepted the invitation to speak at the event. When I began sharing with my urban friends about my upcoming Dantewada visit, they were all ready to say goodbye with a 'Nice knowing you, Naga!' citing how dangerous Dantewada's reputation was as a place packed with extremists. That's exactly what I felt needed to be addressed and definitely, entrepreneurship was one of the ways to do it. So, I decided to visit.

From Vizag, we were to take an overnight train to Chhattisgarh. When I landed in Vizag, I was told that one train had been cancelled and the other one was running twenty-four hours late. Two vehicles had been arranged for around ten-plus people who were all supposed to be attending the conference. On the way, we picked up a few of them and reached Dantewada in the morning. What followed was a very interesting experience with people scrambling all over for accommodation. This had been arranged at an under-construction local college. In the confusion, I managed to locate a friend, Saquib Nabi, who was part of Change Alliance, Bangladesh, and was also scheduled to speak at the event. He came to my rescue, as he had already worked there for two years and knew how to navigate the procedures of government-organized programmes.

I was pleasantly surprised by the turnout and the fact that many social entrepreneurs who had been trying different innovations across the country would be presenting their work. I had never before attended any programme with such a visible presence of security forces around us, as this one. It was apparent that the administration and officials had pulled out all the stops to make us feel secure, as Dantewada is one of the Naxal hotspots of the country.

The various initiatives taken by the young collector and other officials to bring development in the region through entrepreneurship could be seen as soon as we arrived. The electric autorickshaws that drove us from our accommodation to the event venue were driven by women drivers. Many young people had studied and established themselves well in cities who were attending the event to consider how to contribute back to the region.

The conference started with a very powerful performance by the tribals wearing their traditional attire, with a headdress adorned with bull horns. It was mesmerizing to watch! I have spoken about the Nativelead Foundation and their efforts at creating systems to help locals with the help of locals and people from elsewhere who have settled there.

Bringing pride to local products, I saw the collectors' initiative around a local delicacy branded and sold as

Imli Chaska. This is a tamarind-based product, part of the traditional tribal kitchen and it has been branded and marketed with help from the government. Similarly, there was the Bastar Honey team, a group that trains tribal youth on wearing protective gear and following safe practices while going into forests to collect wild honey. From the tribal youths, I learnt that they take only certain portions of the hive where the honey is stored, without harming the bees. The young man explaining to me gave the example of our homes—just as in our houses, food is cooked in the kitchen, they know which part has the honey, and take only that portion and don't harm the honey bees.

Lunch was also a fabulous experience where I tasted their delicacy of 'Ant Chutney' for the first time. My Dantewada adventure was coming to an end as I was returning that night. I was leaving early, set to attend an event in Bengaluru the next day. So, I was travelling alone at night with a young driver from Vizag, who was a college student working part-time. I had slept off, only to be awakened by the driver at midnight. He was very scared and told me, 'Sir, there is no road.'

Conscious of the heavy Naxal activity in that area, we both were scared and we just stayed put. There was no mobile signal for the Internet; his phone GPS was pointing to a road, but there was no road ahead. This was also the first time he had come to this part of the country. After some time, we saw a bike rider coming towards us; we quietly started following him. We were very scared, as we had heard and read a lot of stories about incidents in that area. Following the bike rider took us along a way where there was no proper road at all—it was just a mud path. After a while, we noticed in the pitch dark around us, that we were moving through the forest. The bike rider stopped and parked his bike, turned and started walking towards us. Both, the driver and I were very worried. He asked us why we were following him, speaking in the local language. We both didn't understand, as the driver spoke only Telugu and I can manage a little broken Hindi.

I pointed to my conference badge and told him we were lost. At the event venue, we had been warned by several people not to mention that it was a government programme to anyone. Somehow, he got convinced and allowed us to follow him. After quite a while on the mud path, we reached the proper road and he rode away. What an experience that was! It was an eye-opening reminder of the vast differences and disparities in our country. After that nerve-wracking ride through the forest, reaching Vizag airport at around 6 a.m. seemed like a different world. I caught my flight back to the start-up capital and Silicon Valley of India, Bengaluru, to speak at an event organized by the Confederation of Indian Industry (CII) on entrepreneurship. When I narrated the experience of the night before, many in the audience couldn't believe this happens in India. That's a part of the problem as well. So many in the corporate ecosystem have little idea of vast sections of India and how their fellow Indians live in those parts.

Wrong Side or Right Side?

Udyogini was a name I had heard quite a lot about from Srikrishna of Sattva Consulting—one of my investments. It had also been supported by Change Alliance and Phia. Every time I visited a place, I would check with Change Alliance about the projects that were being supported in that region and they would find a project nearby for me to visit. One time, they took me to Udyogini.

I was returning after attending a regional consultation in September 2014 in Bangladesh arranged by Change Alliance and caught a Shatabdi from Kolkata to Ranchi to visit Udyogini's work. Bundu, 41 km from Ranchi was the hub of Udyogini's work, also in one of the country's top ten Naxal-affected areas. Poverty pushes people in different ways. Some migrate for better prospects; some stay and survive somehow; some get into the cadres of extremist groups.

The Udyogini folks need to take permission to take visitors there. Since they are working for the benefit of the community, they have not faced problems from the locals. They work with tribals who collect lac, a resin that comes out of the tree whenever we scratch the bark or if some insect eats a portion of it. That's how rubber is also produced, by having a cut on the bark from which a sap comes out, gets collected in a bowl and is used to make rubber.

Jharkhand has a large tribal population that makes up approximately 28 per cent of the state's total population. The Asur is one of the most ancient ethnic groups in Jharkhand. The tribal farmers of Jharkhand have long been depending on lac farming for their livelihood. Lac is secreted by insects that feed on the trees like kusum, ber and palash, which are abundant in Jharkhand. This resin-like secretion finds use in a wide range of industries, including food products and processing, and paint. The varied uses of this lac are described as:

'Shellac was once used as a varnish in wood finishing agents across the world till it was replaced by vinyl, electrical insulation as it has very good insulation properties, automobile, cosmetics, adhesive, leather, wood furnishing and other industries. Lac was mainly used for making ornaments like bangles, jewellery.'[6]

In Channapatna toys, named after the town in Karnataka, lac is mixed with natural colours like turmeric yellow and a nice shiny coloured coat is applied. I learnt that during my visit to Maya Organic in Channapatna. Traditionally, lac has been an important ingredient in the crafts industry. Jharkhand alone produces over 50 per cent of the national output of lac.

From being a major source of income, lac production fell dramatically some years ago as a result of lac ornaments becoming unpopular. The projected output dropped from as much as one lakh tonnes of lac per year to under 10,000 tonnes, which affected Jharkhand's status as a lac-producing zone as well. With lac distribution in the grip of middlemen, farmers also failed to realize the desired prices for their lac output. Further, even as the tribal farmers planted more trees that could host lac insects, they found the trees were barely laden with lac, despite multiple infestations. One factor was the climate—extremely hot summers followed by sparse monsoon showers. Crop-growing techniques also appeared to be behind the times.

Earlier, much of the lac produced was exported, with only 20–50 per cent used within the country. The foreign demand also fell away with lac distributors hiking the price exorbitantly, well beyond the usual price fluctuations. More shockingly, lac is underutilized due to the distances that separate the farmers from the markets currently importing raw lac. Strengthening the lac supply chain and establishing market channels continues to be a challenge for the farmers. While farmers can partially process the lac and even store it in their homes, it is a perishable commodity that requires dedicated storage facilities with significant capacity. As a result of poor income from lac, many locals have given up on it and moved on to agriculture, etc., which, found to be not viable, also pushes them further into poverty.

Lac/kh-pati—Old Economy to New Economy

Udyogini started working on the Inclusion and Economic Empowerment of Tribal Women in lac value chain markets. As the locals had lost valuable knowledge of lac and the insects, Udyogini started to look at the scientific cultivation of lac. Not far from Bundu, there is IINRG! The Indian Institute of Natural Resins and Gums (IINRG) by the Indian Council of Agricultural Research (ICAR) in Ranchi is almost a 100-year-old organization that's working on various technologies in improving the production of lac and its processing. They have found lac's use in more industries. With their help, a new lac brood was brought in. This is pretty much an insect developed in the lab. They need to tie this brood on the tree, so the insect will start feeding on the tree for the lac to come out. The first time, there was a setback when the wrong brood was tied to the wrong tree (kusum, ber, palash) so the result was bad. The locals were reluctant to believe in the lac brood and had to be recalled with a lot of persuasion. When the right brood was tied to the right tree, it started producing lac in a good manner.

Tribal Women Entrepreneurs

Now that production had been addressed, a need was felt to fix the market for the output. Udyogini started creating Village Level Service Centres (VLSC) run by rural women trained in I-USE (Intel-Udyogini School of Entrepreneurship).[7] These centres enable women entrepreneurs to help villagers access markets and services in their villages. Primarily providing services of aggregating village produce and then linking them to the market, providing special/social products for improving lifestyles, agriculture inputs, educational products, health and hygiene products and in addition, catering to the daily domestic needs of the village.

The attempt is to select women who show potential as change-bearers and train them at the village level to be Village Level Entrepreneurs (VLE). This training involves a two-month intensive skill and management training programme with a customized training kit, is completed with a one-month internship programme to understand business operations practically. Financial linkages are provided to establish enterprises and market linkages for product/service–procurement/supply. The training also makes the VLEs aware of corporate and government partnerships and gives them a nine-month handholding service to get their enterprise up and running. There is also a refresher training based on the need assessment. Udyogini has a start-up kit for business, R&D and products for scale. They have the means to provide outreach programmes in the business process, develop institutional models, finance, social and gender support services.

A trained VLE[8] aggregates the entire village's lac produce, so that she gets scale of economies and has also been trained to call the Mumbai market where she can check the price of lac. When she finds the price is good, she informs the buyers of the price at which the villagers are selling and the buyers come and pick it up. Premature brood lac could be sold at Rs 300/kg whereas holding it for fifteen to twenty days would fetch Rs 450/kg. This way, the price information arbitrage is eliminated. One VLE was proudly showing me the accounts she manages in the ledger book.

Now, since she is the VLE, she has also learnt enough about business to run a shop to provide the necessary things that a village would need. Thus, she acts both ways—marketing their products and bringing products for them.

With this success of getting production-related knowledge, more people are now going back to lac collection which requires less effort—trim the tree appropriately, tie the brood to the correct tree and spray it a few times, for which a machine has been provided. One person I met had accumulated Rs 1 lakh in the bank, making him a legitimate lac(kh)pati. He proudly told me how he had the money to pay for his son when the latter required a visit to the hospital. Wearing just a towel around his waist, he lives a very simple life and Rs 1 lakh in the bank provides a feeling that if he needs money, he need not run around. It has thus mentally lifted him out of poverty. Several other lakhpatis like him have been created and now some of them are wanting to do value addition activities—lacbrood production, scraping and purifying the lac and other processes.

I was happy to see that many of their houses looked pretty good, with tiled roofs that would have been built a few decades back. Once they have hope for the future, they begin to live well. At the Udyogini office, I saw a spraying machine for lac and more innovations around the value addition of lac.

The next day, I visited Chakkala village where Gramvani, was operating, which is one of my other investments. It is a rural platform for social development that enables over 8,00,000 households across twelve Indian states to create their own voice media, leading to local action, greater awareness and empowerment for development. This gives voice to the poor, where people call a toll-free number and share news, problems, etc. This gets played when someone else calls from that area. Many anonymous calls offering information are shared with the authorities for them to act upon. Today, this system is used in garment factories as well, for people to share anonymous information that affects people.

Every Pocket Has Wealth

On the way back to Ranchi, I saw an Audi showroom. Just a few kilometres from where people living in abject poverty were being pushed to extremities, here was a showroom with evidence that someone could afford a luxury car. What looked like inequality on the face of it also brought, at least for me, a reassurance—that there is wealth in every pocket of India. This strengthened my hope in building Nativelead Foundation, with the goal of ploughing back this wealth by developing local entrepreneurs to slow down the migration. I sensed that this model can work even in Jharkhand and explained this at the partner meeting of Change Alliance (CA)'s Poorest Areas Civil Society (PACS) Programme, Jharkhand. Nativelead's investment arm, Native Angels Network (NAN) was launched in Madurai on 19 October 2014, just a few weeks after this visit.

Four

Enterprise in Every Corner

'I'm encouraging young people to become social business entrepreneurs and contribute to the world, rather than just making money. Making money is no fun. Contributing to and changing the world is a lot more fun'.

—Muhammad Yunus

The year 2020 began with a bang for me and proved to be instrumental in showing me just how much potential for unleashing the entrepreneurial spirit of our people exists in the remotest corners of our vast country. Undoubtedly, our economic growth has been hampered by some regions of the country remaining cut off from the more populated central regions due to difficulties in terrain, infrastructure development and administration.

I was fortunate to be allowed to overcome these hurdles and see first-hand how start-ups in places as far apart as the North-eastern states and Kerala have found ways to use local produce, practices and processes to achieve good results.

What Kerala Did Right

Inequality is one of the two most urgent problems facing the world today, the other being climate change. Social businesses that can build a triple-bottom-line framework may offer a solution to these problems. However, the present model of development, which seems to suggest populating 100 cities with 1.5 billion people, needs rethinking. Villages cannot simply be emptied and their people relocated to cities for work while living in slums.

The alternative, as seems to be the case in Kerala, is to spread development uniformly and ensure that villages offer the same access to resources as towns and cities. Understanding the ideology, systems and processes in place in Kerala can be a good starting point for such an exercise. Another point to remember is that some sections of Kerala's society continue to be matrilineal, just like the Garo people of Meghalaya and a few other communities globally, which contributed to women's empowerment (as enshrined in the United Nations' Sustainable Development Goal 5).

The detailed discussion I had with Prof. Jiju P. Alex, a member of Kerala's State Planning Board, offered interesting insights about the Kerala development model. One view is that the evolution of Kerala's development model has a historical context, with various social reform movements starting from the eighteenth century rendering the society amenable to development. Many of these movements aimed at educating and empowering the oppressed classes and castes and the nationalist movement furthered this renaissance, as did the advent of socialist politics. For instance, the communists won the first state elections in Kerala in 1957, and launched land reforms through the Kerala Land Reform Act, 1963. These reforms

gave agricultural laborers and various tenants the full right
to own the land they tilled, so to speak.

Further, public spending on education, healthcare and
social security has continued unabated despite different
political parties coming to power in Kerala. As a result,
the state has seen the growth of an educated class whose
members subsequently emigrated for employment and
boosted Kerala's economy through remittances. Kerala
also has the highest female-to-male ratio in the country at
1.084 (as per the 2011 census); in comparison, the national
ratio is 0.940. The state's literacy rate, the target of several
major campaigns, is also the highest in the country at 94
per cent.[1]

In the 1990s, India undertook local self-governance
reforms through the Constitution (73rd Amendment)
Act and Constitution (74th Amendment) Act in 1992,
devolving power to local bodies at the village, town and
city levels. In Kerala, however, measures to enhance local
democracy were far more radical, with as much as 26 per
cent of the state's budget outlay directed towards local
governance institutions, which resulted in the creation of
powerful district councils.

The reforms in Kerala, although only enacted in the
1990s, stemmed from decades of discussions through
several committees and commissions, and were seen as the
natural outcome of several socio-economic and political
interactions. Comparing various reforms in Kerala with
those in other states such as Maharashtra shows that
reforms have only sporadically succeeded elsewhere. In
Kerala, local government bodies, which earlier had few
sources of revenue or cash reserves, received at least Rs 4–5
crore each, along with institutional support for handling
this sum. Further, robust mechanisms were evolved to

formulate projects at the grassroots level, enabling people to participate in the planning process.

For twenty-five years, as many as twelve sectors have been handled by local governments, giving people the scope, freedom and flexibility to intervene directly in planning projects and replacing the 'department-ism' pervasive in other states. The experiences of Kerala villages offer valuable lessons for building awareness among the grassroots and leveraging institutions at that level. Implementing these, needless to say, requires the political will to combat or revolt against extant caste and socio-economic disparities and power equations in rural areas. Also, unless the state government itself is transformed, the policies, processes, laws and bye-laws necessary to implement these reforms may not become reality.

Eight States in Six Weeks

Just before the pandemic lockdowns started in March 2020, for the first two months, I had a tightly packed travel schedule across the country, and I ended up travelling through eight states in six weeks. The year had begun with a buzz around start-up activities with chief ministers (CMs), deputy CMs, Union ministers, the NITI Aayog CEO and cabinet ministers in various states climbing aboard the bandwagon of ushering in the visible results of economic activity.

I was glad to sow the seeds of social business everywhere. In Kolkata, I attended the Tata Social Challenge at IIM Calcutta and visited a rural education start-up, Krishworks. While in Kerala, I was at the Value Addition for Income Generation in Agriculture (VAIGA) event organized by the state's Agriculture Ministry at Thrissur and also went to Farmers Fresh Zone in Kochi. Likewise, I was present at the first anniversary of Assam Startup in Guwahati, an Entrepreneurship Summit in Shillong and a field visit to the William Nagar area of the East Garo Hills. I met the IIT Madras Investment Committee and attended the launch of Startup Tamil Nadu's Thedal initiative in Coimbatore, apart from travelling to Rajasthan to visit Craft Catapult in Jaipur, to Nagpur, Maharashtra, to learn about the Lemon Ideas platform, Innopreneurs, and to Karnataka for the Karnataka State Rural Livelihood Mission's field visits to Yellapur, Siddapur and Shivamogga.

Cardamom Coasters and Banana Kurta

On 20 January 2020, I arrived in Guwahati to attend Assam Startup's first anniversary and interacted with their start-ups working on Eri silk, kombucha, purple tea, etc., followed by a visit to the North Eastern Development Finance Corporation (NEDFI). Their CSR focuses quite a lot on the crafts of the North-east and they run a craft gallery on their premises where we can see all the craft wonders of the North-east. I am always impressed by the innovations they introduce me to. Exactly a year back, I had been in Guwahati for the Assam CM's unveiling of the state start-up policy and was very glad to hear that the state was looking at SDG standards. At that time, I had bought banana fibre fabric at the craft gallery. This time, I took home cardamom fibre coasters and left for Shillong, a pleasant ride of around 100 km.

Oxygen Tax

The next day was Meghalaya's launch of an entrepreneurship summit by the chief minister and NITI Aayog CEO. Entrepreneurs can and should play a major role in the development of the region, emphasizing how to play on their strength—nature! Developing this region just like other parts of the country should not be attempted as they have preserved nature very well. I have even hinted to them that the rest of the country should pay an 'oxygen tax' to the North-east so that they continue to preserve their natural surroundings.

The three areas that the North-east could focus on can be tourism, agriculture and crafts. All of these should be targeted at a really premium segment.

That day, I was wearing the banana fibre fabric kurta that I had bought during my previous visit to the North-east. I have mentioned that this could be the first-ever fabric made from banana that is available in the country. Mixed with cotton fibre, my banana fabric kurta looked like silk, because of the golden shine of the banana fibre. This is the potential of the region—valuing their local products, traditional weaves.

Duitara and Haldi

At the entrepreneurship summit, I was very glad to see an eighty-year-old entrepreneur being recognized among other entrepreneurs. I was also happy to note that most of them were working on the strengths of Meghalaya. I learnt that the variety of turmeric from Meghalaya has a higher level of curcumin than the one grown elsewhere in the country—one start-up was making haldi latte. There was another one making Eri silk and one presenting wild apple produce.

One thing that remained with me was the love for music among the people of Meghalaya. In the evenings, their crafts and innovation were on display in a fashion show and a musical performance with the local musical instrument called duitara.[2] This is a guitar-like four-stringed instrument whose strings are made of Muga silk, collected from the wild. All these products deserve to be known and cherished by a wider audience and I had hopes of that from the summit. The next morning, we returned to Guwahati, by driving through beautiful vistas that proved Meghalaya as the abode of clouds.

The Truck Trails

After a session with the Guwahati-based start-ups, I left on a field visit to the East Garo Hills in Meghalaya to see the work done by Sauramandala Foundation[3] towards transforming villages, which was incubated at NSRCEL's social programme. Nagakarthik picked me up, along with another NGO partner, and we proceeded to William Nagar, Meghalaya. We passed through Daranggiri, tagged as Asia's largest banana market, trading place of one of the treasures of Assam—bananas. It was thus no wonder that NEDFI had chosen to work on banana fibre.

The National Research Centre for Banana (NRCB) is located in Assam and the second one is in Trichy, Tamil Nadu. I had seen the banana market in Trichy and wondered about the volume that is traded there, and how it compares with that in Daranggiri. However, I could only imagine this volume; we couldn't see it in action, as we were passing through this place only in the evening. It is located in lower Assam and is near the Meghalaya border.

As soon as we entered Meghalaya, another issue faced by the North-east was immediately evident—the logistics challenge. Trucks were waiting to enter Assam at the border, lining up for miles. I couldn't see many of them with a cold storage facility, so perhaps quite a big portion of the agricultural produce in those trucks could see severe damage and end up as waste.

When we reached William Nagar circuit house, the temperature showed 13 degrees Celsius. We stayed there and the food was delivered by a start-up serving local delicacies.

Areca Nut or Not?

In the morning we left for Bolmoram village, passing a water stream. It appeared as if, on rainy days with the stream full of water, it would be tough to get to the village. We passed a village market where people were selling local produce. It was interesting to see the areca nut was a major item of produce, and a woman was freshly seeding the fermented areca nut on demand for people to buy.

I had been noting that areca nut or supari, is becoming a mono-crop across Karnataka, Kerala, Assam and Meghalaya. I didn't know whether this was a good trend as most of it goes into the consumption of paan! Even while landing in Guwahati, I had seen the wide amount of areca nut cultivation. When visiting a few districts of Karnataka, I saw people seeding the areca nut in villages. Pretty much every house had areca nuts drying on their roof. Similarly, in Kerala, farmers are moving from rubber cultivation to areca nut as it provides more value and they let pepper vines crawl on the areca nut trees. Even though it has some medicinal qualities, since it is mostly used in paan and paan masalas that have been linked to oral cancer, I have reservations about this monocrop taking over so many hectares across the country. In fact, no urban denizen in India could have failed to see drivers on city roads who have paan or paan masala in their mouths and are unable to even talk. They keep opening their car or cab doors to spit out the juice on the roads. This eyesore can also be seen in many public places, especially on the staircases of public buildings.

Now with more growing of areca nut, along with some of its medicinal value, there is also an opportunity for entrepreneurs to find new uses of this fruit. One of the visible products that has made its way to the market is the plate made from areca nut trees. The areca nut plates are made by a growing cottage industry, giving us a good and environmentally sound alternative to replacing single-use paper plates.

Fish Sanctuary

Our journey to Bolmoram continued, with some more insights into the local practices of the region. We stopped at a small pond, where locals fish for their needs and to sell the fish. Overfishing had made everyone struggle to find fish, so the people came up with an interesting concept to address their problems.

They had turned that space into a tourist spot, calling it the Nengmandalgre Fish Sanctuary, with fish feeding being a big attraction for tourists. When we went there, we saw huge schools of fish already grown to good sizes. Once the population has grown too dense for the pond, the villagers catch them and share them among themselves. This is a good example of how communities find out their own sustainable means to retain the diversity and resources of their environment.

When we reached Bolmoram village, we headed to a nice building named Bolmoram Nappakol Knowledge Park. It is an initiative by the Integrated Basin Development and Livelihood Promotion (IBDLP) of the Meghalaya government.[4] It was nice to see that the goal of this programme is to achieve balanced development. They aim for ecologically sustainable and inclusive development by involving people in the process through an entrepreneur-led model that improves livelihood opportunities in the area. Sauramandala has been working with them to bring appropriate partners for the gap. The facility is solar-powered by Selco, which also provides solar dryers for food processing. During our visit, around fifteen people were there to get training on various entrepreneurship opportunities and best practices.

Incubator at the DC Office

We went on to visit the East Garo Hills District Collectorate office.[5] Accompanied by the dynamic Deputy Commissioner Swapnil Tempe, an IIT-Kharagpur alumnus IAS officer, we had a good interaction with the local entrepreneurs and officials, reiterating the importance of playing on Meghalaya's strengths. I was really impressed to see that the DC office had become an incubator and a marketplace.

There was a shop inside the campus with the tagline 'SHG corner—Come partner with us . . . support local entrepreneurs.' This is where some of the local entrepreneurs were displaying and selling their products. I bought a shawl there made of Eri and Muga silk. When I closely examined the shawl, I realized something about the power of Eri silk. It gave me the answer to why, after many visits to the North-east, I had hardly seen wool products which are a normal sight in every other hilly and cold region. The answer lay in the qualities of Eri silk! Eri has thermal properties that make it unique as a warm fabric for winter and cool material for summer.

Eri comes from 'era', which means 'castor' in Assamese, as the caterpillars that spin the silk feed on castor. Usually, Eri silk is made from the cocoon after the moth has left it, thus producing a non-violent silk with a lustre and a slightly coarse and rough texture like wool. Since the worms are not killed during the process of collecting the silk, it is also called non-violent or Ahimsa silk.

One other development that brought much satisfaction when we learnt of it at the DC office, was that George, one of the local entrepreneurs, had started Ecocraft. This collects all the paper waste of the DC office, converts it into recycled paper and folders on the premises itself and these are used once again at the DC office. A working model of a zero-waste DC office!

Beautiful Dakmanda

The Dakmanda is a traditional dress of Meghalayan women. We went to see a weaver, Mina Marak, who owned nine looms and provided work for four weavers to make this traditional dress. Usually, across the country, I had tended to see only an older generation of men and women in weaving as it's not remunerative. Here I was surprised to meet Sonamoni, a young girl who could not afford to go to college as there are seven members in her family. She had become a weaver just four months ago since she couldn't find any other work and was earning Rs 3000.

Sonamoni was working on a very intricate floral pattern woven into the fabric that would take around three weeks to finish. This work of art sells for around Rs 9000. This seemed to bear out my controversial statement that

'Crafts should not be affordable to the middle class. If they are, it means that someone (weaver) is living in poverty.' Also, we must take care to make sure that the products are more authentic. I saw the shiny threads around the floral pattern and learnt from Mina that it was plastic or metal-covered plastic thread.

Bolmoram—the Place of Souls

Our night stay had been arranged at Bolmoram centre. By the time we reached our quarters, we saw that people who had come for the training had already started a campfire and were sitting around it and chatting in the cold night air of around 10 degrees Celsius. We joined them and enjoyed a wonderful evening made special by their singing their special songs.

By the time the food was ready, we had all become more familiar with each other and thoroughly enjoyed the local delicacies. After our dinner, Andrew, who takes care of the centre, started telling us stories about Bolmoram. He was originally from this village and had migrated to Delhi because of a lack of local opportunities. But after some time, he didn't like his life in the city, where he worked in a bar. He managed to study while working and came back to his village as a trainer at the knowledge park. He was clearly very happy to be able to return to his village and help others with their livelihood.

This was a typical example of what I call 'city-returned'. These are the people who come back from cities knowing both good and bad aspects of city life as well as the good and bad aspects of living in the village. They are more easily able to bridge the good of both places and make rural livelihoods better. This also removes the feeling of the other side being greener, a feeling that is quite natural to humans. Unless you have also experienced the other side, you don't begin to appreciate what you have.

We continued to sit in the kitchen after eating our dinner, enjoying the warmth of the hearth. Andrew told us about how, in an earlier time, his grandparents would have to walk for weeks to market their produce. The name of the village was then Bolbokram (that has turned to Bolmoram today), meaning 'souls'. This is because the villagers believe their forefathers' souls reside in the nearby hills and as a pagan society, they used to worship them. He went on to talk about the matrilineal, matriarchal Garo society and the Jhum cultivation system that they practised. Listening to his accounts of these three embedded traditions convinced me once more about how the past already had answers to most of the current problems.

Women Rule

I was aware of Kerala having a matrilineal society,[6] but it was fresh learning for me to know that the Garo people practised it as well. Among the Garo, kinship is passed on through the mother's side, making it matrilineal and the head of the household is the mother, making it matriarchal as well. After marriage, men come to live in their wife's home. Children use the surname of the mother instead of the father's. The first daughter becomes the head of the family and the last daughter inherits the property.

Since most of us are conditioned to think of society in patrilineal and patriarchal terms, it is important to understand social arrangements that are just the opposite. In a matrilineal and matriarchal community, the women lead the society and hold political leadership. The head of the village is a woman and her daughters inherit that. Every year she assigns areas to cultivate for the farmers; thus she can exercise control over the Jhum or Jhoom cultivation.

Today, there is much talk about gender equality in the SDGs that have been outlined by the UN. Goal number 5 out of 17 goals is: 'Achieve gender equality and empower all women and girls'.[7] But the Garo have been practising this for a very long time. This was one more instance where I felt that Bharat had the solutions for the sustainable future, without needing to emulate only Western models of social arrangement and inclusion.

> *'The surest way to keep people down is to educate the men and neglect the women. If you educate a man, you simply educate an individual, but if you educate a woman, you educate a whole nation.'*
> —James Emman Kwegyir Aggrey

Of the ten living matriarchal societies of the world, two are from India—the Garo and Khasi tribes of Meghalaya.[8]

Jhum or Jhoom

The Jhum or Jhoom cultivation that Andrew described to us is a form of slash-and-burn agriculture where portions of the forest are cleared and the felled vegetation is left on the cleared area for rains to convert it into a form of waste that is burnt after it dries.

This burning leaves a residue of ash that is rich with nutrients to make the soil fertile and has cleared the ground of other pests and weeds as well. Cultivation on such a ground has good results and the locals have the experience to judge when the area has lost productivity over a period of five years or so, after which it is left to grow back as forest and another portion is marked for clearing.

In effect, the practice of Jhum cultivation is similar to other ideas about regeneration and repair that I have heard among tribals in places as far apart as Jharkhand, Maharashtra and Andhra Pradesh. Take a little portion of the forest, claim it for some time, return it to its wild and natural form and come back to it after it has had a chance to regenerate its life-giving properties once more. It is practices like this, with their scale, that have enabled communities like the Garo to exist alongside forests and mountains since their living memory.

Across the world, what takes the place of such a community's sensitive approach to their surroundings are large corporations and entities who have mapped out the returns they want from their efforts on a much larger scale. This is when things turn critical. From small pockets of forest cleared for Jhum, big tracts of denuded hillsides vulnerable to avalanches become visible. We need to better understand the sustainable practices that have brought communities like the Garo properly, without perilous and destructive side effects.

High-End Tourism

Expanding the tourism market must not always mean replicating the ultra-modern or luxurious amenities for visitors at remote locations. The beauty of the North-east can remain unspoiled by an increased number of visitors, only if people can stay in these surroundings similar to how the locals stay. Bolmoram can be experienced in a simple cottage, a clean village surrounding it and the many possibilities for walking and trekking in the beautiful hillsides.

In the morning, as we started walking around the village to interact with the villagers who are benefiting from the knowledge park, I saw young girls walking with brooms. When I asked where they were going, the answer was 'jungle cleaning'. We visited one elderly man's home, a beautiful bamboo house with a nice courtyard where they were drying the broom grass to make brooms to sell. He makes rice wine in a traditional way. He was showing us the process and we had it with our breakfast!

Such are the possibilities. Simple living, food grown locally, houses uniquely suited to their environment—what we eat, what we wear, where we live need to be sustainable and people living like these people in Bolmoram need to be celebrated and not tagged as poor. If we were to calculate the carbon of people in Bolmoram with me, you and people living in New York or London, I'm sure the Bolmoram denizen will emerge far richer. So, as we move forward in the era of climate change, we need to ask—what makes you rich: money or sustainability?

Ginger Trail

I met Siddhi Karnani of Parvata Foods at Aarohan Ventures, CIIE-IIMA-Last Mile Accelerator, in Goa in May 2014. As an IIMA graduate not opting for placements, she took up the Young Maverick Fellowship from CIIE, IIMA for pursuing entrepreneurship. She became an entrepreneur with her batchmate, Anurag Agarwal, building a value chain of organic produce from Sikkim with an aim to elevate the living standard of the farmers. On the way to Dhaka via Kolkata, in February 2016, I took a detour and went to visit Parvata's ginger-processing plant in Jorethang. I reached Siliguri by Shatabdi from Howrah—an amazing train journey of just over eight hours. I love to take Shatabdi trains in the daytime wherever possible, as this means I can really enjoy the views and it increases my understanding of the terrain and its people. It was the potato-harvesting season and all through the journey, I could see farmers busy in their fields. By the time the train reached the famous Farakka Barrage that feeds the Hooghly River from the Ganga through a 42-km feeder canal, it was 6.30 p.m.

Teesta Darshan

After staying that night at Siliguri, I started the next morning towards Jorethang, an 82-km ride, with the Teesta River giving us company along the way. When I looked at the satellite map of this path, I noticed that the road was built exactly in tandem with the river route, as that's the only way it is possible to make a road in such hilly terrain. This also makes the roads tough to maintain, with repair work going on, due to the massive landslides. After seeing the Teesta Low Dam hydro projects, it was good to come upon a magnificent view near Teesta Bridge as the Rangeet River joins the Teesta. We now took a turn towards Sikkim and went along the Rangeet to the ginger-processing plant at Jorethang, which took around four hours.

Himalayan Ginger

The entire factory in Jorethang is organic-certified and the fresh ginger that is collected here is washed and packed, and leaves for markets in Delhi. Also, using the air heat method, ginger flakes are made at the factory that get to various parts of the country and the world. All this started when Siddhi, who has studied in Prof. Anil Gupta's class was part of one of his Shodh Yatras, which gave her an exposure to the issues farmers in Sikkim were facing. As the state was going organic, the farmers were struggling for markets. That's when she, along with her co-founder, started looking at this problem.

They started analysing various produce of Sikkim and narrowed down on ginger. After analysing ginger grown in various parts of India, they found the Sikkim ginger to be unique and started calling it Himalayan Ginger. So, the first step is identifying the strength of your product and every region of India has a strength. We always need to play on our strengths.

The second driest place in the country, Anantapur, may be a good place for an automobile factory. But the North-east or Kerala cannot aim for that. Their strength is abundant rain and nature. How to play on that strength, take pride in that strength, amplify it, bring science and technology to it and make it climate resilient, that is the road to prosperity and happiness. Otherwise, quite a lot of migration will be happening from the hills.

After the product, comes the process. Siddhi realized that the entire ginger harvested in Sikkim is brought to Siliguri, where it gets washed, sorted and sold in the *mandi*. She decided to complete the entire process on the hills itself, so the economy stays there. Again, the need for value addition is important for the farmer to get a better price. The government came forward and set up this huge factory with modern technology for the wash, process and value add into products. Now, the final product reaches the market and is sold in Mother Dairy shops in Delhi directly from the farmers to consumers with Parvata enabling it.

Darjeeling to Gangtok

I was planning to visit Darjeeling after Jorethang to understand the tea story of India. However, a call with Prem Das Ray changed my plans. Ray is from Sikkim, an IIMA, IIT Kanpur alumnus and the local representative in Parliament. He is a big enthusiast of the movement towards organic farming and practices. It is great that everyone— politicians, government, officers and people in Sikkim— feel that way.

In May 2017, he visited Manjunath's Lumiere Organics store and farm in Bengaluru and was very impressed with the work that's happening there. On the way to Jorethang, I had aged Ray telling him that I was visiting his state to see Parvata Foods' work. He called from Delhi just after the Parliament session got over and advised me to go to Gangtok and meet the Agriculture Secretary to understand more about Sikkim's Organic initiative. I cancelled the Darjeeling visit and headed towards Gangtok, an 83-km ride, reaching the Agricultural Department around 5 p.m. Here I met the Agriculture Secretary, who passionately talked about the initiative and explained how they are finding ways to support every farmer in the state.

Sikkim Going Organic

During our discussions, the Agriculture Secretary came to know that I am from Madurai and he said, 'I have a surprise for you.' This proved to be the person who had achieved Organic Sikkim, Anbazhagan from Madurai. It was really awesome to meet Anbazhagan at the Agriculture Secretary's office. He had studied at Tamil Nadu Agricultural University of Madurai and been in Sikkim for a long time as executive director of the Sikkim Organic Mission.

My discussion with him brought many useful insights into Sikkim's journey to becoming an organic practices state.

The mission had begun way back in 2003 under the leadership of then Chief Minister Pawan Chamling. The idea underlying this move was concern for the environment and to conserve nature. One of the ways this could be done was by promoting organic agriculture. By preventing the use of chemical fertilizers and pesticides, the soil, water and air could be protected. Backed by political will, the idea was discussed in the Legislative Assembly and a resolution was passed to promote organic agriculture in Sikkim in mission mode. The next six to seven years were spent on preparation—this included setting up the required infrastructure and institutional mechanisms. Infrastructure included the creation of on-farm and post-harvest infrastructure, such as manure pits, vermicomposting units, soil testing and processing facilities and so on.

Institutional mechanisms included firstly, the constitution of the State Organic Board that was responsible for laying the road map for implementation. State-level steering and apex committees were formed, headed by the chief minister and the chief secretary respectively to oversee operations and to guide the entire process.

At the field level, farmers' groups were formed for certification. The state bore the cost of infrastructure development, capacity building of farmers as well as certification. A total of 196 farmers' groups were formed for certification purposes. The state has varied climatic zones and hence all kinds of crops are grown—cereals, pulses, fruits, vegetables and spices.

Many rounds of training programmes were held to train farmers and create awareness among the farming community as well as the political and bureaucratic ones.

All such costs—for awareness building, capacity building, infrastructure development and certification—were borne by the government.

Thus, after six to seven years spent in preparation, in 2010, the Sikkim Organic Mission was launched with the clear mandate of converting the whole state into one where all agriculture activity is completely organic.

By 2015, the state was able to achieve a complete transformation. In January 2016, Sikkim was declared as a completely organic state—the first state in the country to be declared thus. Of the 77,000 ha of agricultural land in the state, 76,000 ha have been certified as organic.

One of the advantages that Sikkim had was that the use of chemical agricultural inputs was not very high to begin with. Yet the challenges faced were many—mainly in terms of creating awareness, training farmers, certification and raising resources for these activities.

One of the main benefits of the exercise, according to Anbazhagan, has been the creation of a platform for organic business. They are now in the process of creating facilities for processing, value addition and marketing. Organic trade is not an easy task due to stringent requirements of certification, etc. Individual farmers cannot meet these requirements and processes are very lengthy. Some of the infrastructure, such as farmers' groups, are in place to meet such requirements. There is a huge demand for organic produce, which cannot be met by the state's farmers. The mission, therefore, plans to focus on certain commodities, these being spices such as ginger, turmeric, large cardamom (India is the second-largest producer in the world, and Sikkim contributes most of it) and buckwheat. Like people, such as Parvata looking at ginger, he wanted more such entrepreneurs coming forward for other produce as well.

There are certain intangible benefits such as those to the environment in terms of healthier soil and water bodies and better health of farmers. These impacts are yet to be captured scientifically. There are plans to conduct large-scale impact studies to assess impacts on farmers' incomes, production and productivity as well as benefits to the environment.

Anbazhagan also told me that in order to effect such a change, the primary factor is conviction. While he does not deny the value of inorganic methods of farming (he likens inorganic farming to allopathic medicine and organic farming to homoeopathy and other traditional forms of medicine), he says that organic agriculture is a well-established system in India and in order to revert to it, the state and community need to be convinced about the approach and helped to get there in a systematic manner.

I impressed upon him the need to share his insights of working to get the state machinery moving in his part of the country, too, when he met his family back in Madurai. I was keen that he should address the start-ups in Madurai and we arranged one session in December 2019 when he visited Madurai and made people there aware of how to turn organic on a mass scale.

SIMFED

I stayed that night at Gangtok and Anbazhagan cautioned me to start as early as possible the next day to catch my 4.30 p.m. train at Siliguri, a 114-km ride away, to go back to Kolkata, stating there could be slowdowns with road repairs, etc. Again, I was made aware of the logistics problems in these mountainous regions. So, what comes out of there should be very expensive and the value addition needs to happen there only, as much of it as is possible.

I woke up early the next morning to a beautiful view of Kangchenjunga, the highest peak in India (8586 m—Mt. Everest is 8848 m high), almost 35 per cent of the state is covered by the Khangchendzonga National Park—a UNESCO World Heritage Site. As we started climbing down, at Gangtok, I stopped by the shop saying 'Organic Vegetable Outlet' by the Sikkim State Co-operative Supply and Marketing Federation Ltd. (SIMFED).

Manoj Kumar Gupta, the shop owner, told me that SIMFED meets his entire vegetable needs. Still, some people ask for vegetables that are not organic and he gets those from Siliguri. Non-organic cauliflowers are sold at Rs 25 while organic cauliflower from Sikkim costs Rs 35. As we proceeded downwards, we stopped by Radang Village in Namli where farmers Pradhan and Gangaram were ploughing their fields in the terrace garden style. Gangaram has been doing organic farming for fifteen years growing paddy and vegetables. He complained about water, since that year they hadn't had rain. These are the visible effects of climate change—we see flooding in some years and no water in others. With the Teesta flowing across the state, water is still an issue. Gangaram feels more needs to be done for marketing the produce. Passang Tamang, organic regulatory inspector of the Sikkim government, who was visiting the farmers, was there to motivate them not to use chemicals. As the Organic Act is in place, they also impose fines if farmers don't follow it strictly. On the way, I stopped for river rafting on the Teesta. The youth who were operating the rafts told me that this was the only revenue source for them. Also, I noticed that stone and sand mining seem to be another revenue source, with people sitting in the river breaking down big boulders.

Tribals in God's Own Country

My meeting with the Garo in the North-east was preceded by other journeys and encounters that have shown me how much there is to learn from different corners of the country where tribal and farming communities still follow sustainable practices that have seen them through millennia.

One afternoon in February 2018, I received a call from the Institute of Societal Advancement (ISA), Thiruvananthapuram, Kerala. They had noticed an article in *Mathrubhumi*, a leading newspaper, that featured my work titled 'Money from Angel'. The caller requested me to see some agricultural work in one of the tribal belts of Kerala—Attappadi. I was not familiar with this place, but his urging and explanation made me curious and I decided to go.

Attappadi is a few hours away from Coimbatore and planning a visit was not so difficult along with Sriram Sankaran and P.K. Gopalakrishnan. Pradeep of FarmerFZ planned the whole trip with ISA.

I found that Attappadi is a cluster of several hamlets where the river Bhavani originates, nestled just below the enchanting Nilgiris of the Western Ghats. Even though very little rain is received in most parts of Attappadi, compared to the rest of Kerala, things are not that bad with perennial streams around. The population consists of tribals like Kurumbas, Irulas, Mudugas and a lot of Tamils and Keralites who have migrated from their respective places. Out of the several hamlets here, we had planned to visit Mele Mully and Kele Mully. Apart from agriculture, tourism also contributes a small portion to the local economy of Attappadi.

We had planned our visit so that we could meet people. Pradeep and the ISA had arranged for us to meet a few farmers, who were new entrants into agriculture. We also wanted to meet those individuals who were keen to interact with us. The response from those who turned up was quite positive and gave me hope for constructive change. First, we met around thirty people in Kele Mully, one of the tribal hamlets there. The restrictions imposed by the Indian Forest Act have made life difficult for these people and we heard how the laws have impacted their lives. I feel that we need serious study on how such legislation affects the communities who have lived all their lives in the forest, depending on and safeguarding its resources. One fine morning they wake up to find that they are denied access to their own habitat.

I had seen a skit enacted by the tribals in Deogarh, Jharkhand during one of my visits, which emphasized this well. How can we expect them to adapt to 'development' when their very existence is being threatened? I had observed this in various parts of India—Jharkhand, Chhattisgarh, Rajasthan, Tamil Nadu and Madhya Pradesh—and now I was seeing it in Kerala. I appreciate the initiatives that several individuals and organizations have taken so far to support tribal communities here but am unable to vouch for how productive the results have been.

Since we were coming with our specific areas of interest, we first examined the simple irrigation system in Attappadi. The team of experts from ISA and NABARD had put Herculean efforts into this and it seemed to be working fine. The farmers grow banana, turmeric, thinai (foxtail millet), cowpea (karumani) and other crops. Pradeep was thrilled to find some really good samples too! Wild honey, gooseberry, herbs, organic food produced by the farmers, good air and unpolluted water—these define how good life is in Attappadi. Then, what's wrong?

Murugesan, a farmer, told me, 'We work hard and we love it. Each harvest is a joyful experience. We do not want to lose this. But we feel that the reputation and remuneration is no match for our efforts.' The lack of hope about his livelihood that this reflected was sobering. To me, this was the usual scenario of any Indian farmer, where dignity for labour and a fair price for the produce has always been the biggest challenge.

'Where are your children?' I asked the elders who were at the meeting, as we found no young attendees. The answers were disappointing. Free education schemes of the government had helped most of the children complete schooling. After this, a few pursued and completed college education. Many of them were back home with exam arrears and little knowledge. They had also become least interested in joining their family at work. So, in effect, they had seen the outside world and begun to yearn for it. But since they were not qualified, they roamed around jobless! 'My son is sitting at home for the past four years. I do not know how to convince him to work,' we found one of the mothers talking about her twenty-five-year-old son. If you ask me, this is the biggest challenge for our society in the twenty-first century—a huge young population who are educated but unemployable.

One of the women attending the meeting was Vadugi, a very enterprising woman. Soon after the discussions she invited us to visit her home. She offered us boiled kappa (tapioca), a mouth-watering dish for any Keralite! She explained to us how a water tank had changed her life for good. She grew vegetables with the help of that irrigation system. She was just one of many enterprising women in the rural parts of India. All they need is empowerment and hand-holding at the right moment, to move themselves, their family and the community forward.

Our journey continued a few kilometres uphill to visit Mela Mully. Here we met Rangan, who was trying his luck with farming for the first time. He used to be a daily wage worker and turned full-time farmer after receiving support. He was cultivating bananas. I was amazed at his enthusiasm; he was even experimenting by nurturing an apple tree on his farm. The villages of our country have abundant resources of skilled labour who can work wonders with the right kind of support and appreciation from society.

As we wound up our visit, a resolve to continue associating with these people had arisen in our hearts and minds. Pradeep has visited them again and our team's visit motivated some of the youngsters to get in touch with Pradeep. A few of them have already promised to become agripreneurs. I hope this will have a cascading effect to improve the situation for Attapadi's tribal farmers. We need more entrepreneurs coming forward taking the wonders of the hills to the rest of the country.

India at Railway Stations

In October 2014, I was invited to a Change Alliance partner meeting at Deogarh, Jharkhand. I had visited Bundu a month back in Jharkhand and had seen Udyogini's work. I also wanted to learn about other partners' work in various low-income states. Reaching Kolkata, I went for a food walk organized by one of the start-ups that won IIMB's Buzzwing competition. A young college student with a great knowledge of traditional Bengali snacks took me around. She said a car would be of no use for the places we were visiting. She asked my driver to wait at a spot and just started walking—we hopped into an auto to the next place, Tasty Corner in Ballygunge and went to Apanjan in Kalighat for fish fry and to Srihari Mistanna Bhandar, operational since 1912.

Loaded up on the sweets and snacks of the rich Bengali culinary tradition—that I had known nothing of before beyond the rosogulla—I felt very content. As it was the festive season around Durga Puja, the whole city was lit up and in a festive mood, including Howrah station, from where I was to catch the train to Jasidih Junction railway station (JSME), Jharkhand.

The train reached Jasidih around 2 a.m. It was tough to come out of the station, as so many people were sleeping on the station floor. There, I saw someone being entrepreneurial, providing plastic sheets to sleep on the floor. These plastic sheets are the quality rejects of various brands' packing labels. This is the situation in every railway station across the country. At the Acumen India Fellowship programme interview, one of the activities I always look forward to every year is the stories I get to hear from the many different kinds of people I meet. Some stories would be so motivating. There was a person one year, who is running a successful school today, but had been thrown out by her family and husband, as she couldn't bear children. She told us about living at a railway station for three months!

That's what I tell many start-ups and students—you don't need to read 100-page reports to understand India's inequality and its varied segments of people; it's all around us. I urge them to go visit any railway station at midnight, any mandi early in the morning, and look at every road in India carefully—you'll see a luxury car, Maruti Alto, modern bikes, the good old TVS 50, a bicycle rider with all the gear and helmet as if he is going to Mars. Next to him, there will be a cyclist riding a rusted BSA cycle, probably a security guard coming pedalling a few kilometres. This man too, has the potential to win a bicycling competition, but he will never be asked to. That's the problem: inequality makes what is a hobby for some a desperate struggle for survival for someone else.

Indigenocracy

I stayed at the Hotel Rameshwaran in Deogarh, Jharkhand, where the partner meeting was being held. The morning started with tribal songs and traditional ways of greeting with flowers, organized by Samvad.

Jharkhand, meaning land (khand) of forests (jhar), has been inhabited since the Mesolithic-Chalcolithic (9000–5000 BCE) period, as shown by several ancient cave paintings in Isko, Hazaribagh district and also the stone tools from Chhota Nagpur Plateau region.[9]

The state is endowed with natural resources and tribals constitute a large segment of the population, as 76 per cent of the state is rural. This brings inevitable conflict between 'development' and traditional lifestyles. Samvad envisions a society where relations between human beings and nature are balanced for the preservation of indigenous social values and the creation of sustainable livelihoods for people towards the establishment of a society that accepts the diversity and differences among human beings. This is the society of 'Indigenocracy'—Village Republic.[10]

When Ghanshyam articulated this, it was the first time I had heard this word and I really admired the vision behind it. The pandemic has brought the word self-reliance into common use. Samvad strives for a self-reliant and self-respectful egalitarian society based on an equality, gender-equity, labour-oriented universe and self-governance by strengthening the communitarian lifestyle of the indigenous and downtrodden people. Efforts are on to empower gram sabhas and traditional governance systems in the villages of Adivasis, Dalits, minorities and the poor as a whole. It ensures equal representation and participation of women and men in community-level decision-making and development processes.

They have already achieved 58 per cent of panchayats having women leaders. It was great to meet some of them. With various livelihood opportunities, including making puffed rice, mahua value-added products and, of course, handlooms that were showcased in the evening, they've reduced migration from the area by around 20 per cent. I was very happy about the focus on climate resilience and the partners spoke about the Leisa (Low External Input Sustainable Agriculture) principle in agriculture. In the evening, we saw a nice performance of dance and a skit about deforestation. With over fourteen regional recognized languages spoken by various tribals of the state, an interesting one is Santhali—one of the oldest languages of the country. I met a few people who spoke only Santhali.

Kalvarayan Hills, Tamil Nadu

In December 2015, after visiting Nativelead's Salem activities with Rajesh, we drove to the Kalvarayan Hills, a part of the Eastern Ghats. Along with Pachamalai, this was a part of the region that I had visited before to see the toilet projects with GUARDIAN.

We passed the Vashishta River on the way where water had been released from a small dam and a lot of greenery could be seen all around. We reached in the evening and stayed in Karumandurai. In the morning, we started meeting the locals and visited the Kalvarayan Hills. As it is a reserved forest area inhabited by the locals, it remains unspoilt, with a bounty of natural resources. The Karumandurai Fruit Orchard by the Government of Tamil Nadu's Horticulture Department is the second largest in South Asia spanning 1054 acres. A lot of tapioca grows here and there are a few coffee and pepper farms, where locals work for daily wages. However, there are wild products like harra, bought by merchants, but there is no value addition to any of this.

Pachamalai, Tamil Nadu

After the GUARDIAN AGM in August 2013, I travelled to Pachamalai, an hour-and-a-half drive from Trichy, to visit some of the tough projects of Gramalaya's toilet-building in the most remote part of the district. Along the way, the hills were full of tapioca plantations. Pachamalai is part of the Solamathi reserved forest, and you pass the forest checkpost before you can start climbing the hills. As it is a protected area for tribals like the Kalvarayan, no one else can buy property here.

I asked about what happens to all the tapioca (cassava) grown here. Almost all of it is bought by mills from Salem, where the thriving tapioca processing happens, converting them to textile starch and sabu dana/sago—a popular ingredient in dishes across the country, especially Maharashtra where sabu dana khichdi and vada are famous.

In the south, we consume mostly fresh cassava. Kappa in Malayalam is Kerala's favourite dish. Kappa is eaten in many forms; the best is with meat and fish curry. I still remember a rainy evening near Mala, when Pradeep and I were having kappa with meat accompanied by kattan chai (black tea) on a roadside overlooking vast farm fields and getting soaked in the rain!

It was very interesting for me to know that Salem supplies the bulk of sago. Even though there is a huge demand for this product, it is not processed in the hills, depriving locals of the opportunity to earn better returns on it. I asked why no one was processing tapioca on the hills so that they could keep the returns from value addition and would be able to sell at a higher price. They were otherwise selling at a very cheap price to buyers. Thus, even with a lot of natural resources and being well-protected from the rest of the people, they were still not able to achieve much prosperity. I felt a lot could be done by entrepreneurs here who could introduce a decentralized manufacturing facility to process tapioca on the hills itself or connect them with buyers directly, similar to what is happening in Karanthamalai, Tamil Nadu, where local medicinal plants are now directly procured by European buyers.

Mandi, Himachal

In June 2019, after attending Craft Catapult by Startup Oasis round table in Delhi, I headed down to Kashmiri Gate to catch the 8 p.m. bus to Manali to visit Thapasu Foods. Amshu, who had been part of the second cohort of the women's start-up programme, is one of the 100 women entrepreneurs that NSRCEL has been incubating across the country. She is from Karnataka and was interested in working in Himachal, looking beyond the apple to do interesting work around local treasures.

Amshu had asked me to get down at Patlikuhal, just 25 km after Kullu on the way to Manali. The bus reached two hours late, by 11 a.m., given the hilly terrain but that was also good, as I could pack in more daytime travel and enjoy the scenic route. The Beas River was flowing alongside our route and many tourists were paragliding.

We went to Naggar where Thapasu's office-cum-house is located. It was such a beautiful house, overlooking the snow-capped mountain across the Dhauladhar range of the Lower Himalayas and inside an apple orchard. This is a good homestay place, where people can be invited for immersion programmes. Amshu had introduced me to the rhododendron flower a few years ago, when she met me for a mentoring session for her start-up. She is a driven entrepreneur who joined the Women Startup Programme (WSP) and is today committed to her cause of establishing herself in the Himachal region, almost like a local. Entrepreneurs like her are very valuable, who operate from the ground instead of operating from the city, relying on local brokers.

My first recommendation to every social entrepreneur I meet is to go to the ground and understand. It would be the same for people who would like to come to the social ecosystem also. The ground-level conditions teach us a lot—more than anything else. Another habit I am happy to see with most of the women entrepreneurs in the WSP programme is taking notes. After every meeting, I get minutes with action items and follow up on the contacts that I mentioned with their names. Otherwise, I get an email saying, 'Please connect me with the people you've mentioned in the call.'

Apart from this, what really impressed me was the report I received subsequent to my visit, wherein each Thapasu member had added a line as the takeaway from my visit. The one I liked best was, 'Being grounded and the grand importance of commitment to our surroundings, while retaining the curiosity to know about every little thing around me, have been some great takeaways for me from our meeting.' I felt really good that this young team member of Thapasu, just graduated from a city college, understood the ground very well.

Reaching this beautiful place, I was given a complete itinerary for two days. After freshening up, we went to see the local museum that had quite a lot of history and the display of Pattu—women's dress of Himachal with colourful and intricate craftwork even in their woollen socks. After that, we visited Tripura Sundari Temple, which is a wood and stone marvel. I had never seen such intricate wood-stone interleaved architecture before. This three-tier, pagoda-style massive wooden structure is full of intricate wooden carving showcasing local wood craftsmanship. The next was Naggar Castle, with a similar architecture and a fantastic view of the town and Beas River. This is now a heritage hotel run by the Himachal tourism department.

Kath-Khuni

Later that evening, Amshu arranged a meeting with local entrepreneurs working in various areas. When I was exclaiming over the intricate architecture of the Mashu castle and the temple, one of them explained to me that it's called Kath-Khuni—vernacular Himalayan architecture. It is a traditional technique that uses alternating layers of long thick wooden logs and stone masonry, held in place usually without using mortar. It has been transmitted orally and empirically from one generation to the next, through apprenticeships spanning a number of years. The technique was devised keeping the seismic activity, topography, environment, climate, native materials and cultural landscape in perspective.

Most of the oldest temples in the region are built using this ancient system. This unique construction technique has led to the formation of a vernacular architectural prototype known as Kath-Khuni (cator-and-cribbage). Learning about this reiterated for me the point about how much we can learn from the past. Learnt over the years through word of mouth without any written documentation, this architectural style has been around for thousands of years. It has evolved given the climate and terrain, withstanding the high seismic activity of the Himalayas with occasional tremors. The castle survived the 1905 earthquake. Even the roofing is with slate stone shingles. Of course, wood and slate stone means more to take from the earth for us. But, as Gandhi once said, there is enough for everyone's need, not for everyone's greed. With regenerative systems in place, we can look at our consumption and build and use only what is needed!

Red Rice of Himachal

After eating a Himachal thali, I went on a farm visit to see the red rice cultivators of Chanala village, Jagatsukh region, Kullu. Thapasu's focus is to bring Himachal's local treasures beyond apples into focus, bringing back naked barley, buckwheat, kullu jatoo red rice, sea buckthorn, rhododendron, rose hip, amaranths (white), finger millet, black peas, artisanal jaggery. I met Chaveram, a seventy-six-year-old farmer who recalled how the climate is affecting the apples growing at the lower altitudes and farmers have to keep moving up slowly. Like many of the farmers, he has also started growing nectarines now. He is trying red rice in a small area with Thapasu.

The movement from apple to red rice happened in this area over the years, as climate conditions have changed. Earlier, Chaveram and others grew the Royal Golden apple variety. Three families depending on 12 acres would make around Rs 11 lakh a year getting around Rs 40 per kg for apples at the mandi. No value addition for these was being done. The labour costs around Rs 500/day. We saw nectarines all over the floor that would go to waste as no processing is being done. We ended up eating as much as we could of those tasty fruits. Chaveram showed us with the gradient, how in earlier times, they used a water mill, as water flowed down the hills, for grinding the rice and rajma they used to grow. Nowadays, they are not using it, as the next generation is not keen on it. Here was a valuable asset powered by the natural stream of water—sustainability at its core. It was around 6 p.m. by then and had started to get chilly. We chatted for some more time with him at his house, having chai, and looking out at the snow-capped mountains.

Child in the Front, Fodder in the Back!

Here in Himachal, I saw a woman carrying fodder for cattle in a big bundle on her back, even as she climbed the hills carrying her child in a sling in the front. This is a common sight I have seen in hill regions from Meghalaya and Manipur to Himachal, as the women need to keep their hands free. They usually tie things on their back or carry them in a basket hanging from their head and infants are carried tied in a sling in front. This is an example of women entrepreneurs at work. Balancing work and family.

During the ten years I was resident mentor at NSRCEL, I have seen the women entrepreneurs programme growing quickly, with one batch of twenty to thirty a year. When the WSP was launched, we saw hundreds applying and incubated ten of them. Next year, with thousands applying after taking Prof. Suresh Baghavatula's online course, 200 of them went on to the next stage across the country. A total of 100 were incubated with regional partners across India, from millets to machine learning. Amshu was one of those chosen 100 in WSP2.

The current batch has 16,000 applicants enrolled for the online five-week course with 2000 of them moving to the next stage, around 245 in the launchpad and 100 of them moving to the next step. Working with many of them is a joy and a lot of learning, as the belief in the country grows that the GDP can go up by 2 per cent if we have more women in the workforce. It is great to see many of them coming forward. I have seen women entrepreneurs (WE) from nineteen- to sixty-year-olds applying with qualifications ranging from completing Class 10 to PhD, from eighteen states of India. I travelled to the regional partners in Visakhapatnam, Nagpur and Indore, and wherever I travel, I try to meet hundreds of our WE there. With 10,000 women programmes as the eighteenth cohort gets going, we have entrepreneurs with Rs 30 lakh to a few crore rupees running amazing ventures. There is no limit to what one could achieve. One WE whose example I give of what women can do is the Goodbye services. This entrepreneur helps relatives bring the human remains of their loved ones who have passed away while travelling overseas. During the Covid-19 pandemic, she did great work, bringing dignity to saying goodbye to those who had succumbed to the virus. Since I am surrounded by start-ups, I often call on one of them for something I need. For instance, at one of my portfolio investment companies, the founder's father passed away. I asked the woman entrepreneur to help him. He called me a few days back, thanked me and told me what a support her team had been during that time of grief.

I have seen WE saying, 'From March, I won't be able to focus on my venture as my child appears for a board exam that month,' or, 'I'm a WE with an 8 a.m. to 3 p.m. system while my child is in school.' As we get more nuclear, the support system in families seems to be waning away. I have seen parents and in-laws away from married children since their lifestyles are conflicting. How do we find a way to bring that cohesion back, so children are taken care of by their grandparents as opposed to paid caregivers?

I remember growing up with an entire street of relatives, so most of the time I ended up eating or sleeping at my aunt's house where my grandfather was. Why don't we want that in our current environment? If we want more WEs to succeed, the most important element is the man's need to change. I explain it this way to my son: 'I'm the last generation of men that can survive without entering the kitchen.' The boys and sons of today need to be sensitized that we are moving towards a more gender-equal society and they need to be trained. At many of the women entrepreneurship conferences, I say we need to bring more men into the room, so they know what they need to change in order to support you. I've also seen a WE saying, 'I had my husband take up the CTO role when my father-in-law retired and I took over the company as CEO.' I am very glad they were supportive of her role and decisions! As we promote more women entrepreneurs, we need better support systems; perhaps someone in the family to carry that child?

Osan—a Village or a Family

From Naggar, we left early to have a traditional breakfast with the farmers of Osan, 45 km away. All eighty households of the village are part of one family of Dadwal Sharma Thakur, depending on 250 bighas (154 acres) of land. If they had kept dividing per family, they would each have around 1.9 acres per family. This is one of the reasons why India has so many marginal farmers with small holdings. As per the family inheritance traditions, the land is divided among the children and it gets divided further among their children. If the child is not able to increase his holding, then what he inherited is further divided among his children.

Of course, we also have landless farmers and farmers with just 1–2 acres. What this Thakur family has done is amazing and proves the power of a collective! The cooperatives, and farmer-producer companies, all bring the same concept of 'United we succeed, divided we fail!' They are experimenting with many products beyond apples— Kullu pomegranate, rajma, walnut, mariposa plum (Rs 80/kg) and tomato. They've been doing cash crops since 1992–93; before that, they grew corn. Ten bighas provide them with Rs 34 lakh worth of pomegranate and tomato.

After seeing the farm, we sat for breakfast where sattu was served and continued the discussion with family members Jai Singh, Yogendar and Hari Lal. Hari Lal, who is part of the younger generation is also a journalist at *Divya Himachal* and is working to start an FPO Chetna Sumriti to produce medicinal plants. This is another example of

Thapasu's focus on retrieving lost wisdom, positioning Himachal's pride, bringing thousands of years of wisdom to others, reviving handicrafts and getting GI tags!

We went on to explore more local produce other than buckwheat and amaranths, which are available elsewhere. On the way, we saw a slate stone, part of the rocky terrain and I picked one up that still writes well on the slate we have at home—a natural writing tool. We also saw a nectarine tree with fruits on the ground not being picked up. One elderly woman showed us the sun-dried nectarines and pulp she was making. We have traditional value-addition processes with simple decentralized models; these resources getting wasted can bring more revenue to farmers. Today, they are under pressure to sell the raw produce as soon as it is harvested, putting them at a disadvantage. The elders know processing; we've been losing their wisdom. While we were talking, I saw our team plucking apples and nectarines from the trees and we all started eating. This is another activity I have recommended to Thapasu. Let the tourists come to farms and pluck and eat fruits themselves. This will expose them to a Himachal beyond snow and paragliding. I'm glad Thapasu has now started agri-tourism as well!

Rhododendron Trail

We travelled towards Mandi, which is 91 km from Naggar, where we were meeting Narakali who was coming from the tribal village Katindi in Mandi district, Kamand region. A bike stopped in front of us. This was Sandhya with Enabling Women of Kamand Valley (EWOK), IIT Mandi, who had brought Narakali from her village. Narakali, being a widow, needed the village's permission to travel out. She had brought one sack full of the dried rhododendron flower collected from the wild. To collect that one sack, it takes her a few days.

We went with the two women to Shaadla village in the Kamand region. After some distance, their bike could not go further as there was no proper road. They started walking down the hills as we drove on in our car. They had reached the village before us, waiting with the SHG women. That village viewed from the top is such a beauty. Houses are dotted across the region. I told them their village itself was a tourist spot. We were received by Anjali Shongi, an entrepreneurial lady whose family runs a textile shop in the city. Anjali invited us to her house. At lunch, we began discussions with Parveen Lata, Meena, Kavita, Dharma, Lata, Veena, Hema, Anita, Subhadra and Raj Kumari. These women were part of EWOK who had been trained to convert these flowers into tea bags that Thapasu sells as rhododendron infusion, a kg for Rs 2500. Converting the local treasures that the tribals have been enjoying into something that everyone can enjoy, bringing livelihood and adding value at the source, the economic benefits stay with them. We left for IIT Mandi to interact with their start-ups. I had stayed back at IIT to catch my midnight bus to Chandigarh. The 181 km journey was delayed by five hours and, instead of reaching at 6.30 a.m., we reached at 11 a.m. I had missed my flight and had to take a later flight out of Chandigarh, experiencing again the uncertainties of travelling in the hills.

Restart, Renew, Remember

Amshu, as a dedicated entrepreneur, sent across the visit report with all the things we had discussed and regularly followed up on those activities. This is the drive which is important to entrepreneurs. Every connection I made for her, she would be able to convert. She launched sea buckthorn infusion in 2020 after analysing this local treasure with scientific information. Often, with many products that we have used for years, we have almost forgotten why we use them. Saying something is good for health as per tribal knowledge is not enough in the present day. We should present it with scientific updates.

I received her brochure on sea buckthorn with these details:

'This wild thorny plant produces orange-yellow berries, which have been used over centuries as food, traditional medicine and skin treatment in Mongolia, Russia and northern Europe, which are its regions of origin. Tibetan healers or locally called 'Aamchis' have been using these wild golden berries to heal mankind from various ailments since the 8th Century. It is an exceptionally hardy plant able to withstand winter temperatures as low as –43°C (–45°F). Because Hippophae (the genus of sea buckthorns, deciduous shrub) develops an aggressive and extensive root system, it is planted to inhibit soil erosion and is used in land reclamation for its nitrogen-fixing properties, wildlife habitat and soil enrichment. For scientists and researchers this produce is a never-ending powerhouse of constant discovery, for tribal farmers it's their source of livelihood, for birds it's a source of food during harsh migratory flight, for nature it's a boon which has the power to reverse the ecological imbalance in the Himalayas and for you it is a berry with tremendous storehouse of vital body nutrients.'

In March 2021, I received an invitation to speak at the National Seminar on 'Creation of Sea Buckthorn Value Chain in the Trans Himalaya' organized by Thapasu and G.B. Pant National Institute of Himalayan Environment and Sustainable Development. It was amazing to see Amshu's ability to bring scientists, farmers and us together on how to take this local treasure beauty to the rest of the world. The farmers had questions about FPO that I encouraged them to form for our collective benefit. She has already started Agri Tours, taking to TraceX to bring blockchain traceability! Right now, she is in the process of setting up an FPO for sea buckthorn in the Lahaul and Spiti regions. Pandemic or not, she is driven to make a difference in the lives of many farmers with a goal to Restart, Renew, Remember!

Five

The Homes We Build, the Cities We Inhabit

*'Development consists of the removal of various types of
unfreedoms that leave people with little choice and little
opportunity of exercising their reasoned agency.'*
—Amartya Sen

As populations swell, urbanization is inevitable—
that's what we hear. However, when cities become
disproportionately bigger than other human clusters
around them and there is a lack of amenities in rural areas
contrasted with easy availability of all facilities in urban
areas, we have to acknowledge that development has been
skewed. This unequal development inevitably leads to
more and more people leaving rural areas to live in cities,
adding to the pressure on civic infrastructure.

If there is one thing that has become clear in the last
three decades, it is that measures must be initiated to
slow down the rate of rural–urban migration in India.
The rapid growth in urban populations has put a severe
strain on infrastructure, such as roads, transport, housing,
water supply, sewerage and sanitation, drainage and waste
management. How can we take pride in urbanization, if it
is at the cost of great hardship to city dwellers, as well as
the neglect of rural areas?

I have read many reports that state that India's urban population is likely to increase to 590 million by 2030 from approximately 340 million as it stood in 2008.[1] Around sixty-eight cities will have a population of one million plus, up from forty-two today. 700–900 million square metres of commercial and residential space needs to be built to accommodate this growing demand for space in our cities. Nearly one-third of India's 1.35 billion people live in cities and their numbers grow every year.[2]

Urbanization happens mainly due to migration. Two kinds of people are coming into cities—people who can afford urban amenities and products, and those who cannot afford them. The people 'who can afford' live in 'India' as part of the 250 million English-speaking population and the 300 million who can afford the Internet. The people who 'cannot afford' are the majority in the India we call (Bh)India, or Bharat–India. This has often been referred to as the India–Bharat gap!

Those Who Can Afford—India

Take my example. I'm a migrant from Tamil Nadu and now live in Bengaluru. Earlier, I was an overseas citizen of India (OCI), who went to the US for higher education and work, and I even acquired USA citizenship. I was one among 17.5 million Indian-born people who live abroad. India continues to be the main origin of international migrants, according to the World Economic Forum.[3]

I lived in the US for ten years before I came back to India in 2006 to look after the India operations of the US company I worked for. With the skills that I had acquired, I found opportunities in Bengaluru and I had arranged everything—the job, the place to live and all other necessary conditions—before I landed in Bengaluru to live and work. So, the first thing people *who can afford* look at is a house to live in. With land being scarce in the city, the only way out is going vertical. This means a greater number of people settling to live on a small land area, increasing the population density exponentially. More demand means that land prices go up and so do the flat prices. The Floor Area Ratio (FAR) or Floor Space Index (FSI) keeps increasing to accommodate more people.

The ratio of a building's total floor area to the land on which it is built is an important element in urban planning. The numerical value of the FAR defines how the floor area of the building must be only a portion of the land area.[4] If a plot has been designated as 0.1 FAR, the total area of all the floors in a building built therein should not exceed one-tenth of the plot area. FAR, or FSI as it is called in India, is also used to create zoning limits, around metro rail lines or alongside streets and roads. A higher FSI is allowed in Mumbai along the metro rail line. In Bengaluru, plots along streets that are 40 feet wide have an FSI of 1.75 and streets that are 100 feet wide have plots alongside whose FSI is 3.25.[5]

One way is going vertical, another way is going horizontal. Thus, we can see the spread of many cities expanding and taking over the nearby villages. As residents of Mumbai, Chennai, Bengaluru or Hyderabad, we have seen the gradual conversion of villages into city neighbourhoods, with the same name. The gram panchayat becomes a municipality, then gets merged into the bigger municipal corporations of a metro.

More people living in a smaller area, in the cities that are growing denser every year, need municipal services that cover everything from electricity, sanitation and garbage collection, water, good roads, transport, regulation and inspection of food, besides the police, fire department and hospitals. Schools, libraries and public recreational areas are also important, as is the factor that has proved to be most important during the 2020–21 pandemic—health infrastructure and hospitals. Highways and access facilities have to be kept in good order for food and passengers travelling long distances to arrive in the city.

Those Who Can't Afford—Bhindians

I come under the category of skilled labour and I migrated to the city and am living comfortably. On the other hand, we have people coming into the city from rural areas who have lost their livelihoods and have been forced to migrate. Most of the migration in India is due to economic reasons. They either move permanently, or temporarily, during summer and drought times. Almost 2000 rural farmers and many weavers leave the occupation of agriculture daily and migrate to urban cities to end up living in slums as they cannot afford a better dwelling.[6] Unlike a skilled labourer like me, they don't have everything set out for them before they reach. Sometimes, someone in their village might have already migrated and put down some roots in the city, or some agent may be offering them daily labour work. I have seen NGOs providing house-help skills to women in villages and offering them domestic help jobs in cities. We had a person working in our home as a house help, who had 20 acres of land in her village in Dharmapuri— just a few hours from Bengaluru. The father had to marry off four daughters, for which he sold off the land and all of them migrated to Bengaluru. A person who was living happily and could have continued to live in her village ends up working as a house help, curtailing her own dreams and aspirations. They are not paid adequately so they live in slums in miserable conditions. A Tamil film called *Kakka Muttai* (crow's egg) depicts people who left their villages for the city and how their children crave the smallest of treats. Many of the people living in India's slums are people who have lost their livelihood from rural India.

They are paid low wages because there is an oversupply of them from places like Bihar, UP and the North-east, north Karnataka and other low-income states. Every day there are trainloads of people that are migrating into the city due to the lure of jobs. An overwhelming number of people who migrate to the city without high-paying skills are treated as unskilled labour. They have other skills, such as farming, weaving and other rural craftsmanship. Unfortunately, those are skills not highly valued in the city. When a very high number of unskilled labourers begin to flow into the city, they are exploited by being offered very low wages. This operates on the simple economics of supply and demand; the more the supply, the less the price. People have the freedom to live wherever they like, but if they are migrating, I want them to come to live in India of the cities, not in slums!

I always say, after running a software company for a long time that pays very well, that everyone in the software industry is not a genius; it's a pure supply–demand equation. The turning point for this came at the turn of the millennium, with the acute need for more software experts to fix the Y2K problem—as the world was entering the twenty-first century, computers didn't have space to store four digits of a year (example: 1999). We had always used two digits to mention the year (for example, 99 instead of 1999). So, every computer in the world needed to be fixed to accommodate the year 2000. If we had mentioned 00 for 2000, as we used to write 99 for 1999, the computer programs would have got confused. This sudden demand for software experts created today's $250 billion Indian software industry. The more the demand, the more the remuneration for software engineers.

To test this, we can let every domestic helper in Bengaluru leave and have only around 100 available and they would easily fetch a monthly salary of Rs 1 lakh applying the supply–demand theory. With no skills (according to the parameters set by the city), the rural migrants end up as construction workers, domestic help, drivers, etc. A person working in the software industry in Bengaluru today, who can afford a house help, driver, cook and babysitter, paying them very little while they get two weeks of leave a year, two days a week off and annual increments, is not willing to offer similar benefits to their domestic helpers.

These domestic helpers, with their low wages, cannot afford the city lifestyle. Around 99 per cent of India should not be able to afford a domestic helper; if they can, then it means that the person working in their homes is herself/ himself living in poverty. So, the people who arrived from rural areas, considered 'unskilled' and working as domestic helpers, end up living in slums or wherever possible in the city. Bengaluru alone has two million people living in slums. Whenever I land at Mumbai airport, I get depressed by the sight of the slum dwellings covered with plastic blue sheets, spreading in every direction. Can we, in our lifetime, uplift and improve these conditions? Is that possible?

It Is the City That Struggles as a Result

Increasing Thirst—Where Is the Water?

The increased urban population causes a strain on urban infrastructure that is felt by city dwellers across the country. We see it in the reduced availability of water, as the first sign of scarcity. Water supply will drop from an average of 105 litres to only 65 litres a day with a large section of the population deprived of potable water. Almost 80 per cent of the sewage in our cities is untreated. These are such scary numbers, particularly when seen in the context of public health challenges such as the Covid-19 pandemic.

Bengaluru is expected to run out of groundwater by 2030.[7] We now see apartments with borewells trying to get water at a depth of 900 feet. In summers, the trucks selling water to apartments are increasing and so is the price of water. Bengaluru metro water is accessible to some portions of the city, but as the city grows faster, many newly developed areas of Bengaluru cannot access metro water. Where does the metro water come from? It is from the Krishna Sagar Dam of Mysore across the Kaveri. When I visited farmers in Hunsur near Mysore, they complained about not getting enough water, pointing at the big pipes going to Bengaluru!

As Bengaluru takes more water from the Kaveri, the downstream farmers in Tamil Nadu get affected along with farmers in Mandya of Karnataka. Whenever there is less rain, we can see the problem of Karnataka and Tamil Nadu getting into a tussle over water and sometimes Bengaluru city comes to a standstill with a bandh on this issue. There was no problem in the city of Bengaluru itself, but the problem existed in the Mandya district of Karnataka and Thanjavur district of Tamil Nadu—then why were buses being burnt in Bengaluru? People living in horrible conditions use such opportunities to vent their anger. Who knows the deprivation and exclusion behind such rage that makes people throw stones at bikes and cars? Who knows what the families of such violent youth were like twenty years ago in their place of birth? There is a lot of resentment at deprivation and being denied what seems to be easily available to others, which comes out at times like these. In cities, it is burning buses and throwing stones; in other remote parts, it could even lead to becoming extremists. So, the social and economic reality of India needs to be faced head-on by entrepreneurs who want to solve some of these problems.

Mountains of Urban Waste

According to the World Bank, 2.01 billion tonnes of solid waste were generated by the world's cities in 2016. This meant a footprint of 0.74 kg per person per day.[8] Since then, the increase in population and urbanization is expected to have increased annual waste generation by 70 per cent to a projected 3.40 billion tonnes in 2050. The World Bank report notes that:

> Compared to those in developed nations, residents in developing countries, especially the urban poor, are more severely impacted by unsustainably managed waste. In low-income countries, over 90 per cent of waste is often disposed in unregulated dumps or openly burned. These practices create serious health, safety and environmental

consequences. Poorly managed waste serves as a breeding ground for disease vectors, contributes to global climate change through methane generation and can even *promote urban violence.*

Managing waste properly is essential for building sustainable and liveable cities, but it remains a challenge for many developing countries and cities. Effective waste management is expensive, often comprising 20 per cent–50 per cent of municipal budgets. Operating this essential municipal service requires integrated systems that are efficient, sustainable and socially supported.[9]

We see the worst effects of this in India. A *Deccan Herald* report describes this:

> . . . with a population of over one crore, Bengaluru generates more than 6,000 tonnes of waste per day, or 20 lakh tonnes each year. The residents of Bengaluru get away with their waste as the Bruhat Bengaluru Mahanagara Palike (BBMP) auto tippers collect the waste at regular intervals. However, the residents of the neighbouring villages—Mandur, Mavallipura, Bellahalli—are forced to live with the foul smell of waste that Bengalureans created. We've seen people from Mandur village coming to Bengaluru protesting as Bengaluru waste has contaminated their water bodies and agricultural lands and affecting their health as well. After heavy protests by the villagers the dumping of waste in Mandur stopped in the year 2014 but still the aftermath continues. Similarly, Mavallipura village saw 40 lakh tonnes of Bengaluru waste dumped in their village from 2003 to 2015. The toxic leachate from the unlined landfill site polluted the local lake and groundwater, resulting in deaths of villagers by kidney failure, cancer and a range of illnesses.[10]

Silk Bored and What It Reveals

There is a famous junction in Bengaluru called the Silk Board Junction. I remember seeing an advertisement saying 'Silk Bored?' while waiting to cross that junction in my car. There are numerous jokes on the Internet, as people started taking this problem of traffic congestion on the lighter side, including comparing the March 2021 Suez Canal blockage with Bengaluru traffic.

I have, of course, noticed how it takes three hours to cross a few kilometres in Bengaluru. I tell people you can have only breakfast-lunch-dinner meetings in Bengaluru if you are venturing out to meet people; the rest of the time is spent in traffic. In Delhi, I remember people saying it took thirty minutes to two hours to reach a place. Indian cities are facing crippling traffic conditions today. I lived in Atlanta, where, with fourteen lanes, one area still had a traffic problem. Where is the place to lay fourteen lanes in Bengaluru?

As we grow, beginning from Bengaluru's inner ring road, outer ring road or peripheral road, traffic is still a problem. In the US, there are about 980 cars for every 1000 people, while in India the number is close to twenty-two cars.[11] Among Indian cities, though, Bengaluru has around 100 cars per 1000 people. If we have such a problem with just 100 cars, imagine when and if we reach 980 cars per 1000 people. Public transportation is definitely one way, but the metro, which was started with a goal to reduce traffic, is hardly a support, since by the time it went operational, the traffic went up manifold.[12] Also, London is celebrating 100 years of their Underground, something we are just copying. If London's Underground also did not solve their problem, then what's the solution?

The Way Forward

On the flip side, it is important to understand that no one would migrate to a city to live their life in a slum unless there were compelling reasons to do so. Those who live in slums would not live there even for a day if the rural situation was marginally better. Similarly, people who are driving cars around in Bengaluru also complain about the increasing traffic and pollution. So, does it mean our cities are not for both the Bhindians and Indians? Then again, where are we heading with such urbanization, I wonder? The root cause of this is rural livelihoods being lost, forcing migration into cities and city resources being managed in a non-sustainable way! The other reason is that the development of public amenities and facilities is concentrated in cities, rather than throughout the country.

Whose Land Is It Anyway?

Property disputes and family conflicts clog our judicial system with around 66 per cent of all cases being property-related litigation. The land is limited and has no means of growing. Coupled with the ever-growing population, the scarcity of land is going to get more acute. Those who own land and want to sell it are going to keep getting a better price, especially since it cannot be produced. Then why are we treating real estate like it's a commodity? A commodity which in short supply and artificially increasing its monetary value? Has India truly engaged with its future, its urbanization future? Since the land price is expensive, the poor are not able to afford houses; thus, slums are born. Can we cap ownership of land? Or make land in city limits available only on lease, not on ownership? Will this reduce the skyrocketing land/house prices in the cities?

I never bought a house in Bengaluru because I felt that the price of the house I would like to buy is ridiculously high compared to our GDP because of the demand for land, whereas our villages are empty. For the price I would pay for a house of my choice in Bengaluru, I could buy many acres of land and build a very spacious house in a village.

The Kiribati Way

The Kerala government has, to a certain extent brought in land reforms, with a cap of a single farmer not owning more than 15 acres of farm land and Bihar has done that in the past. The Bhoodan movement[13] of Acharya Vinoba Bhave in the 1950s–1960s saw thousands of acres of land that were donated for the landless! While attending the Environment and Sustainability Festival,[14] Bengaluru, organized by Grammy Award-winner Ricky Kej, who brings awareness about climate change through music and songs that he performs across the world, including at the UN, I remember a professor from Africa telling us about a beautiful mountain in his country and said someone put a value to the mountain. He was wondering how someone could put a value on a mountain. If a value has been placed on that, then it means that there is someone out there who could buy that too. There are some things in life that are priceless. We saw history being made when Alaska was bought by the US from Russia. Donald Trump wanted to buy Greenland, the country![15]

At the same event, I met Anote Tong,[16] the then President of Kiribati, a small island in the Pacific that is seeing the effects of climate change already. He stated: 'We are not polluting the world and living peacefully with nature, but we are sinking and Kiribati will be gone soon.' He had bought land in Fiji to migrate to his country! Where would this migration end? Instead of fixing Earth, we already see efforts are on the way to find another planet to spoil, the Hollywood way—*WALL-E*, *Tomorrowland*, *Interstellar*.

The Singapore Way

No country in the world has not experienced this shift in population from agrarian dwelling to urban living. Though the pace has varied from country to country, it has been inexorable and irreversible. The only difference between countries is that some seem to know how to deal with it and others don't. Can India deal with urbanization?

According to me, we have a good example in what Singapore did to address this issue.

Singapore had the worst housing crisis imaginable. Post the crisis, 90 per cent of its citizens own their own homes and homelessness is virtually eliminated. It is just one example of what can be done in India. Following independence, Singapore needed an effective housing policy to solve the housing shortage and accelerate economic development. Government bodies were set up and equipped with the legal powers to implement policies. Expenditure on housing was about 8 per cent of the GDP in the 1970s and rose to as much as 15 per cent in the 1980s and 1990s.[17] In the 1960s, the government ensured it had enough land to build homes by enforcing compulsory purchase orders and capping land purchase prices, which prevented landowners from profiteering from sales. By the end of 1965, Singapore had exceeded its target for house-building.

How did they do it? A compulsory pension scheme for workers forced everyone to save money that the government decided should be used for a down payment on a new home. Four years after purchase, homeowners could sell their property at the open market price. And for those who still could not afford it, the government offered subsidized rents and grants. Singapore had approximately 2,40,000 squatters,[18] mostly migrants from Malaysia, who refused the housing given by the government. We've seen this in India as well, where the slum rehabilitation projects are not able to attract the slum dwellers to relocate. One of the reasons is that the slums located in the heart of the city make it easy for the dwellers to access their workplaces. When you build a house for them on the outskirts of the city, it ends up being unattractive to them. Wherever possible, if it is possible, people prefer to be in the same location; it's natural.

The Kerala Way

I have crisscrossed Kerala by train and by road many times, from the Land's End of Poovaru near Thiruvananthapuram all the way to Kannur, Kozhikode and Kasaragod in the north! But I see a uniform development across the state. I've never seen a village. Instead, there are numerous smaller towns with almost all the amenities of the city. So, there is less need to migrate to a city.

Sustainable Dwellings

According to Kiran Keswani, an architect of repute known to me and someone who has developed knowledge over the years on how and where we live and extended it to sustainability, there are possibilities to reverse the role that architecture or urban design plays in making our lives and our habitats sustainable.

On the architectural front, in the past, vernacular architecture was used in rural areas. It was based on the use of local materials, indigenous building skills and local climatic conditions. In recent times, we seem to have moved over to building in cement-concrete, often stating that we cannot build any more with mud, bricks, timber, stone, etc. In Tamil Nadu, where Kiran had spent time investigating this, she found that the skills are available and will continue to be if we manage to find work for the traditional building artisans. This would mean that contemporary architecture will need to find new ways of using local materials and the skills. If we were to marry the modern skills of technology and the Internet with the traditional forms of architecture to build, sustainably, an online portal that connects contemporary users or an architect to the rural building artisan, we will ensure the continuing of his skills. Encouraging the use of these skills and these artisans has the double advantage of leading to lesser migration from these areas, as well as building houses and buildings that are more sustainable.

Currently, the ecosystem of what constitutes Indian heritage is fragmented. However, there is a need to create continual work for artisans. The traditional form of building or the skill of the artisan was never really documented but rather handed down from one generation to another. More opportunities for entrepreneurs on solving this!

Learning from the Past—Haveli's Nawalgarh

While I was looking into what we eat—I was happy to find organic farming. On what we wear—I found khadi and handlooms. But finding out more about where we live was a quest that wasn't finding its answer until I met the couple who started the venture Kaushal Bhaav Skill Solutions (KBSS).[19] They took me to Nawalgarh, Rajasthan. I was amazed to see havelis built 150-plus years ago were still standing tall. In summer, they are cooler inside, beating the Rajasthan heat. No cement or steel was used in their construction and they are still in a pretty good condition. I was told this town was filled with traders once upon a time. I could see a similarity of structures in Karaikudi, Tamil Nadu, which is also one of the driest places in Tamil Nadu. The trader community has built beautiful homes and palaces that are well-preserved even today. These typify the Chettinad tradition of building.

KBSS started to learn from the past, calling it reverse learning. They searched and found people like Mohammed Syed, who is a UNESCO-awarded seventh-generation lime mason. He became their teacher, who taught Junior Heritage mistris. Today they've built a zero-carbon low-cost house from that knowledge with zero cement and steel. I was proud to inaugurate their first house in Nawalgarh, where the whole village was curiously watching, to see what was in that house. That's exactly what we need—when people feel proud of what has been created through artisans in their midst. We need them to feel a personal engagement in creating sustainable solutions! Now I've asked them to calculate the carbon saving of this house compared to others and the owner of this house should get carbon credits, rewarding them for doing good.

Earthship

Anurag Maloo, a young start-up enthusiast, mentioned Earthship Biotecture Academy[20] in New Mexico (USA) to me after his friend had learnt to build Earthships with Michael Reynolds. That was really inspiring and I found that one Earthship was in Karuna Farm at Kodaikanal, Tamil Nadu. As my wife is from the Kodai hills, on our next visit there, we stayed at Karuna Farm. This place has minimum amenities. We visited the Earthship built by Alex Lee from Europe, who was living there. It was in such a nice place in the Kodai hills.

An Earthship dwelling uses waste materials like tyres and bottles for the wall, and it is easier to build the dome-like structure using rammed earth. You have wind and solar for power, rainwater harvesting for water and grow food around and inside the dome, so it can be off the grid.

Proto Village

Another model of housing and living was mentioned to me by Ricky Kej, where he had performed with his wonderful team. It is a two-hour drive from Bengaluru on the way to Anantapur, so I dropped by at the Proto Village when I was returning from attending the Annual Maha Sabha of the Farmer Producer's Company of CCD. I saw that Kalyan and his family have done good experiments in creating structures for housing and living, including building a school with mostly waste materials. The roof of the school is made of recycled Tetra Pak. Tetra Pak has seven layers and the shiny side of the roofing sheets is kept on the top so that they can reflect heat in a place like Anantapur, which is the second-driest place in the country.

Political Will Needed

As far as town planning in India is concerned, it suffers from a lack of a single, effective, central urbanization plan. State-level urbanization plans also are sketchy and ill-developed. And till recently, India lacked effective, functional district-level comprehensive urbanization plans. Though there have been ministries and departments, their power to make deep dents in the system has been negligible. It is shocking but true that the only plans we have had so far have been after random, haphazard growth in Indian cities has done enough damage.

PURA—an Important Blueprint Ignored

In terms of many factors, including waste management and the availability of land and resources, while we can try to fix the city, the better alternative is getting rural areas *Back to Bharat* where there is uniform development and rural migration can reduce significantly. With uniform growth, both the Indian and Bhindian need not migrate. For example, we are spending over Rs 14,405 crore in Phase 1 and Rs 27,000 crore in Phase 2[21] to improve traffic by investing in the metro. But can this money be spent in northern Karnataka, so that the livelihood could be improved there and migration could be reduced? The model of the MNREGA[22]—the 100 days of work for people in rural areas—has proved that even if it is just 100 days in the year, people prefer to stay in their villages rather than migrate. That's the reason our beloved former President Abdul Kalam had a vision for India to be achieved by the year 2020 called PURA—Provision of Urban Amenities to Rural India. He had made significant efforts in documenting many aspects of it. But sadly, we have been unable to build a single example of that vision.

Six

Working Models of Positive Change

koottuppuzhu kattikkonda koodu kallaraigal alla
sila pozhudhu poanaal siragu varum mella
rekkai katti rekkai katti vaadaa vaanam undu vella
vannachchiragin munnae vaanam peridhalla

a caterpillar's cocoon isn't its prison
as time passes, wings sprout gently
bring together those wings, conquer the skies
let these colourful wings put the sky to shade

—Lyrics by Vairamuthu in the
Tamil film *Citizen* (2001)

So many ideas to make the world a better place remain at the stage of visualization. Since I made the decision to assist enterprises with social impact, I have been fortunate to have invested in many ventures that bring real change for people and the quality of lives they lead. I have also had the good fortune to meet and appreciate individuals and groups who have demonstrably made a positive impact on communities and society. I have seen, as a resident, the waste menace of Bengaluru and how Saahas Zero Waste and Carbon Masters are tackling that problem.

Also, while we fix the city, what initiatives have Anandwan and Nativelead taken in rural areas, which can reduce the need to migrate to the city?

My Portfolio and the Circular Economy

On World Environment Day 2020, I proudly mentioned something to a group of people: 'I am very proud that four of my investment portfolio companies are demonstrating the circular economy. Very soon, the food waste I leave at IIMB will come back to my home as Lumiere Organics papaya!'

Saahas Zero Waste (SZW) is making IIMB a zero-waste campus. Around 95 per cent of every tonne of waste that the institute produces gets recycled. With me spending most of my time at NSRCEL, IIMB as a resident mentor, I was hoping that soon the waste I leave at the IIMB canteen bin gets collected by SZW. Now, all the wet waste SZW collects is going to Carbon Masters—another company from my portfolio that converts waste into Carbonlite Bio-CNG and Carbonlite Organic Fertilizer.

Next, Lumiere Organics—again from my portfolio—started selling this Carbonlite organic fertilizer at the store and also at the Lumiere Organics farm in Thali. As, for the past ten years, all my weekly supplies of groceries, fruits and vegetables come from Lumiere, it's most likely that one day I will get a papaya from Lumiere farm that has been grown using the Carbonlite made from IIMB waste. With so much concern about the disposal of city waste, I am glad these three start-ups are closing the loop in making good use of it. Farmers Fresh Zone, which works with farmers to grow safe-to-eat vegetables, also signed an MoU for their farmers to use this organic fertilizer. I am hoping to get a CNG vehicle that would run on Carbonlite Bio-CNG and perhaps also replace LPG at home with Carbonlite Bio-CNG. Since this is at higher pressure, we need the piping to be done for this, but I hope to see that one day as well. For now, I've gone with an electric vehicle that costs 2.5 times its internal combustion engine (ICE) counterpart! This proves again that sustainability is a luxury for the affluent, whereas the poor are living more sustainably than many of us. With an electric vehicle, even though I'm not polluting Bengaluru, I'm polluting Raichur, Udupi, Neyveli, Bilai, Bokaro, etc., as more than 80 per cent of India's electricity comes from coal. Again, an opportunity for entrepreneurs to make electric vehicles more affordable and find alternative power sources!

In July 2021, we ordered recycled notebooks from SZW, as we wanted to get recycled ones for The Valley School work. The SZW team worked diligently to get us long notebooks in ruled, unruled, interleaved and drawing varieties, with higher gsm paper. When the books arrived, we were very happy and an interesting thing happened that day. Som of Carbon Masters called and said they had been growing vegetables at the Malur factory with our organic fertilizer. At this model farm, farmers could see the benefits of going organic with Carbonlite. He said they had their first harvest of tomatoes and beans and were sending it across. Both the vegetables and notebooks arrived in the same week, making me realize once more the power of the circular economy that SZW and Carbon Masters have made their business and practice.

The dry waste SZW collected got sorted and paper waste came back to me as notebooks. The wet waste got converted to organic fertilizer and I received tomatoes grown using them. It proved to me most convincingly that there are entrepreneurs who can make this happen. Now, I want them to work on sharing the data and calculating carbon so that we can measure the tomato that I am eating and the notebook I am using in terms of how much carbon they are saving. Collect carbon credits and share them with everyone—the customers, farmers and recyclers—rewarding them for doing good as they exercise their individual social responsibility. Carbon Masters and SZW proved this by building the Koramangala plant using carbon. Yes, a company funded the plant in lieu of carbon credit for the next three years.

Go Zero Waste, the SZW Way!

I met Wilma at a corporate event where she was standing at the SZW stall, explaining passionately about recycling. I tried to introduce some of her recycled notebooks at the company where I was then. When I plunged into the social entrepreneurial arena, Wilma was one of the first people I met in June 2012 over a coffee. I had then been very impressed with her clarity of thought and the cause. It started with an email I received in June 2012 inviting me to the Kasa Rasa inauguration and Greenstorm by SZW. She also introduced me to Srikrishna of Sattva Consulting, whose work supports non-profits. That first cup of coffee was so strong, that the journey with both of them still continues and I've invested in both Sattva and SZW. Sattva Consulting,[1] started by Srikrishna, Ratish, Aarthi and Vikram, has become synonymous today with delivering impact at scale, with over 400 employees supporting CSR, donor agencies, foundations, the government and NGOs through knowledge and data. They translate ground reality into a language that the government and donors understand. I enjoy Sattva board meetings where I always emphasize the question: 'Can we eliminate poverty in our lifetime?' Even after this great growth, the founders are very grounded in taking the vision forward, the Sattva way.

For-Profit/Non-profit Social Enterprises

I joined the board of GUARDIAN by Gramalaya in 2012, which helped me understand the hybrid model of social enterprises. Gramalaya works on a non-profit model supporting community toilets and awareness. GUARDIAN, on the other hand, is a microfinance entity providing loans to build toilets for individual houses and it was one of the first in the world to do so. This experience brought me clarity—wherever social enterprise is able to find a business model, that portion can be made into a business so that it need not rely on donations any more. It can sustain and grow on its own if the product-market fit has been established.

This was also the idea of Aid vs Market that Jacqueline Novogratz at Acumen had been talking about then. The social business would be able to raise impact investing as well. Acumen was able to provide debt to GUARDIAN for giving microfinance loans to people for building toilets and we saw a 98 per cent recovery of the loans. Similarly, my thought with Wilma was the same: Waste is my problem as well, why should my waste be managed by donation dollars? If I feel my waste is managed properly, is not adding pollutants into the environment nor spoils the livelihood of the villages where waste is being dumped, I would be happy to pay. I mentioned to Wilma that while living in Atlanta, where we segregated our waste at home, the more we segregated, the more we had to pay to waste management companies.

We spent two years shaping up this thought in SZW with the help of Sattva and slowly SZW was able to identify how the B2B part could be made into a for-profit venture, while B2C and working with the government could be made a non-profit. I visited SZW's Kasa Rasa in Koramangala to understand how they were operating the non-profit side working with the community. The segregated waste from homes was coming there, dry waste was getting sorted and baled for recycling, while the wet waste was converted into vermicompost at the site. Similarly, at the IIMB campus, one of the early customers of SZW for-profit, their processing unit was inside the campus itself. Awareness has been created across the campus and multiple bins have been kept to segregate at the source—which Wilma vehemently promotes and today, it has become a law. The segregated waste is taken to the campus processing site. Here, SZW employees who have now got a dignified job, compared to some of them being ragpickers on roads or at dump sites, prepare the waste for recycling. They are paid the state's minimum wages and provided with due benefits, working on campuses like IIMB and Britannia. Out of the 6000 tonnes of waste Bengaluru produces every day, around 40 per cent comes from businesses that can help sustain the for-profit.

Within two years of having had that coffee with Wilma, by June 2014, I was convinced of the for-profit model that was named Saahas Zero Waste. I had Wilma pitch her business ideas to our angels at IAN. It was a great moment to see Wilma in those years, evolving from the hardcore activist who started SZW in 2001 to becoming a social entrepreneur in 2014. Then came the tough decision of handling both entities. I still remember the discussion I had with Wilma in the IIMB canteen, asking her to choose between the two entities so that she could focus 100 per cent on one of them. Wilma decided to handle SZW and we went ahead and hired a CEO for SZW the non-profit.

In 2015, the proud moment of SZW investment came around when I joined the board of the company as an IAN investor member and Upaya Social Ventures also came on board with their investment.

The Swachh Bharat Abhiyan announced by the PM on 2 October 2014 had brought the focus on making cleanliness, sanitation and waste management a top priority. This was particularly important for cities groaning under piles of urban waste. SZW, as a company that worked on organic waste management, including collection and recycling of packaging waste and e-waste, also helped build capacities of public institutions like the municipal corporation along with supporting progressive policies around waste management.

SZW drew investment because of the policies they had followed and their growth strategy. I had seen Wilma Rodrigues as a veteran in the ecosystem who deeply believed in the cause since 2001. SZW had pioneered the zero-waste campus very well with a triple bottom line focus and successfully delivered onsite waste management services to bulk waste generators. They directly addressed the daily waste from Bengaluru that usually ends in landfills, affecting the lives of people around the area and contaminating water bodies when not properly segregated. By segregating at source and recycling most of it, SZW addresses this in a unique way. They were also able to provide dignified employment to over 200 former ragpickers and people from the bottom of the economic pyramid. Bulk generators of waste have been able to become zero-waste campuses by outsourcing their waste management to SZW.

Such bulk-waste generators included corporate offices, apartment complexes and educational institutions, where SZW provided integrated solutions for managing waste close to the point of generation. As an aggregator of e-waste and packaging waste, which enables a reverse logistics system whereby producers of this waste can fulfil their Extended Producer Responsibility (EPR), SZW in 2015 was managing 20 tonnes of organic and recyclable waste per day across thirty locations in Bengaluru and Chennai.

The investment made in 2015 and further investments by C4D partners and others helped SZW to scale up from 20 tonnes per day (TPD) to 100+ TPD in 2023. They introduced simple technology to enhance efficiency in their waste management processes even as they continued to provide safe livelihood options to a large number of people.

The Producer Pays—A Valuable Lesson

The for-profit model that SZW built revolutionized the waste management space because it forced people to think differently.

All of us are used to thinking of the waste we generate in terms of how much value it would bring us in terms of money. We pile up newspapers, PET bottles, milk pouches, etc., and there is a *kabadiwala* or an app-based start-up willing to pay a price. But all this is valuable waste, collected and resold to someone who recycles them with a margin.

Many entrepreneurs come to me with ideas and apps to collect old newspapers and PET bottles and give customers money, points or mobile minutes in exchange. I call them traders, not waste management start-ups. So then, what is a waste management company? It is a company that manages waste that does not have value as well. That's the waste that's contaminating the water bodies and is dumped at sites, creating problems for people living in close proximity.

I ask the waste management entrepreneurs who come to me if I have soiled sanitary napkins, soiled diapers and a plastic grocery bag with a half-eaten idli inside, would you take these items and pay me money as well? That's when they realize the nature of the problem. These non-value/low-value waste items are the problems that no one wants to deal with. When a cow trying to eat half an idli ends up eating the plastic grocery bag and dies from eating too many of them, these are the dead bodies that end up on our roads or floating in our water bodies.

This is why I always tell entrepreneurs to look at the root cause of a problem and solve the toughest part of the problem. If it is easy to solve for you, it also means that it is easy to solve for many others. That's why there are hundreds of people entering the space targeting the valuable waste.

In sheer contrast, the very first time Wilma meets a customer, she tells them, 'You are responsible for creating this waste, so you need to pay me for managing your waste. I'll manage all your waste—valuable and non-valuable.' This is the approach that pioneered the term 'producer pays'. When bad behaviour is punished, people will reduce that behaviour—if someone is paying me for my waste, I would keep creating more waste. If I have to pay money to someone to manage my waste, I will find ways to reduce the creation of waste. Thus, SZW enforces the motto of 'Reduce, Reuse, Recycle'.

Even though my customer pays me for waste creation and every extra bit of waste he adds means more money for me, I still tell him to reduce. Is this bad for business?

That's when the triple bottom line focus of the company comes in. You are not just focused on your revenue and 'Profit' alone, you also ensure that you take care of the other 'P'—the 'Planet'. Today, I can see at IIMB that we all carry water bottles and the students are given water bottles as well. Earlier, I used to see bottled water everywhere, even one in front of each student in class. From there to a generation of students carrying their own water bottles is a good demonstration of the change a social business can bring about by being good for customers, business and our planet. On top of this IIMB Prof. Suresh Bhagavatula's case study on SZW is now available at Harvard Business Publishing and taught in many countries.

Reduce

It took me some time to adopt different practices as well. I used to argue with Wilma, if I'm carrying my own bottle or using plates that are washable, am I not using more water and soap to clean? The answer was: first reduce. Every action you do can ensure that you are reducing the creation of waste. This formula is another essential for social business: how to define the DNA of an organization and how to make it simple for the team to follow. Otherwise, everyone will interpret things differently and over time, the DNA is lost. This simple way for everyone to reduce first, then reuse and then recycle gives an example of setting the business DNA for your company.

Getting to a Zero-Waste Campus

People question the SZW model when I relate it to them, telling me that there is always competition from someone who pays a little bit more for the waste and they will lose business if they say that they have to be paid for the waste instead of giving money to the customers.

This is where the positioning of the offering is important and moving the discussion beyond the price to the value of what is being delivered is important. When SZW gives out a Zero-Waste Campus certificate, that has quite a lot of intangible benefits. When I sit in my office which is under the 'Naga Tree'—a gigantic sishu tree (we lost this big tree during the pandemic due to a heavy storm; the Naga Tree has been replanted now)—and tell people about IIMB being a zero-waste campus, they can see it in action. So, every visitor to the campus can see the effort that IIMB is putting into making the campus zero-waste.

SZW has provided RMZ, one of the famous builders in Bengaluru, with a sustainability report that the builder shares with their IT company clients. Those IT companies share it with their employees, emphasizing the importance of becoming a zero-waste campus.

RMZ are tech park developers and managers, who envisioned becoming the first zero-waste tech park campuses in India. The problem was 20 million sq. ft of assets under their management in beautiful and clean eco-campuses with 180 clients, which were generating 10 tonnes per day in waste that was dumped unscientifically, with valuable resources lost. SZW led the design and execution process for a holistic, end-to-end waste management system to help them reach their goal. Their corporate tenants were given regular feedback to help improve waste-management practices. This began to have an effect, visible year on year. The reject waste reduced from 60 per cent in 2015 to 6 per cent in 2018. Today,

94 per cent of the waste from RMZ, Bengaluru is recovered. RMZ Ecoworld has been certified 'TRUE Zero-Waste' in 2020.[2] There are thirteen RMZ properties in three cities with eleven dry waste units and nine wet waste units.

Just one company taking the zero-waste route has resulted in an environmental impact where 10.9 tonnes of waste are diverted from landfills every day. Around 869 tonnes of CO_2 emissions are averted every month, and thirty-one trees are saved every year via recycling paper. The social impact can be seen in the employment of people from lower socio-economic groups, gender equality and equal growth opportunities. This is what enables SZW to showcase the intangible benefits of making a zero-waste campus. They send their customers notebooks and T-shirts made from the waste they've collected from the campus, thus closing the circular-economy loop in a very visible way.

Recycling as Routine

SZW kept looking at ways to sort all the waste coming to them and ensured it found the appropriate recycling partner. Tetra Pak is a great example of recycling, as those juice packets once thrown out to landfills now get recycled into sheets that can be used in place of medium-density fibreboards (MDFs). The SZW office has bookshelves and chairs made of recycled Tetra Paks. I have a tray and photo frames at home made from recycled Tetra Paks. The proto-village school roofing was done using Tetra Pak recycling. Now, with a layer of plastic used in wrappers, chips packets and chocolate wrappers are not recyclable. SZW is looking for partners and scientists who could find ways to recycle these. I have found reCharka[3] that upcycles these to make hand-woven bags and they are working with both SZW and GoCoop.

Own the Waste

The SZW goal was to own the waste so that we can manage it scientifically. Otherwise, it reaches the unorganized sector where methods that are harmful to both people and the environment are used in its disposal. I have found that there are many recycling plants in Bengaluru that can powder the printed circuit boards (PCBs) used in electronics and extract rare metals from the powder. The problem is that many of these recycling plants are unable to find waste to run to full capacity. On the other hand, poor children are using soldering irons to try and get the metals out in a very unsafe way. When people collect waste that they don't process, they simply throw it away. That leads to mountains of trash to be sorted by poor and ill-equipped ragpickers. By relentlessly focusing on waste at the source, SZW ensures each and every bit of waste is segregated as much as possible and reaches the appropriate recyclers. And when there is no one to recycle a particular waste, SZW tries to get help from technologies/scientists to find ways to recycle them and train the partners.

This approach calls for a razor-sharp focus on only one thing, which is 'own the waste' so that the people generating it are themselves thinking of its safe disposal. I use this as an example of the kind of learning necessary for entrepreneurs: define your focus area and keep finding partners for other things. So, if you end up wanting to do everything, then you lose focus and everyone will treat you as a competitor and not a partner. With SZW, the focus is not on owning the waste, as much as it is on teaching people to own responsibility for their waste. It works with many partners who function on other parts of the value chain. SZW focuses on deeper solutions for their space—the use of technology and the automated material recovery facility.

Material Recovery Facility

Many businesses that throw up more than 500 kg of waste per day had a space to process it on their premises. But SZW was moving towards businesses with less space for processing. So, they began to look at building centralized processing centres, where this waste could go. Here, they wanted to introduce the best technology.

On 30 April 2019, the SZW Material Recovery Facility (MRF) was operationalized at the Jigini Industrial area on the outskirts of Bengaluru. After seeing many other processing plants, this one didn't look like a waste management facility to me at all. It looked like a hi-tech factory. There was segregated dry waste coming from various places that was moving upwards on a conveyer belt. Here, the SZW team picked up different kinds of dry waste and kept segregating it in different categories, such as coloured paper, tissue, low-value multilayer plastic, low-density polythene (LDPE), etc. They segregate seven different types of plastic. Each segregated item category is compressed into bales for shipping to recyclers.

I saw a bale of green plastic bottles. The team explained to me that this particular colour of plastic had some other ingredients and they were still trying to find people who could recycle it. The search for appropriate recyclers is relentless so that they can be prevented from becoming pollutants. Today, this MRF with a 40-tonne/day capacity is helping to provide decentralized processing. Traceability of material and improved manpower efficiency through mechanization and aggregation help in better price realization (increased selling rate) of dry waste. In addition, the supply is to authorized end destinations, skilling the bottom of the economic pyramid and providing dignity of labour, establishing careers in the waste management industry and providing safe working conditions. The highest level of occupational health and safety (OH&S), a hygienic work environment, employee welfare and social security, automated fleet management and scrap inventory management with reduced pilferage are other features of the SZW story. No wonder they were featured as Planet Healers on the Discovery Channel.[4] SZW has also invested in robots for the segregation of waste as it moves along the conveyor belt at the MRF. Dry waste is sorted; what about wet waste, that's 50 per cent of the generated waste?

Wet Waste—Carbon Masters

In May 2016 at IAN, I met Som Narayan and Kevin Houston pitching their idea of converting wet waste into bio-CNG (compressed natural gas) and organic fertilizer, and I was really impressed with their story of how they had made progress. This space is very close to my heart as I strongly believe that the biogas potential has not been fully realized in our country. I remember growing up puzzled, wondering why gobar (the Hindi word for cow dung) gas plants in my town, which converted cow dung into cooking gas, had not taken off in a big way. I have also seen big biogas plants lying in a non-operational state at Madurai, at the CCD campus, near Kasa Rasa of Bengaluru and in many other towns of various sizes.

In October 2012, I finally found the answer through a few IIT students. They told me the problem was the lack of input discipline and the inefficiency of the output gas. On the input side, people were greedy and put in every possible biomass that killed the bacteria. On the output side, the gas not only had methane but it also had carbon dioxide, hydrogen sulphide (H_2S) and moisture. Those students told me they had a scrubbing technology that could purify the output gas, so the efficiency could be improved. I was really happy and issued a term sheet to invest in their company but it didn't materialize. Since then, I had been waiting for some entrepreneur to crack this space and was glad Som and Kevin had done it. I told them I was keen to understand more and wanted to see their plant in action.

Tracing the Carbon-Neutral Idli

In June 2016, after visiting Uzhavan, an FPO that works with turmeric farmers supported by Kumar of Nativelead's Erode chapter, I reached Bengaluru in the afternoon from Coimbatore. Som picked me up from the airport and we went to visit a poultry farm near the airport at Doddaballapur. On the way, he started telling me the Carbon Masters story. Som had been working in the area of climate change for ten years. In 2008, he had gone to Scotland for his master's in carbon management at the University of Edinburgh. Here he met his co-founder Kevin, who was his batchmate. Kevin's is an inspiring story and he is the oldest entrepreneur in my portfolio, breaking the myth about age for an entrepreneur. At seventy-five, he is as young as Som, who is half his age. The pair are such amazing co-founders and work very well together. This is Kevin's third avatar as he calls it—first selling soaps, then software and now soil. Som also holds an environmental engineering degree and a postgraduate diploma in environmental law from the National Law School of India University. In 2012, they set up Carbon Masters India Pvt. Ltd and have successfully combined their engineering and carbon domain expertise to launch Carbonlites—India's first Bio-CNG brand.

The poultry farm we visited had a biogas plant, but as the farmer didn't have a use for the biogas, he just flared it, as his interest was in the fertilizer. He made the fertilizer and started using it in the village as well as selling it. Som had found this plant and worked with the farmer for almost two years, taking the biogas and purifying it. He also helped the farmer to control the pH value of the biomass that was going into the digestor. How does a digestor work? The biomass—biodegradable wet waste—such as kitchen waste, food waste and dry leaves are fed into the digestor, which is nothing but a huge balloon or a floating tank. As the biomass decomposes, the work of anaerobic (without oxygen) bacteria causes it to release the gas, which is captured in the digestor. This gas has a high amount of methane in it, which can be used as fuel. Som started applying discipline and rules to what was being fed into the digestor.

A big reason many of the biogas plants don't work is because they are captive plants—meaning a biogas plant installed inside a campus of a factory or college to process their waste. They may not have enough waste generated for them to get a constant supply of gas. Also, the pressure of the gas isn't high enough to give them constant heat. Because of this, I've seen in some places that the gas is only being used for heating water in one burner or they just flare the gas. Som ensured the Doddaballapur plant is running with a full supply of waste fed in with the highest level of discipline. Once the input part was streamlined, he started working on improving the efficiency of the output gas and started removing the hydrogen sulphide (H_2S) and moisture from the gas. Now the gas that emerged was of high methane content, thus increasing its caloric value to be as good as LPG (liquified petroleum gas)—the common cooking gas in Indian households.

In our homes, as the LPG is in liquid form, when we open the cylinder valve it gets turned into gas. The biogas coming out of the waste was in gas form. Now, with this good gas becoming available, the farm was unable to consume all the gas. Som then started working on how the gas could be transported, so work began on compressing the gas, to be bottled in cylinders and sold to customers who would want the gas.[5] After quite a lot of experiments, they created a cylinder cascade that can hold very highly compressed purified biogas. They named this Bio-CNG as there was already a gas called CNG, or compressed natural gas. CNG is 'natural' in the sense of coming from the earth, but it falls into the fossil fuel category. To differentiate compressed biogas made from waste, the name Bio-CNG was used.

Once Carbon Masters got their explosives licence and started bottling the bio-CNG into their cylinder cascade, the next challenge was, where to use it. They bought a CNG truck from Mumbai, as in 2016 there were no CNG stations in Bengaluru. They fitted the truck with Carbon Master's cylinders marketed as Carbonlites and the truck started running well with Carbonlites bio-CNG. So, it was proved that the Carbon Master's bio-CNG could run vehicles. This story evolved into something really big—we will see that in a bit, hold on!

On the cooking side, they started reaching out to restaurants and found that Konark Restaurant at Sree Kanteerava Stadium, Bengaluru was ready to try them out. They began supplying them with the Carbonlites Bio-CNG cylinder cascade that was feeding into their existing LPG chain and it started working pretty well. There were savings as well—as the regular LPG cylinder is in liquid form, there is an energy loss as it converts from liquid to gas.

Also, there is always some amount of liquid left at the bottom that doesn't get converted to gas. Since Carbonlites Bio-CNG is in gas form, it burns completely and there is no energy loss. Its unique cascades of two or four cylinders plus pressure-reducing systems/piping and burners also improve efficiency. The total cost in use is 5 to 10 per cent less than LPG because bottled bio-CNG has more than 90 per cent of methane. The calorific value of Carbonlites (kJ/Kg) is 47,000 versus the calorific value of LPG (kJ/Kg) is 46,000.

After visiting the poultry farm, we headed out to the Green Konark restaurant, which had added the word 'Green' to its name after they began using renewable energy for cooking. In the kitchen, we saw Carbonlites in action. Carbon Masters use Agnisumukh burners as they are more efficient and give out a red flame. I had met the Agnisumukh entrepreneur on the jury at the Global Cleantech Innovation Programme (GCIP) organized in October 2015 by United Nations Industrial Development Organization (UNIDO) in Delhi. Agnisumukh is a very nice invention that has changed the way burners have been designed so far. Distinct from the blue flame that we are familiar with, Agnisumukh burners provide a red flame, and it has been successfully implemented in commercial kitchens. Designed for convection-cum-radiant heat cooking, this burner provides uniform heat across the vessel, with higher thermal efficiency, resulting in lower gas consumption. Also, there is lower ambient heat in the kitchen with no emission of carbon soot. This lowers water and detergent consumption to clean the vessels.

I was glad to see Som had already brought those burners to their customers and further improved the experience at the restaurant. Less ambient heat in the kitchen made it more comfortable for the chef and kitchen workers. After visiting the kitchen and seeing the lovely food being prepared, we were naturally hungry. The menu had an interesting 'Carbon Neutral Idli' listed and we ordered that. Emissions from burning 1 kg of LPG is 3 kg of CO_2. Emissions from burning 1 kg of Carbonlites is ZERO CO_2.

What is carbon-neutral and how is zero emission reached? A gas is being burnt here as well, just as we burn fossil fuels such as petrol, diesel, LPG and natural gas. Why is this better? Fossil fuels are made over millions of years by living organisms getting decomposed and leaving carbon deposits inside the earth. So, it takes millions of years for those carbons to be captured and now with the demand for energy, we are unearthing the fuels at a faster pace that produces a carbon imbalance in the atmosphere.

How Carbonlites works instead is more immediate. A banana plant that is growing and absorbing carbon now gives fruit for us to consume. After eating that banana, we throw the peel away. That peel gets collected by SZW and goes to the Carbon Masters' digestor and gets converted into biogas. This gas is captured and bottled and it's what is being burnt to make us the idli. So, the carbon that the banana tree took in, came out and was used. Thus, there is no net new carbon emission—it's neutral.

Another by-product of Carbon Masters is organic fertilizer. After the gas has been captured in the cylinders, the slurry is let out and dried to make organic fertilizer. There is carbon there as well, going into the soil, thus sequestering the carbon into the earth. On the other hand, if that banana peel is left in a landfill, it decomposes and the gas is released directly into the atmosphere. By capturing it and being put to proper use by SZW and Carbon Masters, we get both a cooking gas and organic fertilizer that can grow another banana tree.

The Gloom and Doom Today

Pollution of the atmosphere happens when greenhouse gases like methane from landfills and carbon dioxide from vehicles and factories are let out into the air. This disturbs the ideal situation in the atmosphere that has naturally been for the benefit of living creatures. Without the addition of carbon dioxide due to human activities, nature also produces 750 gigatons from volcanoes, decomposition of organisms, ocean release and respiration. Along with this 750 gigatons,[6] humans produce only 32.5 gigatons, which means there are 782.5 gigatons of carbon dioxide in the atmosphere due to humans and other forms of nature. Even though the carbon dioxide produced by humankind is less than nature's, it is the 32.5 extra gigatons that are doing the damage since the earth is capable of only holding what nature releases.

We cannot blame the earth's capability when it is the extra carbon dioxide and methane produced by people that is the problem. Also, this is because natural sinks remove around the same quantity of carbon dioxide from the atmosphere as that which is produced by natural sources. This had kept carbon dioxide levels balanced and in a safe range. But human sources of emissions have upset the natural balance by adding extra carbon dioxide to the atmosphere without removing any.

Pollutants of air are generally classified into five categories—primary, secondary, gaseous, natural and man-made. Primary pollutants are those which are directly let out into the air, such as smoke, dust and radioactive compounds. Secondary air pollutants are those that chemically react with components in the atmosphere, such as smog and ozone. Air pollution is also caused by gases such as hydrogen sulphide, sulphur dioxide, nitrogen oxide, methane and carbon dioxide released into the air. Methane is let out into the air mostly from the 11.2 billion tonnes of waste that is dumped and collected every year in landfills.[7] Methane from landfills represents 12 per cent of global methane emissions. In the case of India, 50 per cent out of the sixty-two million tonnes generated annually is either organic or biodegradable, meaning the remaining 50 per cent ends up in one of the many landfills that contribute to air pollution.[8] Methane is the second-most common greenhouse gas after carbon dioxide but has a twenty-one times stronger potential for pollution. Carbon dioxide exposure has rapidly increased since the Industrial Revolution; human activities like burning of oil, coal and gas, and deforestation have increased its concentration. Around 87 per cent of human-produced carbon dioxide comes from the burning of fossil fuels, 9 per cent from deforestation and 4 per cent from industrial processes such as cement manufacturing.[9] Other man-made air pollutants include vehicles that release carbon monoxide and hydrocarbons, fire extinguishers, deodorants and cleaning agents in refrigerators that are made of chlorofluorocarbons (CFCs).

Carbonlites in a Box

While Doddaballapur is a good example of how existing investment in biogas plants can make them more viable, Carbon Masters also experimented with a small model called Carbonlites in a Box. They finished implementing that model pretty quickly and took me to see it in action at Akshaya Patra at ISKCON in north Bengaluru in December 2016.

Akshaya Patra runs one of the largest midday meal programmes for many of the government schools of Karnataka and it has scaled up into other states as well. I was curious to see what Carbon Masters had done for them. We went to the parking lot where two 27-foot shipping containers in Carbon Masters' green colour were stacked. Som told me that this was the Carbonlites in a Box process. It had become an attraction for people visiting the temple complex. Around a tonne of food waste that comes out of the kitchen is mixed/crushed to an appropriate pH value and fed into the digestor. A balloon inside the top box collects the gas.

The entire purification and compression process happens inside the box. From the box, a line has been put out directly to the kitchen. We went to the kitchen and met the chef who was very happy with the pressure. It was interesting to hear that, as they follow very strict quality control of the food that's being cooked for thousands of children every day, sometimes the food gets rejected, not passing the QC standards. As there was no place to keep it until it got picked up, in order that the food does not spoil and smell, they used to keep it in cold storage. Now, within twenty-four hours, all the food waste gets converted and comes back to the kitchen for cooking.

The World Wildlife Fund (WWF) recognized the efforts of Carbon Masters with the WWF Climate Solvers 2017 award for GHG (greenhouse gases) emission reduction efforts.[10] They have gone on to say that were Carbonlites to expand globally, it could reduce global GHG emissions by twenty-seven million tonnes of CO_2e (carbon dioxide emissions) from 32.5 million tonnes today.

What about Water? Zero Waste, Zero Discharge Water Communities

While very happy with waste to bio-CNG, organic fertilizer and recycled and upcycled options with the wet and dry waste, I was wondering about water. The amount of water we consume every day in the cities is increasing as we have the modern way of handling ourselves with flushing out toilets and showers, etc. I remember while growing up, when we took a bath in our grandfather's house, the bath water got into the home garden where vegetables were being grown. I've seen this during many Gramalaya visits where we encourage people to build toilets and bathrooms together. The toilet waste converts into compost by the twin-pit anaerobic model. The water from the bathroom is channelled towards growing vegetables. I've seen beautiful gardens and moringa and banana trees as well, growing in many villages like Dalmiapuram and Lal Gudi. Now, with all the water we use, how do we reuse? The sewage treatment plant (STP) is mandatory now in every apartment in Bengaluru. In some of these apartments, recycled water is used in flushes and gardens. In many places, given the cost involved in running these STPs, people just let out water into the storm drain that finds its way to the lakes. The result is the foaming lakes that we have seen in Bengaluru caused by the excess detergents in the wastewater. Vikas Brahmavar and Gowthaman Desingh have come up with an interesting solution. Since many of the apartments do have a basic STP, they tell the residents, give us STP water and we'll convert that into drinkable water. As people are very superstitious and not able to fathom drinking bath water or using it for growing vegetables, this model is yet to take off. So they take the water, purify it and sell it outside for various other uses. I would like them to launch recycled drinking water one day in India!

When Vikas pitched his idea at World Research Institute (WRI), he brought the water and I have drunk it and it was pretty good; I couldn't tell the difference. I remember watching a documentary *Inside Bill's Brain*, where he drank recycled water. But the behaviour change takes time—Singapore drinks recycled water sold as NEWater (rightfully named).[11] NEWater is the brand name given to highly treated reclaimed wastewater produced by Singapore's Public Utilities Board. More specifically, conventionally treated wastewater (sewage) is further purified to produce NEWater by using advanced treatment technologies (microfiltration and reverse osmosis membranes and ultraviolet irradiation). The water is potable quality and is added to drinking water supply reservoirs where it is withdrawn and treated again in conventional water treatment plants before being distributed to consumers. Currently, however, most of the NEWater is used by industries requiring high purity non-potable production water.

Vikas found a different use—in August 2018, after inaugurating the Lumiere Organics HSR Layout store in Bengaluru, he took me to an IT park where he had taken the STP water, further processed it and sold back the pure water, which they are using in their cooling tower for air conditioning. They are saving 3,60,00,000 litres of water every year.

Bengaluru, nearing a population of two crore, needs 400 cr. lts/day. Today, metro water from the Cauvery provides 145 cr. lts/day and borewells provide 80–100 cr. lts/day.[12] Around 200 cr. lts of partially treated water is sent to drains (equivalent to thirteen lakes) each day. However, Bengaluru needs around 77.7 cr. lts/day now and

Cauvery Phase V is spending Rs 5520 crore for that.[13] With Boson Whitewater spending half of that, Rs 2500 crore, it can recycle the water and we need not draw more water from the river that the Mandya and Tamil Nadu farmers are asking for. We Bengalureans, instead of recycling our used water, are asking for fresh water. So I've made Boson Whitewater my twenty-fifth investment.

So SZW, Carbon Masters and Boson Whitewater show the way to making the city liveable today. What models are there in rural India that are worth emulating for reducing migration to the cities?

Anandwan—A Self-Sustaining Village

I was struck by the words of Baba Amte and by reading about him in Rajni Bakshi's book *Bapu Kuti: Journeys in Rediscovery of Gandhi.*

'I took up leprosy work not to help anyone but to overcome that fear in my life. That it worked out good for others was a by-product. But the fact is I did it to overcome fear,' Baba Amte had said.

Anandwan, the village community created by Baba Amte, was a place I had wanted to visit for a long time. I was able to visit on 1 March 2017. I had landed in Nagpur and was received by students from Lemon Ideas. My baggage hadn't arrived, so I went ahead to Anandwan without it—a good test for the self-reliant village. We reached the place, around 100 km from Nagpur, and checked into the guest house. Then we went for a simple lunch, shared by the whole community, and prepared to go around the village.

Anandwan, or the forest of bliss, was singlehandedly set up by Baba Amte, who arrived with his wife, a few followers and the lepers who had been outcasts from society after they had become disfigured and disabled. Founded in 1949, this self-sustaining village has built livelihood capabilities for thousands of downtrodden people. Persons with disabilities like leprosy or who are orthopaedically handicapped, vision and hearing-impaired people and those from oppressed and marginalized tribes have been able to improve their circumstances with their self-respect intact.

Baba Amte had visualized and developed Anandwan to be a self-contained community, where residents never fear social exploitation and ostracism. Today, its residents are self-sufficient in terms of meeting their basic needs through what they grow and produce. Various home-based, small-scale industry units run by the residents also generate income for additional requirements.

From the beginning, Anandwan was shaped as an environmentally aware community to practice energy utilization, waste recycling and minimizing the use of natural resources that might otherwise lead to their depletion.

At Anandwan, there are two hospitals, a college, an orphanage, a school for the blind, a school for the deaf and a technical wing. We visited the hospital area where a banyan sapling planted by the Dalai Lama in 1990 has grown into a huge tree and someone was taking rest in its shade! When leprosy levels started going down, Anandwan, which had initially been founded to give lepers a place to live with dignity and self-respect, started to help with other disabilities. We visited the school for the blind and later saw those with speech and hearing impairments learning computers and tailoring.

When they learnt I was missing my baggage, they offered to stitch me a kurta from the fabric that was handwoven there. I collected the kurta the very next morning. I was most intrigued by how people with impaired hearing were practising a dance, learning steps with signs from their instructor, who was also hearing impaired. I watched them just follow the counts and signs. Then we went to see the reservoirs that they've built for rainwater harvesting. This brings them enough water for all their agricultural activities. We passed acres of paddy, wheat, vegetables—cabbage, tomatoes and a big orchard (*vanavihar*) with many trees.

On the way, we met people who had just harvested the tomatoes and were sorting them to send them to the market. All the excess produce beyond feeding the 2500 inhabitants of the village is sold in the weekly market of Warora town. It is indeed an irony—Anandwan was formed to shelter those whom society had rejected and now the vegetables they grow are in high demand because they are of such good quality. I saw that many of the vegetable sorters had lost fingers to the disease, but their will to overcome any handicaps had proved unstoppable.

One very interesting feature was the eco-friendly dwelling called the Nubian Vault. Another jaw-dropping sight is a structure housing a humongous solar concentrator that can track the sun from sunrise to sunset. The water that passes through the concentrator gets converted to steam that is capable of cooking 3000-plus meals every day, backed up with a 5-tonne/day biogas plant, a complete renewable energy system for cooking!

Anandwan was made self-sufficient for the families of the inhabitants by ensuring that education is available to them close at hand. There is a school, college, polytechnic and agricultural college on the campus. In the evening, I met Dr Vikas Amte who shared stories of how people arrived at Anandwan as outcasts and became proud and productive members of the community. 'People who were rejected by society are contributing to the GDP today,' he said. Amte also spends time with the Anandwan orchestra that tours towns and cities for outstation performances. In fact, at Anandwan itself, there is a huge auditorium for cultural performances and the buses parked there to transport the residents to other locations had the slogan 'Give them a chance not charity' painted on their sides.

My stay at Anandwan[14] would have been incomplete without visiting the Anandwan shop where I bought a handwoven dhoti, towel, T-shirt, cap and a bag to keep all of them—everything was made in the village. The next morning, we visited various craft-making workshops and saw greeting cards, framed crafts, woodwork, the vocational training centre and a factory where sheet metal work was being done. Due to a spinal condition, Baba Amte was unable to sit in the later period of his life and a vehicle was fabricated at this factory that enabled him to lie down and navigate around Anandwan.

Self-sufficiency defines the place. The textile mills on the campus manufacture all the bandage cloths and hospital bedsheets, besides huge handwoven rugs—dhurries from 10 feet to 50 feet long are hand-woven. Screen printing units are available as well as a printing press for notebooks and a bag-making unit. This makes the requirements of school- and college-going children also accessible close to home.

I was overwhelmed after seeing so many activities, to which Dr Sheetal Amte—the third generation to be looking after Anandwan, proudly said, 'We are India's first smart village, taking the vision way ahead!' She told me jokingly that except for sugar and diesel, pretty much everything they needed was available right there. I was sad when she passed away in 2020 and recognized it as a big loss to the social sector. I had spoken to her just a few months before that, saying that with the pandemic taking many rural youths back to their villages, the Anandwan model should be replicated. After my visit, I shared my wonder and appreciation in a social media post: 'Reimagining rural India through self-reliant Anandwan SMART Village—built by, built for people shunned by society, that is today a model village for the country, that we could replicate—2500 differently-abled people have been taken towards becoming self-reliant, carbon neutral, towards SDG. Education, Healthcare, Agri, Industry, Crafts, Renewable Energy, Environment—I was blown away by a vision and its execution for decades.'

Nativelead Foundation

In 2013, I visited Madurai for an angel investing session organized by Sivarajah Ramanathan and others from the city's Software Industries Development Association (SIDA). After the session, Sivarajah mentioned their initiative to promote entrepreneurship in the region, which began as a CII initiative and evolved into the Nativelead Foundation. He thus started providing entrepreneurship skills to the students of various colleges with the help of CSR.

I was impressed by this and told him, 'It's a great initiative,' and, as a person from Madurai, I wanted to support it. I asked him to come and visit me at NSRCEL, IIMB. Sivarajah and Ashwin Desai then came to visit me in Bengaluru. During that visit, based on my experiences with many organizations that are focusing on awareness or mentoring or incubation or investment, I charted out on the board at NSRCEL that, in small regions, we need all four for us to support an entrepreneur.

Thus, the model of Nativelead Foundation with Enable, Nurture, Incubate and Invest was born. However, whichever town we are placed in, we look at the strengths of that town and if any organization is working on any of these aspects, we don't need to repeat them. This way we can partner with everyone and plug in where support is needed. So, the entrepreneur who comes into the system is taken care of. This is different from what is happening in the ecosystem today, for example, when an entrepreneur pitches to an angel network. If the angels present in the meeting are not keen on taking it forward, they would just reject it.

Enabling

But in a place like Madurai, such rejection would be counterproductive, especially when we wanted to encourage people to look at entrepreneurship as a viable option. With a programme like Enabling, we wanted to bring confidence to people, that they could start something on their own. The tendency of people to think that entrepreneurship is for someone who is already into business has to change. We could see how people from families who had some exposure to business were the ones starting businesses. Others felt that settling down in life meant finding a job. Providing potential entrepreneurs with the confidence that they could start and that we are there to support them was the first part of our task with students or those who were employed and wanted to start something of their own.

With Enabling, we were able to start campus programmes in colleges, running sessions on entrepreneurship and partnering with organizations such as CII, Young Indians (YI), Madurai District Tiny and Small-Scale Industries Association (MADITSSIA), Tamil Nadu Chamber of Commerce (TNCC), FICCI, Coimbatore District Small

Industries Association (CODISSIA), NASSCOM, The Indus Entrepreneurs (TiE) and others. From there, we identified entrepreneurs who were interested and figured out a way to nurture them.

If they needed space, there were plenty of colleges that we worked with, to offer them the place to operate. Also, many of the towns where we were operating already had a Department of Science and Technology (DST) and National Bank for Agriculture and Rural Development (NABARD)-supported incubators. As for investment, this is the part I am very proud of today—over 240 angel investors are part of Nativelead and ready to invest. When I thought about mentoring in the regions where there were no thriving first-generation entrepreneurs, I came across the mindset of, 'Why should I help that person to grow?' Places like Bengaluru have become the hub of thriving entrepreneurship and acquired the label of start-up capital because there are quite a few of us who have seen success as the first generation in the information technology (IT) space.

Since we know the problems we have faced while growing as first-generation success stories in this space, we could connect very well with someone who is just starting. To overcome that, I've started telling people that they should invest in a company to support them in growing, without worrying about whether the person you helped to grow will acknowledge your support or not. A Tamil saying captures this: 'ஏறி வந்த ஏணியை எட்டி உதைப்பார்கள்—*Eri vantha yeniai etti uthaippargal*—people kick off the ladder that helped them to go up!'

Another way to look at it is that if you invest in a company, then you are a part owner. If the company does well and grows, you will also benefit, so there is an obvious interest to support them. Today, I've seen our investors providing their CFO to help with the finances of the company they have invested in. They open doors, asking start-ups to implement their ideas in their college or company. They provide expertise, like in the food industry, about what regulatory items need to be followed. So, the investing arm works very well to provide a win-win for entrepreneurs and investors. On the nurturing part, we now bring in experts to help them in areas like finance or marketing or sales.

So much potential exists in Tier II and Tier III towns! I am skilled labour who left my home town. Unskilled labourers regularly leave the places they are from as they perceive metros and cities as the places where things are happening. This major migration skews the development across the country. Once, I visited CCD's project in Sevayur, where Muthu showed me villages that were empty as their residents had moved to towns nearby. I've also seen conditions around slums in Trichy when Gramalaya was helping them build toilets. So, I am all for encouraging entrepreneurs to start wherever they are and giving them all the support to make it easy for them to grow wherever they are.

This is what Sivarajah also felt, starting an IT company in Madurai. He realized he had been doing the business equivalent of driving blindfolded. He had no knowledge of the nuances of entrepreneurship, such as business strategies, business models, financial planning or raising investments. He was concerned that entrepreneurs in non-metro cities such as Madurai lacked exposure to the know-how of new-age entrepreneurship and knew that they could not compete unless the playing field was levelled.

Nativelead was born of Sivarajah's passion and commitment to creating an ecosystem for new-age entrepreneurship growth in non-metro locations. The name 'Nativelead' also had a nice resonance, as among Indians, it's common to call our home town our 'native' place, a place associated with fond memories. By capturing those feelings, it draws support from people who left their hometowns and are doing well elsewhere. It provides them an opportunity to give back to their 'native' place. This is also what attracted me and I became the co-founder of Nativelead, as my home town is an hour from Madurai and all my childhood was spent there, which will always remain dear to me. I welcomed the opportunity to give back to my home town. Similarly, Ma Foi K. Pandiarajan, the successful entrepreneur from Virudhunagar based in Chennai, also an angel investor, came forward as a co-founder and we strengthened Nativelead further along with Palani Kumar.

To bring in good standards and processes, I've had Nativelead incubated at the 'Incubate the Incubator' programme at CIIE, IIMA. Nativelead has partnered with IAN as a knowledge partner for investing processes. In October 2014, Madurai's native entrepreneurs proved their commitment to developing this ancient town, when twenty-nine HNIs came forward to join the initiative on the first day, a remarkable development in the entrepreneurial history of Madurai. This first-of-a-kind model has now gained prominence all over the country. Many enthusiasts are coming forward to replicate Nativelead in their respective regions. The Trichy wing was launched in April 2015 and the Coimbatore chapter in July 2015.

Today, Nativelead has completed fifteen investments, touched over 25,000 students, and has operations in Madurai, Karur, Erode, Coimbatore, Trichy, Tirunelveli and Tuticorin, enabling 240-plus angel investors to become models of how successful entrepreneurs can come forward to support the development of other entrepreneurs in their home towns. As Kris Gopalakrishnan, co-founder of Infosys said, 'USD 3 trillion of wealth in India is in private hands and only 1 per cent is invested in start-ups here. I invest 10–15 per cent of my wealth in start-ups.'[15] When our focus was on non-metros, what became evident was that people in Chennai wanted to connect with their original hometowns as well, as many had migrated to Chennai from the towns further south. Thus, a Native Connect chapter was started in Chennai and this feeling of wanting to connect with and support one's roots has only been strengthened during the pandemic. We have now started Connect chapters in Japan and the US.

Super Side Effects—Nativespecial

What can be more evocative for a person to be reminded of their home town than the taste or smell of food unique to the place where they grew up?

Nativelead collaborates with YI, CII or TiE every year to conduct start-up events like Arambam (Madurai), YuTry (Trichy), Startup Mania (Erode), Ohli Mayam (Salem) and The Pitch (Coimbatore). At the Erode event, the simple idea of people who had moved away from their hometowns yearning for the snacks and sweets of their region led to the creation of Nativespecial.[16]

The idea was simple: To make native delicacies, such as Tirunelveli halwa, Manapparai murukku, Nashik chivda and Andhra pootharekulu, available worldwide, with the majority of the customers being from the US. We have already got a partial exit from them, as a few of their overseas customers came forward and invested in the company. During the pandemic of 2020–21, they were able to ship

Kabasura kudi neer and other Siddha immunity boosters overseas and grew 400 per cent in this period. Started by the simple fact of Karur V. Baskaran sending snacks to his brother V. Parthiban who was in the US, the company grew by leaps and bounds when Parthiban's friends really liked those authentic products. Baskaran quit his job in Chennai, went back to Karur and started Nativespecial to provide authentic snacks from the place where they are made directly to the US. His brother, who initially helped him from the US, also returned home. Parthiban is now in Karur, having left the US along with a friend. He employs over twenty people, bringing employment to their home town as well as helping those cottage industries that were struggling, unable to compete with the marketing of bigger corporates selling chocolates and biscuits. The success of Nativespecial is a true testimony to Nativelead's vision.

Providing more opportunities to old economy professions, so that migration slows down from smaller towns and villages, agri and allied sectors continue to be important areas for Nativelead. We have supported Mathuranthakam Vetrivel's UzhavarBumi providing fresh dairy milk directly from farmers to customers in Chennai, Coimbatore Selva's VillFresh providing a similar service in Coimbatore, Tirunelveli Palani Rajan's Rural Basket connecting traditional products to customers and Madurai Sakthivel's RainStock. With more investors looking to invest in bigger deals, Nativelead has today invested in six other ventures from Chennai and Bengaluru as well.

Oru Kodi Oru Medai (one crore one stage) was the only thing on our minds in early 2020. We were scouting for at least 100 entrepreneurs from towns in Tamil Nadu. On the final day at the *Oru Kodi Oru Medai* event, we were going to announce on stage Rs 10 lakh of investment for ten finalists, making it Rs 1 crore to be invested on that day.

I was very happy to see the Chennai Native Connect chapter under the guidance of Latha Pandiyarajan, taking this initiative across many small towns of Tamil Nadu and we were about to witness the outcome on 12 March 2020. Then we were hit by the Covid-19 crisis of the century that shell-shocked everyone across the world. That's when we immediately started Nalay Namathe (Tomorrow is ours) online, to provide moral support and bring in positivity. In the first Nalay Namathe, as an Ask Me Anything (AMA) format, I was encouraged by the kind of participation and questions. Nalay Namathe went on non-stop for thirty-seven episodes, positioning Nativelead as a thought leader in entrepreneurship amidst the global crisis. I was there at their last session too, and it was so heart-warming to hear the impact Nalay Namathe had made in entrepreneurs' lives. Given that boost, virtual Startup Tamil Nadu '20 was launched, which was a very bold move that again turned out to be a runaway success. I remember Rajan Anandan, a prominent angel investor in the country, who spoke at the event, telling me, 'Wow, 200-plus people are eager to listen to us.' I had been telling him it was around 2000-plus in the morning.

The prelude to that was non-stop pitching by twenty of the shortlisted ventures to our forty-plus angels attending every day. This saw four shortlisted ventures beating our Rs 1 crore target—we were able to commit Rs 2.5 crore beyond the initial goal of Rs 1 crore. Another unexpected consequence of the lockdown was many people returning to their hometowns/villages. This reiterated our belief that by supporting the non-metro small-town entrepreneurs, we could improve employment opportunities there. Now, with this reverse migration (I call them city-returned), there is more work cut out for us and it is providing a great opportunity to Nativelead. Our focus has been strengthened to promote non-metro start-ups with Enable, Nurture, Incubate and Invest—that have seen an unprecedented three investments happen worth Rs 6.5 crore. We also saw the emergence of new leads for Rural Basket and Sankar Kanagasabai of Karur chapter leading three deals—Carbon Masters, Happy Hens and UzhavarBumi—making Nativelead an even stronger institution.

I have been invited by NITI Aayog to explain the Nativelead model of how locals can help solve local problems by investing themselves, without the support of the government, in various incubators supported by the government. I've spoken to people in Nashik, Nagpur, Bhubaneshwar, Ahmedabad, Mangaluru, Jaipur, Udaipur, Guwahati and Kannur and am happy to see that the Malabar Innovation Zone has been born based on the model of Nativelead. We made our first investment in the Farmers Fresh Zone along with the Angels of Kerala and Nativelead. Every pocket has wealth in the country and how we plough that back for development with locals solving local problems brings cheer!

You Build, the Government Will Come

I always say to social entrepreneurs that they are picking up problems that the government has not solved yet. Governments cannot innovate, but you innovate and show scale and the government will pick it up. Be it the environmental studies subject for every student, 108 ambulances, Prof. Yunus's Microfinance into NBFCs and small banks in India, Damodaran's thirty-five-year effort of building toilets to Swachh Bharat. Similarly, as I write this, I'm very happy to share that Sivarajah Ramanathan has been offered to be the first CEO of TN Startup and Innovation Mission (TANSIM), a new initiative of the Tamil Nadu government, asking him to replicate what we did at Nativelead within the government.[17] We are also transitioning Startup Tamil Nadu to the government. Also, I see today the Prime Minister talking about strengthening start-ups in Tier II and Tier III towns, which was the objective of Nativelead. Nativelead will continue to work on the gaps.

Part II

Individual Social Responsibility:
What Can I Do?

Seven

Healthier Choices, Happier Outcomes

'*People don't realize the great happiness there is in living to be very old and together all the time.*'

—Gunnar Myrdal

The increase in awareness of better dietary choices over the past few decades was accelerated as a result of the limitations imposed on us by the Covid-19 pandemic. As millions of people hunkered down in their homes to ride out the pandemic, the food they chose to eat—at a time when their activity levels had come down considerably—became even more important. It was natural for people to pay more attention to calories and ingredients, to organic produce versus processed foods.

Unfortunately, even here we seemed to be looking at Western models to decide what could be considered good eating practices. From TV shows like *MasterChef* becoming hugely popular and getting everyone from twelve-year-olds to grannies interested in pasta and crème brulée, to food stores stocking artisanal breads, balsamic vinegar and other exotic ingredients, we were gravitating to international diets and patterns of consumption, at least in the urban areas.

For me, this was the right time to ask: Wait . . . what are we eating?

We need to build different models around consumption, eat locally available produce and more of it during the season in which the produce is harvested.

Making the Most of the Season

Seasonal produce skews the supply-demand equation as the supply goes up subsequent to a harvest and causes prices to drop. However, because a particular crop can only be cultivated in the appropriate season, the production cost does not decrease, making the crop less viable for the farmer. Sometimes, we end up seeing farmers dumping huge stocks of their produce on the roads as even transporting the produce to the market may not be worthwhile considering the low-price realization.

In terms of eating produce, if we align what we eat with what nature provides in a given season, we can actively boost our health and well-being. For example, oranges are plentifully available in India during the winter. So, we should eat more oranges in winter when there is more supply, ensuring more demand in the process. Importantly, oranges are a rich natural source of vitamin C, which we need more of during winter to guard against catching a cold. Humans are among the few species whose bodies do not produce the required vitamin C[1] and therefore need a regular intake of vitamin C-containing foods. While there may be many fruits and vegetables that contain vitamin C, not all may be as easily available in winter as oranges.

To emulate Westerners and particularly Americans who may prefer drinking orange juice throughout the year, we would need to preserve fruit artificially during the non-winter months. For this, we would have to rely on the processed food industry instead of buying freshly harvested oranges from the farmer.

On a wintry day in November 2015, I was in Nagpur for a Lemon Ideas mentoring programme. We travelled around the so-called Orange City, named for the local mandarin orange variety called Nagpur Orange, and visited Paliwal farms in Kalmeshwar. The Nagpur Orange is grown first between September and December, and later in January. The former crop is characterized by a somewhat sour taste, while the latter crop is considered sweeter. It received a GI tag in 2014, with the Maharashtra government also creating a brand, MahaOrange, to promote exporting Nagpur oranges and to market them better within the country.

Since we visited during the peak harvesting season, workers were sorting loads of oranges, but the farmer, Paliwal, realized that the entire crop could not be sold fresh, so he started processing and storing the pulp. We also met Ashish Gaikwad of Khumari village in Kalmeshwar who had arrived with a load of oranges. We proceed further to Kitol, where a farmer, Manoj Jaunjal, was growing oranges in a completely organic way using *panchagavya* (the five products either directly or indirectly given by a cow—urine, dung, milk, curd and ghee). He intercropped the oranges with marigold, which gives the soil a natural, pest-repellent property. Manoj now supplies to Lumiere Organics as well.

Fruits like mango, watermelon and palm fruit are consumed in the summer with similar nutritive advantages. The mango is also our national fruit in whose production we are world leaders, accounting for nearly 40 per cent of the global output. In India, we consume the mango in various forms even during the harvest season, offering a fantastic example of how seasonal produce can be consumed in great variety. From a nutritive perspective, a 100-gm serving of the average mango offers 60 kcal of energy, with cultivars like the apple mango providing an even higher caloric count. The mango can provide 44 per cent and 11 per cent of our daily requirement of vitamin C and folate (folic acid), respectively, with the pulp and peel also containing several phytochemicals and carotenoids.

Among the popular ways in which the mango is consumed is the traditional drink called aam panna, made using raw mango pulp and believed to help counter the effects of the summer heat. Aamras, made with the pulp of ripened mangoes, is another common drink that is also eaten with rotis and pooris. Pickling and making chutney out of mangoes also ensures they can be eaten all year round, often as part of a regular meal.

Go Local

To understand the traditional modes of agriculture in India, the example of Tamil Nadu is instructive, where people in drier areas like Ramanathapuram, which receive lower rainfall, would grow millet varieties as these consume less water. Meanwhile, farmers living in the Kaveri River delta around Thanjavur grow the water-guzzling paddy. These and the other five landscapes (Ainthinai)[2] can still be compared to the descriptions in Sangam-era literature written between the third century BCE and the third century CE. Even the diets and preferences of the people living in these different regions are indicative of the landscape and the produce grown on those lands. Similarly, in West Bengal, mustard is grown almost everywhere and used extensively in their cuisine.

In Himachal Pradesh, during a visit to Thapasu Foods, I remember noticing how ghee would be poured generously over the local Himachal delicacy siddu, just as in south India, we pour sambar over rice. With most of the energy released via digesting our food being used to maintain the body's temperature, we need more energy in colder climates, which can be more easily produced from fat. Amshu, Thapasu Foods' founder, took us to a local restaurant to try siddu and ghee and one of her friends joked about how I should tell the waiter to stop serving me ghee. Instead of saying 'stop', I was supposed to say 's . . . t . . . o . . . p' and he would keep pouring the ghee until I finished saying the word. We enjoyed it along with jatto (a red rice variety) and also had makki di roti (maize flour rotis) and sarson ka saag (spiced mustard greens). Kullu, located in the higher Himalayan ranges and mentioned in legends as *Kulant Peeth* (end of the habitable world), is home to much of the organic produce that Thapasu Foods offers, such as red rice, amaranths, finger millets, pulses, etc. Thapasu Foods aims to popularize other local treasures from Himachal Pradesh apart from the apple. In today's globalized world, everyone wants to eat all kinds of food throughout the year, due to which we may be missing out on locally available and seasonally grown produce.

We appear to have lost our pride in eating our traditional food and this may be costing us more than we realize. We need a balanced diet, but we end up eating a few items excessively. In a typical Tamil meal that starts with a sweet, sambar (dal that has protein), rasam (pepper water) and curd (probiotic) give a complete balanced diet. When I was at the 2017 Tribal Entrepreneurship Summit in Dantewada, Chhattisgarh, I was served chaprah chutney, a tribal delicacy made from red ants and their eggs. Eaten in moderate amounts, the chutney can apparently provide proteins, calcium, zinc and vitamin B12. The internationally famous chef Gordon Ramsay also travelled to Chhattisgarh to try this chutney.

Rajasthani cuisine includes dry pulses as they cannot grow vegetables in desert regions. This is a key part of arguably the most popular Rajasthani meal—dal (lentils) baati (wheat roll) churma (a pulverized mix of jaggery and ghee). During my visits to Jaipur, I usually stay at the Jaipur Rugs guest house at the request of Nand Kishore Chaudhary, which allows us to converse about life. He ensures that I have a nice dal baati churma meal during my visits. Similarly, in Manipur's Senapati district, I have had a Naga Thali with plenty of vegetables and fermented delicacies when visiting L. Elijah Raiveio's Hill Garden initiative. According to Elijah, no one in the North-east goes to bed hungry as plenty of vegetables are grown everywhere in Manipur. Eating locally available food also helps lower the carbon footprint as those foods need not travel across the globe.

I have been fortunate as a mentor and investor to meet and interact with several businesses that address issues of how we grow, procure and consume our produce. I now discuss some ventures that have set new benchmarks and can show us the way ahead.

The Customer Is the King/Queen

When I talk to people about making sustainable choices, the common question I get asked, from nineteen-year-old students as well as highly mature entrepreneurs, is, 'What can I do? There are these big brands advertising extensively and offering big discounts. We are helpless.' Consumers have more power than they think they do and can take actions such as rejecting the brand, asking questions about the product, reading the ingredients label and digging deeper into any asterisked items. The reverse of the product label typically contains more crucial information than the front. Many broadcasters now have to include scrolling messages in television advertisements which state that, if you find that an advertisement is misleading or contains misinformation, you can inform a regulatory authority. Around 70 per cent of GHG emissions can be reduced if the consumer chooses what they are buying and how they use it and how they dispose of it.[3]

Fair or Glow?

If you rely solely on celebrity endorsements, you are likely not fully aware of what you either buy or consume. 'Boost is the secret of my energy,' announced Kapil Dev then, as does Virat Kohli now. Do you think they played well just because of consuming Boost (a malted beverage brand)? How many times a day would they have drunk Boost mixed in milk? We are not able to differentiate between the actual and the acted-out, even if several advertisements now include disclaimers about casting models and that the claim is based purely on lab tests. Even this is the result of customers questioning the brand. The cosmetic brand Fair & Lovely had to change its name to Glow & Lovely[4] following outrage about promoting a narrow vision of what might be considered beautiful. With people becoming more aware, 'cause marketing' is on the rise, with some advertisements mentioning how much of the product sales are donated to various causes. The question to ask here is, how much do they spend on their advertising and how proportionate is that to the amount donated?

Sale, Sale!

Another aspect of marketing and sales today is the discount culture. In India, we now have discount sales coinciding with practically every festive occasion. Traditionally, in India, during the Ashada/Aadi month (July–August), many traders and shops start their new accounting process. So, before they start the new accounting year, they want to clear the inventory as much as possible, so they will have room to bring new products for the Diwali/Deepavali celebrations in the next few months. Since there won't be many sales, they have introduced the discounted sale to get consumers to buy. So, the Aadi/Ashada sale was the only discounted sale we've seen before.

But now, we have sales for pre-spring, spring, summer, winter, Friendship Day, Mother's Day, Father's Day and Valentine's Day. Alternatively, there could be a clearance sale or innovative ones like 'buy one get one' (BOGO) sales. To be able to provide discounts around the year, manufacturers either have to forgo a part of their profits or suggest a higher maximum recommended retail price (MRP). Alternatively, the cheaper, discounted products may not be high-quality products, with the cheapest products likely to be adulterated.

Adulteration in Various Ways

Consumers' eagerness for cheaper products often results in some manufacturers and distributors indulging in sharp practices to make a quick profit. One of the more common—and continuing—cases of adulteration involves contaminating milk with substances like urea, detergent, caustic soda, etc. While such practices do not go unnoticed, consumers have to be vigilant and learn how to confirm the quality of milk or other foodstuffs procured from the market. Organizations like the Consumer Guidance Society of India[5] have stepped in to make consumers aware of testing measures as well as collectivize their grievances and seek official redress from the relevant government agencies and courts where necessary.

Adulteration is not simply about contamination and can also involve removing ingredients or mislabelling products. For instance, given consumers' growing preference for organic produce, sellers are adding labels like organic, natural or fresh for produce that is not organically grown and selling them at lower prices than actual organic produce. Here too, customers have recourse to check whether the produce is certified organic; for instance, by using the label India Organic, etc. Likewise, packaged foods are regulated by the Food Safety and Standards Authority of India (FSSAI) and, when checked and approved for quality, carry the FSSAI mark. Consumers should realize that they can dictate terms and change what they are buying, which will force manufacturers to change their methods of production and distribution.

Be the Change

The US-based charity, the Association for India's Development (AID), where I volunteered as a website coordinator, has helped further an understanding of the problems people face in India in tandem with global changes and the impact we can have. The AID logo features a hand-drawn outline of Mahatma Gandhi's facial profile, which I redrew digitally in a higher resolution in 1999; this version is in use even today. I had just read Gandhi's *My Experiments with Truth* at the time and was even more inspired by his life—his message as he called it—as a result. I took away his message to 'be the change you wish to see in the world'.

At AID, we also believed in being self-aware, a term that I understood better after reading the philosopher Jiddu Krishnamurti. Environment degradation was one of the focus areas in our discussions, covering solar power and ethical consumption. I also learnt about organic farming in these discussions, about the corporate irresponsibility that led to the Bhopal gas tragedy and the issues arising from companies selling bottled water.

We began running an 'Ecoshop', offering eco-friendly products and started supporting projects like greening Vellore hills. We trialled several initiatives such as avoiding the use of paper and Styrofoam plates for our gatherings and instead carrying our own plates and glasses. We segregated the waste and paid more money to the waste management company to pick up the segregated waste. Even so, their ability to segregate was stretched when it came to plastic bottles, which were marked with a number ranging from one to seven at the bottom that let the customer know the type of plastic that was used. They picked up some of these bottles and the rest we used to drop in the bin at Georgia Tech.

Be the change, whoever you are!

I returned to India in 2006 as the managing director for CDC's Bengaluru centre. I was then thirty-five and the personal change that occurred within continued even as I climbed the corporate ladder. I started implementing some of those changes in my life between 2006 and 2012. Among the people I met during this time were Wilma Rodrigues, the founder of Saahas Zero Waste (SZW), and Neelam Chhibber,[6] who had just launched Mother Earth by Industree Foundation.

SZW offers waste management and materials recovery solutions, with facilities in Chennai and Bengaluru, while Mother Earth is a social enterprise and 'artisan-oriented firm' that retails sustainable living products. I also learnt about Daily Dump, a composting solution provider founded by Poonam Bir Kasturi, from whom I bought a three-tiered *Khamba,* a stacked set of earthen pots with small ventilation holes. Even now, fourteen years later, my family is still using one of the pots for creating compost at home from kitchen waste.

At Work: CDC Cares

At CDC Software, we encouraged senior management personnel and employees to volunteer for the CDC Cares programme, which involved various social activities both within and outside the office. These volunteers vowed to reduce the use of paper cups in the office, opting to carry mugs instead. They also calculated the office's electricity usage and examined how to reduce it by writing software to check which computers were left on even after people left the office. They arranged for Deepavali gifts which were crafted by autistic children; participated in cleaning up and painting drives organized by The Ugly Indian; supported rural investees through Rang De; planted trees for free; screened *An Inconvenient Truth*; set up handloom stalls in the office; and invited Manvel Alur (founder and CEO, Ensyde) to talk about our carbon footprint.

Encouraging an Intrapreneurial Culture

On the people side, I've encouraged an intrapreneurial culture, with the motto—'I should be able to take a one-year vacation without anyone needing me.' I follow the link of thinking described by Ricardo Semler in his book *The Seven-Day Weekend*. Every job description sheet allows much space for employees to write in. We gauge whether people's work exceeds, meets or falls below expectations. We adopted an open innovation system through which people could submit ideas. I remember, initially, people wondering, 'What is in it for me'. When they saw their ideas had made it into the final product, they felt pretty good that they could contribute to changing the product direction, thus bringing belongingness—the intrapreneurial culture. An open grievance system allows any employee to voice their opinion anonymously. I would be the only one able to read and respond to their grievances. Even if my team suggested discovering the identity of the complainant, I refused to do so, as this would defeat the purpose of the anonymous system.

Further, I encouraged 360° feedback, asking senior management personnel to provide their assessment of me as well, from which I learnt what I needed to improve. For me, an open-door policy has always literally meant keeping my office door open and using the room for meetings when I am not there. After all, why waste precious office space? This intrapreneurial culture resulted in the company being shortlisted for NASSCOM's prestigious Next Practices Award for 'Promoting Innovation and Entrepreneurship'.[7]

Back to India

In 2006, I packed my bags for a three-year assignment and came back to India. I had been managing a team of four in the US and one of my colleagues sarcastically asked how I was going to build a team of a few hundred people. 'I'm going to see you back here in six months,' he taunted. I took that as a challenge and built a large team. After just a year, I saw how the Indian financial system was growing and realized that our company's products would be a good fit. With a few entrepreneurs, I started a sales operation to sell our products in India. One of my bosses joked about whether India could afford our products, which were fairly expensive. I told him I was going to try and asked him for a moderate budget, adding that if I failed, he could fire me. I put over ten years of work credibility at stake. Within a year, we bagged new deals and I beat my targets. From being MD of the Development Centre, I went on to head development and sales. Even that expanded first to south Asia and then to South-east Asia,[8] spanning thirteen countries and by 2012—in six years—I was made president of the region. Typically, most multinational companies have their South-east Asia headquarters in Singapore, but I had Singapore reporting to India. Exceeding sales targets usually meant a Chairman Club award, something I managed twice. As a result, I was asked to oversee the Middle East and Africa as well, which I said I would do once I had stabilized South-east Asia. I just had to say that I don't want more—the reward of being intrapreneurial.

Retiring at Forty-One

I had never bought a house in Bengaluru as the prices didn't sound proportionate considering India's GDP. My mother had inherited an ancestral house in my home town and that was good enough. Again, although our office was housed within a luxury mall in Bengaluru, I never felt pressured to buy luxury goods and get into the mode of earning more to spend more.

While living in the US, I had seen people live beyond their means and take on excessive debt as part of keeping up with the Joneses, so to speak. They would buy expensive houses that were doubly mortgaged and the repayments invariably meant a hand-to-mouth existence. Now I see this trend among younger Indians as well, as evidenced by the steep drops in saving rates. Fast fashion seems to be gaining popularity, partly driven by the desire of youngsters not to appear in their Instagram selfies or TikTok videos in the same outfit more than once, that too in expensive branded outfits. Instead, I chose bespoke clothing with my monogram on it, relatively inexpensive compared to branded!

When people move higher up in your organization and start earning more, they are likely to get more reasons and opportunities to spend, besides getting invites for 'Page 3' social events, luxury home or car launches, exclusive entertainment, premium credit cards, etc. Affluence promises a certain kind of glamour and people can easily get swept away by it. While I've personally admired the glossy magazines and invites that I received, I was not tempted to do anything apart from looking through them.

It Takes Time and Patience

For sixteen years, I stayed in one place and worked with fifteen managers, but I never needed to change. You should not change who you are based on who is on the other side of the table. Eventually, the other side will come around to understanding you, provided you are sincere in what you do. My wife used to joke that I put in an effort worth five bucks for every buck I make. I have always believed that you should be entrepreneurial in your thinking and put in the maximum effort; the remuneration will follow—a highly philosophical stance which may seem unlikely to work today, but it worked for me. To paraphrase Jiddu Krishnamurti, humans have advanced technologically but not psychologically. Consistently doing what we have set out to do over a period of time will definitely yield results as long we can keep driving ourselves and deal positively with criticism.

During one of my appraisals, my manager told me that my spoken English was not comprehensible and that my co-workers in San Diego were unable in understand me. I immediately enrolled for a course in Advanced English at the University of California, San Diego, and requested my manager for feedback on my improvement. If I had chosen to reject his critique or bad-mouthed him instead and perhaps started searching for another job, I would not be writing this book. I studied till Class 10 in a school where the medium of instruction was Tamil and then went on to study Classes 11 and 12 in an English-medium school in a village called Kalloorani, near Aruppukkottai in Tamil Nadu. Later, I went to Thiagarajar Engineering College in Madurai. With twenty-one years of not leaving the Tamil-speaking state, I don't think I was expecting any other kind of feedback. However, no matter how trivial the feedback appears to be, we should take it seriously if it is genuinely offered.

From Engineer to Manager

I graduated as an engineer with technical proficiency, but I wanted to understand the workings of management as I had seen some of my managers who were also technology graduates struggle when appointed to managerial roles. I decided to get an MBA and was advised by a friend at work Leslie Mounts, who lent me her GMAT materials to join a programme at San Diego State University (SDSU). I took a week off work to read the materials and managed to get into SDSU. One of the other managers asked me why I was wasting my time on the course and what I expected to learn. I first and foremost learnt to let my ego go as, until then, I would only remain a technical expert. My long-time mentor and boss Eric Musser used to say, 'You three don't get on the same plane', pointing at me and two of my tech colleagues, Alan Katz and Juan Miguel Rodriguez. This was feeding my ego until then as an invincible technical guru.

All about Teamwork

What the MBA degree taught me was the importance of the team and holding back the urge to say, 'I can do better than you.' I learnt about giving my team space and responsibility; that freedom comes with accountability and responsibility. I found out about enjoying work and spending more time with the family to avoid stress in the office and at home, which is the secret to retiring at forty-one. When my company was sold in 2012, we took stock of what we had. My wife put down her basic needs and I decided that I would do no more running. I was going to retire and let the money work for us, not the other way around. Most of us are in the rat race until the age of sixty or sixty-five and then we retire and start doing good deeds. Why not do that at the age of forty-one or earlier if you could?

Choosing the Right Actions

My nephew studied at the Rishi Valley School run by the Krishnamurti Foundation India.[9] When he was admitted, I had vaguely heard about Jiddu Krishnamurti. In Atlanta,

I found and read his book *Freedom from the Known* but did not understand any part of it. When my daughter was born in India in 2007, we wanted her to study at alternative schools or home-school her. I looked up The Valley School website and, interestingly, found out about their 'Study Retreat'.

The retreat involved spending three nights from Thursday until Saturday there and coming home on Sunday afternoon. I recall booking it and remarking sarcastically that we would be greeted by someone wearing robes, that there would be Krishnamurti statues everywhere with garlands and people would be singing bhajans seated before his image. Instead, I was welcomed by a mesmerizing forest in September, when Bengaluru's second monsoon was just setting in. At the orientation session that followed that evening's dinner, the first message was, 'We are here to explore, we don't have answers. As Krishnaji says, we are your mirror. When you see yourself well, then the mirror is not needed.' No bhajans, no robes, no chants to memorize, no songs to sing.

The roster we were given asked us to assemble at 6 a.m., at which time we simply sat in silence for a few minutes and then went on a nature walk. Again, we just walked in a certain direction without any conversation and were told to observe nature. Later, after breakfast, we gathered and sat in silence on the upper floor of the Study Centre building for some music and a dialogue on the theme 'What is Right Action?' Ultimately, the retreat turned out to be an amazing three days of self-exploration and reflecting on what I am doing and where I want to go. After that first retreat, I ended up going there at every opportunity and have attended almost nine such retreats. This strengthened my resolve about what I wanted and helped me decide to retire at forty-one as well.

From the Cow to the Cloud

In June 2012, I went on a road trip to Tiptur, a few hours' drive from Bengaluru, to understand the workings of Akshayakalpa Farms and Foods,[10] a social business that supports dairy farmers. I wanted to meet G.N.S. Reddy, a veterinary doctor by profession who, after three decades at BAIF Development Research Foundation in Pune, partnered with a telecommunication professional, Sashi Kumar, who had worked at Wipro for thirteen years. The puzzle I was out to unravel was how a vet and an IT professional came to collaborate on a dairy farm which supplies organic milk to consumers without using any antibiotics. In fact, their entire system involves no humans touching the milk at any point.

They identify a farmer owning a coconut grove spanning a few acres, of which Tiptur has plenty. Then, they grow fodder for the cows under the coconut trees, giving the farmer an additional source of income apart from his coconuts. A simple paddock houses the cows with a mat spread over the cement floor to ensure that the cows do not hurt their knees. The dung and urine are cleaned out and the dung is supplied to a bio-digester wherein biogas is produced and used to run a generator, which in turn powers the milk chiller. The cows are milked using a machine that also computes the milk's quality parameters and sends the data via a GSM module—literally from the cow to the cloud. Each cow's details are included along with the quality of milk obtained from that cow. If a cow has been ill and marked for quarantining, the machine is programmed not to milk that cow to avoid the risk of any antibiotics given as medicines to the cow getting mixed into the milk.

The raw milk stored in the chiller is packed and sent to the customer or to organic stores. Akshayakalpa also grows protein-rich algae such as azolla to feed the cows. We didn't invest in Akshayakalpa as they had already raised capital from others, but for the past ten years, my family has been buying milk from them. Dr Reddy told me that most of their milk is sold at Lumiere Organics stores and also introduced me to Manjunath Pankkaparambil who runs the stores. I eventually invested in Lumiere and consume all organic products that they offer.

Someone who bought bananas from Lumiere complained that the bananas did not look ripe when delivered, which exemplified how we have started worrying about the cosmetic appeal of our vegetables than their nutritional value. It is tough to wait until the bananas ripen on the tree before harvesting and transporting them, which is why they are typically brought to the mandi or wholesale market in an about-to-get-ripe state. They are ripened using ethylene or other agents and the last mile vendors pick up the ripened bananas to sell to their customers. At Lumiere, they sell about-to-ripen bananas, which you can eat when they are ripe without the risk of consuming any chemicals.

What the customer wants, the market provides. Customers need to be aware of and support more organic farmers so that we all can consume nutritious vegetables and not chemicals. The organic food space has fairly succeeded in making people aware of the benefits, with the result that more entrepreneurs want to sell organic produce. My first question to them is, 'Did you eat organic food today?' Their answer is mostly, 'No. However, I'm exploring and would like to help people find organic produce.'

To me, the problem is that more entrepreneurs are interested in the market size and willing customer base rather than experiencing the organic way of life themselves. Unless you believe in the product you want to sell, how are you going to ensure the product's quality and confirm that it is safe for customers to eat? I call this 'Eat your own dog food'. If you feel it is only for others to help the planet and not your job and use the word 'sustainability' only in your writings and presentations, then the goal of limiting global warming by 2000, which was moved to 2030, will only move further away. I request such entrepreneurs to start eating organic food all the time first, analyse the space for potential problems and try to fix that gap, rather than start just another e-commerce website or store selling organic products.

The organic market can expand if more people consume organic products. Today, there are three kinds of consumers eating organic food of which the first are the very fanatic, who spend beyond their means on organic products in the hope that they are investing in their future health. The second group has turned to using organic products after they or someone in their family suffered an ailment or when a child is born. I recall meeting a friend who argued that eating organic food is just a fad and there are no proven benefits. The conversation was triggered by a freshly arrived supply of water apples from Lumiere. I didn't counter his arguments that day but, a few months later, he called me to say that he had a heart issue and wanted to know the location of the organic store.

The third kind of consumer is on the fence, who buys just one product and posts about it on their social media claiming 'I've gone all organic' as it is a symbolic way of showing that they practise sustainable living even if they don't really mean it. Also, well-to-do folks who buy luxury products otherwise complain that organic food is expensive.

I once gifted Lumiere's organic nectar to a friend who liked its taste but remarked that it seemed expensive. I had to remind him that he drives a Mercedes car that probably cost much more.

How Can I Afford Organic Products?

My response to this common question about organic products involves this line of analysis. If you can read this, you are already part of a highly privileged class of English readers. Even today, only 246 million[11] Indians speak English, meaning over one billion are not English-educated. This population of English-speaking elite can make a change if only they choose to prioritize eating less but healthy food over eating whatever they choose and staying healthy by burning the excess calories in a gym. In India, the middle- and upper-class population tends to avoid any physical work, which is seen as a low occupation meant for those who could either not afford a good education or make a good living otherwise. This mindset needs to change and people need to recognize that they can make lifestyle choices that are more directly healthy.

Why Are Organic Products Expensive?

1. **Fair price to or fair trade with farmers:** Most organic products' sellers focus on ensuring the viability of farming and believe in paying their farmer suppliers fairly. For instance, Lumiere Organics pays farmers a fair price to incentivize them to continue growing chemical-free food. Customers should confirm that the organic seller indeed pays the farmers better and is not making an empty claim.

2. **No preservatives**: Most fresh organic produce has a low shelf life as no preservative ingredients are added. The farm-to-home time needs to be brief to avoid products getting wasted. Lumiere has attempted various natural techniques such as using earthenware trays filled with water to keep their produce cool. But they still had to install a vegetable chiller for the greens and even then, could not reduce wastage to zero. The only alternative is to convert any product that is not moving quickly into pickles, jams, etc.

3. **Natural tax**: An organic paddy farmer from Mandya, Chame Gowda, once told me that he does not use pesticides. Chame Gowda believes we need the entire ecosystem to thrive and not just us human beings. According to him, if you are healthy, you don't need to visit a doctor often. Similarly, he ensures enough nutrients are supplied when growing plants to guarantee their health, which in turn means healthy food for other creatures that eat some of the plants. He calls this sort of 'crop damage' a natural tax that lowers production somewhat.

A Debt-Free Farmer

One of my interesting field trips involved meeting Chame Gowda at his farm in the Mandya district. At the age of sixty-five, this farmer is walking a lonely path in his village practising natural farming. Chame's father divided the four-odd acres of his land among his four sons and as a result, he ended up with less than an acre of land. But through his relentless efforts over the last ten years, he has produced two tonnes of paddy and proved every agricultural statistic wrong in the process, making a profit of around Rs 1 lakh with zero debt.

His secret is zero use of pesticides or fertilizers, complete ownership of seeds and only incurring labour expenses during sowing, transplantation and harvesting. His multi-cropping technique comprises four and a half months of growing paddy and one and a half months of growing hemp. He mulches the hemp into the field before starting the next cycle and does not even till the land, which consumes only 50 per cent water compared to other paddy farmers in the area. Effectively, Chame Gowda works hardly three months a year in total, as, unlike traditional farming methods, he doesn't need to maintain the crop and leaves it to grow on its own, and enjoys attending organic farming lectures over the rest of the year. He offers a great example of people withstanding peer pressure, with his farm surrounded by those of his brothers who are growing sugarcane using chemicals.

Chemical-Free Cleaning

Dr Gayatri Hela,[12] who earned her doctorate through a study of dietary antioxidants, was part of the Goldman Sachs 10,000 Cohort 2 initiative at NSRCEL. Later, she incubated her idea in the Launch Pad programme, taking up that challenge excellently to replace chemical toilet cleaners. Until then we've gone chemical-free everywhere except for this. She has been successful in marrying the ancient wisdom of Ayurveda with modern science and has developed several AYUSH-certified products such as mosquito repellents, bathroom and toilet cleaners with scale removers, glass cleaner, multipurpose kitchen cleaner, surface cleaner, handwash, sanitizer, etc. When I visited her lab in J.P. Nagar in Bengaluru, she demonstrated how tests were conducted. She could even refer to Ayurveda literature mentioning the herbs that she uses, including soap nuts and holy basil, among others. She has even been working with a paint company to create mosquito-repellent wall paint.

Soaptreez

Balamurali Jaganathan, popularly called Murali, who hails from Trichy, has always been passionate about nature and his father believed deeply in Siddha practices. He once took me to his farm where his father grew several herbs and also installed statues of the Siddha saints. Murali and his wife Jayasri Murali started looking at the various seeds falling on the ground and launched a venture—Jungle Jewels—making jewellery out of various seeds. They also had soap nut trees on the farm and prepared a soap nut-based solution for washing, which they began exporting to Europe. When I met them, they were the only ones who had figured out how to make a liquid soap nut solution. Until then, we were soaking soap nuts in water to generate the lather and then using that solution for washing clothes. Or what was available in the market, which was cotton pouches containing soap nut powder that you can drop into washing machines. The liquid soap nut solution they developed can be used in the machine more easily, bringing convenience to a sustainable lifestyle.

Soaptreez and Reseda successfully won my 'Toilet Cleaner Challenge', which I throw to entrepreneurs to see how they can create products to inculcate sustainable living into ordinary lifestyles rather than treat it as a luxury offering. Lumiere's organic stores also sell Soaptreez products.

Varthur Lake Starts Foaming Up

In 2015, Varthur Lake spewed 10-feet-high foam,[13] spilling scum on to the adjacent Whitefield Road. This problem has continued since, caused by the flow of detergent-laden wastewater into the lake, which is partly diverted from Bellandur Lake. Manas Nanda of Bubble Nut, who visited NSRCEL for a mentoring session, came up with the idea of using soap nut-based products to help tribal communities in Bhubaneshwar, Odisha, who may be able to procure and process them. It would help with the Varthur Lake issue, if more people started using natural cleaning products using soap nuts rather than detergents. I guided him towards using liquid-based products as powder-based products are already available. I also connected him with Jayasri Murali of SoapTreez to license their liquid solution technology, Rajnish of Avani to procure soap nuts from Uttarakhand and Padma at the Foundation for Revitalization of Local Health Traditions (FRLHT). He came up with a liquid-based solution himself after much effort, which I had placed in Lumiere's organic store. Manjunath of Lumiere is someone I consider a resident mentor for piloting many of the products launched by NSRCEL start-ups. He noted that the bubble nut, washing liquid, vegetable wash and dishwash products received good feedback as he introduced more product lines compared to others in the market. It was received well, especially among mothers with newborns, who used it to wash baby clothes. To our surprise, he also found a veterinary doctor recommending the solution as a pet shampoo.

Econut: To Climb a Rock Face or a Coconut Tree?

When I travelled to Mysore, I visited Ramanagara, which is popular as the place where the classic Hindi motion picture *Sholay* was filmed, amid its rock-strewn mountains.

Now, this place has become famous for rock climbing and people throng it to climb the rough cliffs. Rock climbing is becoming popular even among children today and many malls in Bengaluru have set up artificial wall climbing where children compete with each other.

This made me wonder whether Lloyd's commute on the Bengaluru-Mysore Road gave him the solution for the problem he was facing in his venture. Lloyd was working in an IT company and he thought one day, 'Why does a tender coconut that I drink in Bengaluru cost me Rs 35, when my father, living just 3.5 hours out of the city, sells these coconuts for Rs 15 in Hunsur?' He was struck by his situation of being in an IT company writing some code that he had no clue who was using, but someone was selling him this tender coconut at a high price while his father, who grew the coconuts, was struggling. Thus began Lloyd's journey of analysing what was happening in the tender coconut value chain.

The Mandya region of Karnataka, where Lloyd is from, is home to ten lakh coconut trees. However, lately, farmers are not keen on growing coconuts. There are two reasons: one, the price; two, the fact that harvesting coconut is becoming increasingly cumbersome. What is the problem with harvesting coconuts? It costs around Rs 1000 to cut coconuts across an acre of land and the climber brings down around 1000 nuts. As hiring climbers repeatedly is expensive, the person who climbs cuts down Grade A, B and C tender coconuts.

Grade B would have become Grade A in a few weeks, but the cost of harvesting is high, so the farmer would like to do it in one shot. That means he earns less money on the B and C Grade coconuts. He supplies the tender coconuts to the buyer for Rs 10–15. So, he ends up making hardly

Rs 2 on each coconut. With coconut farming becoming less viable, farmers in the Hunsur region started moving out of coconut to tobacco, vegetables, etc.

Lloyd quit his job, went back to his village and started searching for solutions. The rock-climbing craze came in handy; he organized the youth of the village and provided a simple climbing tool given by the Indian Coconut Board. He also started arranging a coconut tree climbing competition among the youth. If rock climbing is so popular, why isn't coconut tree climbing equally popular?

The response by the youth to this new activity was very encouraging. When they reached the top, they cut coconuts. This changed the perception among the youth about coconut-tree climbing, which had traditionally been looked down upon as the exclusive work of toddy tappers. Now, many of the coconut-tree climbers are college students. In India, we often see that people feel ashamed to work on farms after they go to college. Even farmers say to their sons: 'I'm toiling here as I don't have an option. I'm making you study, so you don't need to do this.' This attitude also reiterates their thoughts about agriculture being a non-viable business.

Now, Lloyd used this new-found enthusiasm around coconut-tree climbing and started giving youth earning opportunities by paying them Rs 2 per coconut. The youths, carrying their climbing tools, would visit the farmer every day and cut only Grade A tender coconuts. By visiting various farmers every day and working for only a few hours, a young climber could make around Rs 1000 easily on a good day. This had solved the problems of harvesting. It also brought about a change in people's thinking, restoring the dignity of labour.

When I visited Kuppe, Hunsur, to meet all these farmers and interacted with them about this wonderful initiative, I met Shivakumar who had a master's degree in Kannada and was pursuing his PhD, when he realized that he could make more money with Econut and started working there. Suresh, another youth who has a master's degree in English, was now working as a coconut climber easily making Rs 500–1000 per day. A bachelor's degree-holder Chetan works as a driver for Econut. Sachin, their kiosk operator, dropped out of his diploma and has now undertaken a bachelor's programme. Sudhakar studied BBM with a focus on accountancy and works with Econut.

We went to the village Benkipura, where our young coconut climbers were competing to show me how good they are at climbing. I met Swamy Nayaka, a Class 10 graduate and the son of Econut farmer Annayya Nayaka, who showed me how easily he was able to climb a tall coconut tree with the tool provided. Like him, there are 600 youths available to turn the tables for their farmer fathers and make them tigers. It was amazing and very inspiring.

At the next village, Emmekoppalu, I met Mahadeva, a farmer owning 6 acres who had earlier cut his coconut trees and moved to tobacco farming. Now, he enthusiastically showed me his new coconut plants, signs of his renewed faith in the coconut as he did not personally feel good about growing tobacco. Very soon, he told me that he would be completely back to coconuts and would grow vegetables as the intercrop. At this village, Renuka stopped us to display her share certificate proudly—that she is also the owner of Econut. Her son, Yadhukumar, showed me an airgun developed by him that shoots out paper pellets to chase away monkeys who come to pluck his tender coconuts.

Econut showed me the true spirit and possibilities of farmer-owned entities.

Now, with the harvest problem solved, the next was the market. In Bengaluru, most of the tender coconuts are sold by roadside street vendors. It is cut by a sickle that may be stored in unhygienic conditions, open to layers of city pollution. As consumers, we seek tender coconut water because of its various benefits. According to the Coconut Development Board (CDB) of India, tender coconut water is a natural source of electrolytes, minerals, vitamins, complex carbohydrates, amino acids and other nutrients. The natural carbohydrate content is between 4 and 5 per cent of the liquid. This makes coconut water particularly suitable for the burgeoning sports drink market. According to the Sports Science Institute (USA), sports drinks containing less than 5 per cent carbohydrates are likely to provide benefits while drinks exceeding 10 per cent carbohydrate content (most soft drinks) are associated with abdominal cramps, nausea and diarrhoea. Isotonic and bacteriologically sterile properties of fresh coconut water, straight out of the nut, promoted its use as a direct plasma replacement by military forces in the Asian theatre of combat during World War II. It has a caloric value of 17.4 per 100 gm. 'It is unctuous, sweet, increasing semen, promoting digestion and clearing the urinary path,' says Ayurveda about tender coconut water.

Even though there is sufficient demand for tender coconut, Lloyd wanted to change the way it was being served. He was wondering why the IT parks in Bengaluru did not serve tender coconut at their canteens. When I was heading CDC Software in Bengaluru, I would drink tender coconut water from a roadside vendor every day on my way to work. I also often asked my administrative team to replace the aerated drinks that we provided to our employees with natural coconut water. Their response was that vendors brought 'weapons' (sickles) inside the Software Technology Parks of India (STPI) premises and that they would make a mess within the facility. However, just to satisfy me, during our annual day, they brought tender coconut into the premises.

Lloyd found a solution to this; he created a machine to cut the tender coconut and created a nice-looking kiosk that hides the shells. He convinced IT parks to set up these kiosks inside their premises and is now running over eleven such kiosks. His innovations continued—now that he had brought tender coconut into the campus, what about the boardroom? He started using technology developed by the CDB and started trimming the tender coconut in such a way that it could stand on the table. To avoid oxidation after the trim, the coconut is dipped in an enzyme and wrapped to ensure it stays white in colour. So now people can drink inside their offices without a mess.

Another innovation by Lloyd's friends was a 'pull tab' tender coconut, making even the opening of a trimmed coconut an easier process. The best part of all this is that these kiosks are run by youths, many of whom are farmers' sons and daughters. In the morning, they bring the tender coconuts in trucks into Bengaluru, run the kiosks during the day and return to their village in the evening.

Tender coconut has a high demand in summer as people drink more of it to quench their thirst and to beat the heat. But what happens in winter? Although the coconut tree provides nuts throughout the year, Econut came with a value addition. They now have a licence for selling neera, the drink made out of coconut flower sap. It is a highly nutritious drink but needs to be chilled, so they are using it to make coconut sugar. Econut is today owned by 1146 farmers, 40 per cent of whom are women. NSRCEL's social programme incubated Econut, the first FPO to be incubated for providing initial support and now for scaling up support and grant as well.

While this example from Karnataka was most heartening, I was sad to hear during my visit to Kannur in Kerala that tender coconut farming was moving to Karnataka since farmers felt harvesting coconut is not economically viable with daily wages going up in Kerala. This, by itself, is great news—at around Rs 800 per day, daily wages in Kerala are reaching developed state levels. This provides great opportunities for entrepreneurs to bring technology to address this, as farmers are giving up on the coconut. Shamil Salam, a mechanical engineer and the founder of Kenzon from Areacode, has done exactly that. With his brother, they designed a simple coconut climbing machine, which improves productivity by enabling anyone to climb the trees and harvest the coconuts. The design is so simple that the climber can just sit down and pedal their way up. He has sold over 300 units which, at Rs 2800, are fairly affordable. After meeting him at NIT Kozhikode, where he was incubated, we proceeded to see his work in action at Areacode, where Shamil and his brother have turned their house into a workshop and are already designing other products like an areca nut tree-climbing device and another device to cut passion fruit that has crept all over a tree. Now, they needed to collaborate with Lloyd and Econut to make the educated youth in Kerala climb trees as well. When we visited Kappad on the way back from Areacode, the seed for this book was sown.

During another visit to witness the launch of the Greater Malabar Initiative, which focuses on bringing the Malabar region on to the tourism map with homestays at Kozhikode, we visited rubber plantations set against the backdrop of the beautiful Wayanad foothills. These plantations also provide plenty of opportunities for automating the cutting and collection processes. It is always good to move up in the value chain, as it protects the farmers from price volatility. Entrepreneurial opportunists are interested in the value addition of the rubber supply chain, but it is important to create a local investor community that would support these entrepreneurs through a better grip on the problems. I have had promising discussions with a few high net-worth individuals (HNIs) in Kozhikode regarding this.

The success of Econut and Kenzon serves to underline the importance of our individual choices as consumers too. By choosing produce that has traditionally been a valued part of our diet and lifestyle—by making a healthy choice—we are also supporting our farmers, entrepreneurs and entire communities that can continue living in the villages where they have lived with dignity, instead of searching for employment opportunities elsewhere.

Coffee with Araku

In 2016, I spoke to students on entrepreneurship at IIM Visakhapatnam. Afterwards, I headed to Araku about which I had heard a lot from Infosys co-founder Kris Gopalakrishnan and Prof. Trilochan Sastry, as an example of a well-run producer company. Manoj Kumar, CEO of Naandi Foundation, who had taken Araku coffee[14] to world standards while doing fair trade with the tribals, had mentioned to me that his colleague Vinod

Hegde was also landing in Visakhapatnam that day and would accompany me to Araku. During that two-and-a-half-hour drive to Araku, Vinod told me how the Araku story began. David Hogg, an expert in agriculture and biodynamics taught the farmers about the concepts behind biodynamic growing. Araku is now the largest coffee plantation in the world to be certified organic and biodynamic, using the moon movement with organic inputs. I saw the Cow Pat Pit (CPP) next to the processing plant at Araku where they were making the composite. The coffee growth is taken care of very carefully from seed to tree. By having the processing plant in the hills, over 2000-plus coffee growers work there, thus keeping the economy in the hills. What's coming down is the coffee, that too, to completely export markets, especially France. As France sets the standard on coffee Q rating, I saw a few experts from France in Araku advising on the world standards, so the entire produce doesn't even go to the commodity market but directly to the customer. After their success overseas, they opened their first coffee shop in Bengaluru in 2020.

Having the tribals as part of the cooperative society makes them part of the journey. When I was in Araku, I managed to meet farmer Kondal Rao, the president of the society in 2013. He mentioned to me that in the last five years or so, their ability to make decent returns had improved. He also acknowledged that following strict processes can help avail better prices as well. He grows pepper and mango alongside coffee on his farm, which gives him some additional income.

Sustainability begins with our choices—as consumers, as entrepreneurs, as agriculturists or industrialists. We can look at Econut and Araku Coffee as examples of how much is waiting to manifest as visible rewards, if we just make the right decisions, going forward.

How Socially Responsible Are the Social Enterprises?

I have much admiration for entrepreneurs trying to solve serious problems in remote parts of the country and uplifting the locals' living conditions by exchanging services or products with them. However, something began bothering me after my recent rural area visits and interactions with social entrepreneurs about their priorities. For instance, many of those who work in the water sector use the reverse osmosis (RO) technique for filtering water, resulting in about two-thirds of the water going to waste. In one remote village I visited, the RO plant is near a community pond. The water from the Panchayat pipes is fed into the RO plant and filtered water is sold to people, but the wastewater containing more concentrated contaminants flows into the pond, from which the local livestock drink. For many of the villagers, the livestock are their livelihood and the health of their livestock directly affects their income. Also, if milk-bearing cows drink that water, the milk will also have some residues of contaminants.

Many Western multinational corporations are being watched for their practices of taking water from one location and shipping it to other locations, which affects the local water table. But are today's small social enterprises conscious of this fact? Another entrepreneur mentioned the issue of marginalized communities that opposed plans to set up a water treatment plant. One group of local people threatened an economic boycott if the plant came up on the other side. The entrepreneur simply walked away from that village saying, 'I'm solving only the water problem. If I focus on other issues, I may not be able to survive.'

Eight

Food, Commodities, Pricing—Finding the Way Forward

'In ancient times, we were users; we used the commodities in accordance with our needs. Using is not sufficient for the modern market; it needs consumers. Consuming means consuming things much more than the natural need of humanity or of any living being.'

—Samdhong Rinpoche

These words stuck with me when I heard them at The Valley School retreat with Samdhong Rinpoche ji, held from 25 to 29 September 2017. Food is the key to whether our planet can sustain a burgeoning population or not. Nothing expresses the inequality between humans as the differences in the quality and amount of food they eat. In recent times, we have seen environmental activists the world over attempt to make people more aware of the wastage of food, better methods of cultivation and the harmful effects of chemical pesticides and fertilizers.

But one area where we still do not direct as much attention as we should is how food is treated as a commodity and how this affects its availability and pricing.

For instance, this can be expressed through a simple question—What does New York have to do with Kozhikode?

International Gamble: Coffee and Rubber

Commodity exchanges allow people sitting in New York/Chicago who have never seen wheat or coffee grown in India to make money on both items as they sit at a commodity exchange market and speculate on prices. Why do we really need a commodities exchange and who is it helping? A commodity exchange helps the broker, the trader, the middlemen and those who work at the commodities exchange. Those who grow and nurture the crops on which the commodity exchange is speculating are the last ones to benefit.

Just imagine the scenario—one year the coffee prices go up, and the farmer in India is very happy and excited about it, maybe at the expense of a Colombian farmer who has seen a drought and the production reduced there. Next year, due to the forecast of rains, the coffee price goes down and the Indian farmer is crestfallen. But why should the farmers play this gambling game? People sitting thousands of miles away have looked at the weather forecast predicting rain and the price of coffee has either gone up or declined. The reason a Wall Street broker is making more money than anyone else in the world is that he or she is working on speculations!

I was made aware of this when I went to Kozhikode and was talking to rubber farmers a few years ago. I was told about the prices going down every year whereas the demand for rubber keeps going up! This was puzzling and recently I watched an episode on *This Giant Beast:*

The Global Economy on the value chain of rubber. In this episode, while discussing how many rubber farmers in Thailand are turning to alternative crops because of the declining prices of rubber, the host traces the problem back to the commodity stock exchange.

According to this programme, the demand for rubber is going up 40 per cent every year, but the prices are going down so farmers are leaving their rubber farms and turning to other crops. The corporate buyers, the tyre companies, instead of trying to fix the problem, have started looking at alternatives to rubber. They are experimenting with dandelion flowers as a substitute for rubber. Imagine if this is the fate of rubber—a product which is needed for everything right from planes to car tyres. If rubber can face this because of commodity exchanges, what does it tell us? Can we not trade without commodity exchanges? Yes, we can and we should.

Luxury Cars and Luxury Tomatoes

Another element to keep in mind from the point of view of agriculture is differential pricing. If you look at a car, its basic use is to help a person go from point A to point B. Yet, there is a Maruti Alto and there is a BMW, with vastly different prices. In essence, both have the same use. So, whichever car one uses, one is paying the difference in rate depending on the brand, but getting the same utility. Just consider, what if the differential pricing involved in cars was applied to a tomato? In that case, those who can afford a BMW should also be willing to pay Rs 300 for a kilo of tomatoes. On the other hand, those who can afford only a Maruti Alto would pay the usual Rs 30.

This sounds startling and people begin to shift uneasily in their seats because we have become used to paying a premium on all goods seen as coming from industrial plants with massive investment and backed by huge spends on advertising and brand building. But for the farmer, tasked with the responsibility of sustaining whole generations of humans, we want to give the least and we can get by without punishment.

Also, consider differential pricing in different sectors. When there is a demand, the railways push up the price of tickets, the airlines are doing it for their flights, cab companies are doing it for their cabs within the city. In fact, everyone is doing it, so why not for tomatoes? So, can an entrepreneur do differential pricing for agricultural produce? Should the government be thinking about this?

All this is leading us back to square one of the problems for agriculture—farmers unable to sustain growing their crops in the rural areas of India, abandoning their homeland and seeking to live in the city. As they migrate from agriculture to more productive jobs in industry and services, GDP growth will be boosted but only provided the migrants find jobs. On the flip side, if these jobs do not materialize, the demographic dividend will turn into a demographic disaster. The demographic bulge will come in the form of slums. Is this the development that India is moving towards? An average of 2000 farmers leave their land and agriculture every day to end up in slums.[1] I defy anyone to call this progress.

What are other ways that we can explore to bring more value to the produce? How can we ensure that customers understand this? Let's look at some of the ways in which entrepreneurs are making efforts to solve these questions.

Hill Garden-Treasure Hunt—in Search of Wild Apple

I had the opportunity to see first-hand how the hidden treasures of the Manipur hills are being taken to the world. I met L. Elijah Raiveio from Maiba Village, Senapati District, Manipur while he was studying at IIMB (PGP 2016–18). Elijah started Hill Garden as a student-run venture—he didn't opt for placement after graduation and went back to help his people. Initially, being the first from his region to come to IIMB, all Elijah was looking at was settling into a high-paying job after the course.

But, intrigued by the agriculture start-ups at NSRCEL, he started to explore the possibilities of a student-run venture while studying. I connected him to Lumiere Organics to understand the organic space and he was motivated to bring produce from Manipur that we in Bengaluru don't know about. He spent two years studying seasonal produce and identified twenty-three-plus wild produce that people outside Manipur do not know about. Around 30 per cent of this is consumed during the season in Manipur; the rest is not even collected and goes to waste, as there is no market. The logistics of the hill regions are a big issue to overcome. We took almost a day to reach Mao Gate from Imphal.

One of the delightful discoveries I made then was sougri—pink tea!

From 15 to 23 January 2019, I travelled to three states. After going to Jaipur's Craft Catapult event and seeing the havelis of Nawalgarh, I reached IIT Guwahati for an event and joined the CM of Assam to unveil the state's start-up policy.

Elijah came to the event and we took a flight from Guwahati the next day, the twenty-first. The flight landed at

9.50 a.m. at Imphal Airport. We started around 10.30 a.m. towards Mao Gate and on the way stopped to have a nice cup of sougri tea. It was slightly sour, in a beautiful pink colour. I later found out that this was made using the good old gongura leaves I knew from Andhra Pradesh. Andhra people locally call gongura Andhra matha (mother Andhra) in Telugu, due to its significance in their day-to-day diet. While it has many culinary uses, the most popular is the pickled version.

It was interesting to see that, while the leaves are used in cooking in the south, in Manipur a tea is made out of it. Gongura is part of the hibiscus family called roselle (Hibiscus sabdariffa) or kenaf in English. I have also seen this being grown by tribals in Amale, Maharashtra, who call it *ambadi*. Gongura comes in two varieties, with a green-stemmed or red-stemmed leaf. The red-stemmed variety is sourer than the green-stemmed variety. Gongura is a rich source of iron, vitamins, folic acid and antioxidants essential for human nutrition. It is a summer crop and the hotter the place, the sourer the leaf gets. These leaves are used in south-central Indian cuisine to impart a tart flavour that is believed to build the body's response to the scorching summer heat and prevent illness.

Now I was ready to sample the delicacies of the Naga Thali.

We reached Senapati around 1.20 p.m., a 66-km ride that took three hours. Our lunch was the lovely Naga Thali, containing sticky rice with a lot of greens—three different fresh leaves, cucumber salad, steamed vegetables in hot water, soup, mushroom, pork and the famous akhuni or fermented soya, which is the delicacy of the region. Eating that was an adventure. I always respect the local culture and food is one of the best ways to do so. I remind myself that if I had been born here, all the dishes I am sampling would have been most natural for me.

We continued on our journey at 2 p.m. and reached Mao Gate by 4.20 p.m., taking two hours and twenty minutes for a 44-km ride. By the time we reached the lovely Mao market, the sun had almost set and a chill had set in. On the way we enjoyed wild apples—cut slices of wild apple with pepper and chilly, just like we eat raw mango or guava in other parts of the country.

Wild apple is one of the twenty-three-plus produce that Elijah had identified. Being in season, it was eaten in various forms throughout the day. However, hardly 30 per cent of the total available stock would be consumed during the season. Elijah had identified a cold storage partner at Mao Gate and preserved over 25 tonnes of it. We stayed that night at the cold storage owner Chiisia's home and enjoyed an amazing dinner cooked by her and her son. The son, Thojiio, was keen to come back to Manipur as well if there were more opportunities here.

In the morning, against the beautiful sunrise, we saw frost-covered kiwi fruit growing around their house and the huge cold storage below us. Chiisia's husband was knowledgeable enough to use the AAPDS Integrated Cold Chain Project (ICCP) scheme of the Government of India's Ministry of Food Processing Industries.[2] He had built such a massive facility in the midst of the village. However, it was sad to see that Elijah was the only major customer then, with 25 tonnes of wild apples stored there, along with some kiwi that someone else had stored. There was a need to increase awareness among the locals to use this facility and also figure out the way to use the Warehouse Receipt Financing, so that people who store there can use proof of that to get bank loans. This would free them of the pressure to sell their produce as soon as they need money.

I learnt from them that frequent power problems are hurting them in trying to run a profitable cold storage, and it occurred to me that there was a potential for solar power as well. Once the supply of produce had been secured in the cold storage, Elijah researched for over a year with ICAR institutes and found an agriculture hurdle technology to make value-added products such as Wild Foshy Apple Candy and Santa Rosa Plums Candy, which he markets across the world! He has motivated two of his brothers and a sister to join him in this agriculture venture. L. Michael Khoveio, a veterinary doctor; L. Mevei, an IIMC graduate; and sister L. Leshina—all are working on this. Identifying the hills' hidden treasures, collecting, preserving, adding value with technology and marketing to the world—we need more Elijahs for and from the North-east.

Grama Mooligai—Rural Wisdom: Tamil Nadu's State Flower in Europe

After an incubator meeting in October 2018, at the Tamil Nadu Agricultural College and Research Institute, Tamil Nadu Agricultural University, Madurai, I left to see the work of the Covenant Centre for Development (CCD) under Grama Mooligai (Village Herbals) near Natham. An hour-and-a-half drive took us to V.S.K. Valasai, surrounded by the Karanthamalai Reserve Forest. We walked some distance to meet farmer Kalimuthu, as vehicles cannot go up to his house. He showed us the beautiful red flowers on his farm. Senganthal (Kanvali Kilangu/*Gloriosa superba*),[3] Tamil Nadu's state flower, is a plant mentioned as medicine in Siddha texts, the 2000-plus-year-old traditional medicine system of Tamil Nadu.

Kalimuthu showed us around the mighty hills and told us how he was giving away those wild seeds to people who came and collected them for a very meagre amount. Now that the flowers are not growing wild on the hills, he is cultivating them on his farm, knowing their value. What is the newfound value of this 2000-plus-year-old medicinal plant? A European pharma company found a use for it in the treatment of cancer, making the seed price go up to Rs 3000 per kg at its peak. CCD and Grama Mooligai intervened and ensured that they are now able to sell directly to the buyer.

This was an example of many such items of rural wisdom or traditional knowledge that are being lost, as we don't value them until someone else finds their value and worth. On the way out, we saw some other leaves that had been collected from the hills. I asked them about it and Kalimuthu said that they were a good treatment for cough and had been kept for dispatch to a buyer who had approached Grama Mooligai.

We ended up spending so much time on the hills, that there was no way I could get back to Madurai to catch my train to Bengaluru. So, instead, we decided to go to the next stop, Dindigul, and catch the train there. The contrast between those who engage in sustainable practices and those who profit from them was evident as we were leaving. On our way out of the village, we met an old farmer living in a house with a thatched roof. Clearly, while those wild seeds from the hills were selling at Rs 3000 per kg, none of the money was reaching him. He was worried about his house not having electricity—his granddaughter studying in Class 10 had to finish her homework before the sun went down.

Thinking about the disparity between people—in a fast-growing state, it was still possible to find people without electricity—made me depressed. On our way to Dindigul railway station, the CCD person stopped the car and showed me a plant that grows wild on both sides of the roads. He told me that a buyer had been found for this too.

There is knowledge/wisdom by the side of our roads, but we are searching for it somewhere else. That's the idea that CCD,[4] run by Muthu Velayutham, an Ashoka Fellow, explores by looking closely at knowledge and practices at the grassroots. Earlier, we had supported their tsunami project in 2004–05 through AID India in Kanyakumari, where their Kanyakumari Kalai Koodam had been selling palm leaf handicrafts.

During my earlier visit to a CCD centre near Sevaiyur, Tiruchuli, an hour's drive from Madurai, I found out about the amazing amount of rural wisdom in the local herbals. Many herbs we consider weeds are locally grown by people here and used for medicinal purposes. Grama Mooligai uses the traditional knowledge of these people who would otherwise sell their collected herbs to local healers for very low prices. CCD collects from all of them, does value addition like cleaning and drying and reaches out to buyers like Dabur, Himalaya and others who want to buy these herbs in bulk. So, the gatherers get a good price. In the Sevaiyur centre, they've pretty much emulated all the herbs that grow in the Western Ghats with the support of the United Nations Development Programme (UNDP). It's a valuable initiative that ensures that people know the value of their herbal remedies and don't lose this rural wisdom!

Farmer's Fresh Zone: Know Your Farmer

In July 2017, I arrived in Irinjalakuda, Kerala, by train at 6.30 a.m. and was welcomed by abundant south-west monsoon showers. Hailing from a rain-shadow region in Tamil Nadu, I had never seen this much rain. I joked with the entrepreneurs in Kerala that they should simply bottle the monsoon rain and sell it. However, I learnt that, despite all the rain, Kerala gets its vegetables from outside. My trip to Irinjalakuda was to find out all about this.

After visiting Kodakara, we proceeded to meet a young farmer, Renjith Ravindran, in Ashtamichira. Renjith leases farmland on which he then grows vegetables using safe-to-eat practices. In the summer of 2017, he made a profit of Rs 3 lakh by growing cucumber alone. It was great to meet a few younger farmers like Sreejith and Vijith, as well as the ex-military man Joseph Pallan, who seemed to be their inspiration as he has been growing vegetables profitably since 1998. When I asked Joseph about labour charges, he told me that he never hesitated to share his wealth with his farmers who earn around Rs 800 per day and had been working with him for more than eight years. Compare this with the practice of other farmers to employ migrant labourers from Odisha, West Bengal and other states.

At one of the farms, Alex—who hails from Odisha—told me he earned Rs 9000 per month and received Rs 7000 after deduction for food. He was looking forward to going home for Christmas. I was struck by the fact that he had migrated from home for a mere Rs 7000 per month. Economics is the main reason for migration within

India, with a prosperous state getting people to migrate for a low wage from an already low-income state. While Kerala is losing its people to Gulf countries, workers flock to it from other states. Interesting cycle, but how long can this continue?

Connecting all these farmers is the young entrepreneur Pradeep Punarka of Farmers Fresh Zone, who stays in his village in Kadambode and procures these vegetables as per the needs of his customers in Kochi. He does so without engaging any middlemen and provides a better price for farmers, in the process encouraging more people from the younger generation to take up farming. India needs entrepreneurs like Pradeep to get back to our pre-Vasco da Gama glory days of economic prosperity. We need to play to our strengths.

Every Connect You Make

I first met Pradeep in September 2016 at the Agri hackathon in Kannur, where he was the event's sponsor. He later emailed me in May 2017, which led to my investing in the company a year later, when he had achieved a growth of 15x. In September 2021, over four years since that first email, I put out a press release about investing another Rs 6 crore as pre-series A funding in his venture. I only have to tell him, 'I'm in Kannur next month, let's meet' and he'll come and meet me.

This is an important takeaway for any entrepreneur— the network you build wherever you go is critical but preserving it and remaining connected is even more crucial. Every person you meet is important and you can never tell how helpful they may turn out to be. Pradeep reached out to me eight months after our first meeting and I subsequently met him in Kannur in June 2017. By 1 July 2017, I was already accompanying him on field visits.

And the Drive You Have

Impressed with Pradeep's work, I started connecting with many other people in the organic agriculture space to understand it better. Pradeep was diligent and even travelled to Madurai to meet the CCD team and understand the FPO model and working with farmers. After every one of his discussions with them, I would get an email updating me about the progress. I have met many entrepreneurs in Kerala since my first visit but I have yet to find an entrepreneur who has the same drive as Pradeep.

People often ask me what I look for in an entrepreneur before investing in their enterprise. We usually make an equity investment, meaning that we believe in the entrepreneur and their ability to take his vision forward. The entrepreneur—and their ability—is definitely the most important element for an angel investor, especially since we come into the investment cycle early, when there is less traction from past performance. One of the things I look for is their drive and being brazen in asking for help. Sometimes people call me and say that they reached out to the person I connected them with but they got 'no response'. I believe they need to understand that things won't get done in one email or message and they need to be perseverant.

One of the ways I test the drive of potential investment seekers who meet me at events is by asking them to send me an email at the address published on my website. I have noticed that 70 per cent of these seekers do not progress beyond this step. Earlier, I used to carry recycled business cards made by SZW but I realized that fewer people reached out to me compared to the number of cards I gave out. As I didn't want to waste paper, I stopped carrying the business cards. When people ask for my card, I simply say, 'I'm jobless and don't have a card. However, you can visit my site.' Similarly, among the people who reach out to me on social media, only 50 per cent follow up with me by email. Next, I share my calendar for them to block a time, at which point another 20 per cent drop out, in further self-elimination. In my experience, only people with a high self-drive tend to be successful, which is what worked for me as well.

Attapadi to Cherthala

In May 2018, Pradeep and I visited Attapadi to see how we could get the tribal community there to market their products. In June again, we met at Cherthala where Manjunath was converting his restaurant, Huts, into a fully organic establishment. Pradeep is always curious and builds on his relationships; Manju is a veteran in the organic space and started Lumiere Organics in 2002 when hardly anyone was thinking along those lines! Huts, the restaurant, was his first venture in Cherthala, his home town. When he first started an organic store in Kochi, he struggled to procure organic ingredients as even Kerala was not yet open to the idea of organic food. As a result, Lumiere Organics moved to Bengaluru.

In Cherthala, Pradeep came to know about Lumiere's first organic farm in Kanthaloor near Munnar, from where Manjunath got his produce. Pradeep immediately decided to procure his produce from the farm as well and we decided to go there soon. After an amazing organic lunch at Huts, loaded with fresh fish from the local rivers,

Pradeep took me to visit his store in Kochi. On the way, we visited a fishing village. I had been told that the fishing community was one of the poorer ones in the state. When I saw many old boats lying around rotting, it struck me as a great entrepreneurial opportunity for recycling those boats. Wooden boats can be reused, but the locals had no idea how to recycle or repurpose the many fibre boats.

Tomato Speaks!

After seeing the farmer side of operations with Farmers Fresh Zone (FFZ), I was now curious to look at the front end of it. The storefront had a patch with vegetables growing in it. Pradeep explained to me that this was to keep the children excited and to show them where the vegetable is coming from. Children were free to pluck the vegetable and take it home.

What intrigued me was the QR code on each crate of produce. Scanning the QR code, the customers can get details of the farmers who grew those vegetables and what fertilizer they used. FFZ became one of the first ventures in the country to introduce the 'Know Your Farmer' feature with complete traceability to the source of production. FFZ's safe-to-eat policy follows the Kerala state government's directive on permitted fertilizers. The progressive farmers and agripreneurs in the villages ensure the farmers follow this policy strictly and every batch is sent to the Kerala Agricultural University for testing for chemicals. This process has a great opportunity for entrepreneurs to innovate. I tell them that I should be able to take my smartphone and scan the tomato and it should be able to tell me if there are chemical residues on it. However, this problem is still being worked on, as lab tests take time.

Locals Solving Local Problems

During this time, I made many trips to Kerala to bring in the thought of social business and the Nativelead model of locals solving local problems. I met groups in Kochi, Kozhikode, Kasargode, Kannur and Thiruvananthapuram, and many organizations invited me, including the Kerala Startup Mission (KSUM), KSIDC, Youth Welfare Board, Greater Malabar Initiative, Positive Commune, Kannur Technologies (first private incubator in Kannur) and CII. After seeing their interest, I asked people in Kannur to come forward and invest in FFZ. I announced that I would invest Rs 3 for every rupee they invested so that their risk was reduced.

I was very glad when a few Kannur angels came forward and we invested in FFZ, with IAN, Nativelead and Malabar Angels formally making their first investment jointly with a bigger network. Within two years of being invited by Haani, a young college student in October 2018, we were able to announce the investment by people in Kerala; thus the Nativelead model had taken root in Kerala. In July 2018, the Malabar Angels had been launched officially in the presence of the head of KSUM. Nativelead had conducted workshops for the new angels of Malabar. With KSUM support, Mizone was launched in February 2019 by the CM of Kerala.

Happy Hens—Traditional Wisdom with Global Standards

Ashok Kannan was the winner at Aarambam (meaning 'start' in Tamil), a start-up contest that Nativelead hosts in Madurai with CII and Young Indians every year. At the first Aarambam in 2014, a few of the Nativelead members heard

Ashok Kannan's pitch and were really impressed with the vision of Happy Hens. As per the rules, the winner would be considered for funding from Nativelead. So, at the pitch at Madurai, I first saw and met the Ashok Kannan that everyone had talked about. As the saying goes, don't judge a book by its cover. Ashok shattered my thoughts with his impressive pitch on Happy Hens. Ashok is wheelchair-bound and only one of his hands and head can move; the rest of his body is paralysed. He has never been to school (or maybe schools didn't accept him given his condition). Ashok's knowledge of his subject was amazing.

Ashok is a self-taught guru on traditional herbals, natural farming and herbal medicines. He is also a serial entrepreneur. He had entered the BPO space as well. After that, he had been collecting herbs from the gatherers and supplying them to buyers. As a farmer as well, he had been feeding the herbals to the chickens in his backyard and was surprised to see that the colour of the yolk found in their eggs was orange.

When he had the eggs tested in labs to identify their nutrients, he found that it was these extra minerals and nutrients that were responsible for the colour. As an avid social media user, he met the textile trader Manjunath Marappan, who is based in Bengaluru with roots going back to Karur, Tamil Nadu (the traditional poultry region of the country). Manju had been experimenting with this as well. They shared a common passion for healthy food produced by happy animals. In 2012, in Madurai, the duo started the Happy Hens Farm,[5] for free-range eggs. Free-range refers to the traditional way of raising hens by letting them roam free and forage as they liked.

According to Manju, 'Though backyard poultry was widely practised in India, the high rate of consumption in metro cities and poor connectivity between farmers and consumers and with the influence of the western model, it gave way for factory farming. The rest is history.'

Indian factory farms were confined to approximately 200 million hens in barren battery cages. Each bird lived within a space smaller than a single sheet of paper for more than a year before being slaughtered.[6] Cage-free hens at Happy Hens have more space and are able to walk, fully spread their wings and lay their eggs in nests. The Royal Society for the Prevention of Cruelty to Animals (RSPCA) standards were followed, which define the space given to each bird and not overcrowding them. Thus marrying 1000-plus years of traditional knowledge of herbals to the UK standards, they have formed a unique business model in the good old poultry business.

'Happy Hens' eggs assured one the sunny side, in its true sense, as it was guilt-free food. We do all that is required to keep our hens happy,' said the founders.

In addition to free-range standards, Happy Hens Farm treats its birds with natural and traditional remedies. These include brahmi, basil, sweet flag, turmeric, neem, aloe vera and the like, which have high medicinal value in the diet to ensure the good health of the birds.

The knowledge of rearing poultry with traditional methods is fading. We need to carry forward our rich Vedic knowledge and remedies, which have solutions for many disease-related issues. In addition to traditional methods of farming, the founders are looking to rear the black soldier fly (BSF) worms from unused/surplus vegetables from the market, which will be a breakthrough in the industry.

Happy Hens is the only start-up that operates in the cage-free eggs production industry, which already has established players like Keggs Farm. They are unique, as they rear native Indian breeds while complying with global RSPCA standards and practising traditional and sustainable methods that are different from commercial-scale players.

Being a start-up, Happy Hens faced hard financial times in the initial days, as no bankers were coming forward to support indigenous farming. It was the Native Angels Network (NAN), a forum for enabling angel investments in Tier II and Tier III regions, promoted by Nativelead Foundation, which invested Rs 50 lakh in 2015. This has kept the Happy Hens ball rolling.

After our investment, taking their small experiment to a bigger level, Ashok had moved from Madurai to Trichy and set up a farm on 25 acres in Trichy, with the concept of being a larger version of the backyard poultry. I visited this farm and was super impressed with the fact that Ashok Kannan also lives on the farm with his family—his wife and two children, that too in a shed similar to the one he has built for the girls—how he proudly refers to his birds.

The birds have been freely moving around, with around 1000 birds per acre arrangement. Also, they are moved to the next patch after a few months, so that the ground is freed for it to regenerate. I was introduced to a similar concept of Jhum cultivation, the shifting cultivation of Meghalaya, where the tribals do farming in this way. Their agricultural system is one in which plots of land are cultivated temporarily, then abandoned while post-disturbance fallow vegetation is allowed to freely grow while the cultivator moves on to another plot.

After they perfected this system in the Trichy farm, Ashok and Manju decided to focus on bringing together farmer partners, so the model can scale better. Today, they work with three farmer partners producing over 7500 eggs today. They provide one-day-old chicks to the farmers and their intellectual property is the herbal feed. Also, they focus on traditional breeds that they get from Central Poultry Development (CPD), so that they are more suitable for local climates—Kaveri (Karnataka), Grama Priya (Tamil Nadu), Kairali (Kerala) and Kalinga (Orissa). Once the birds are ready to lay eggs, the farmers take the feed from Happy Hens.

There are also table eggs, or, in other words, non-fertile eggs. A farmer today rearing chickens gets around 50 paise for an egg. On the other hand, Happy Hens provides around Rs 8 to its farmers, thus making the profession very viable for farmers. Besides, there is also a secondary income, as the hens roam freely under coconut or mango trees in a grove or orchard, where their droppings become a great fertilizer. No antibiotics are used on the birds, making this one of the country's first free-range eggs companies, whose birds are fed with natural herbs.

Nutritional facts are printed on the label as well, including why the colour is orange, thus creating trust in customers who are willing to pay a high premium for Happy Hens' eggs. Today, these are the most expensive eggs in the country, enabling the Happy Hens to pass on the benefits to the farmer by providing a better price—fair trade. While country eggs are becoming popular, more people are beginning to claim that the colour of the eggs has been changed to brown by dipping the eggs in tea decoction. Happy Hens differentiates their product not by the colour of the egg, but the colour of the yolk, making it tough to replicate for copycats. I always tell entrepreneurs that solving a tough problem and making it tough to copy also is very important. You need to find easy ways for your customers to see how and why your product is different, which Happy Hens has done very well.

One of their successful farmer partners is Madhavan[7]—
an engineering graduate who left his job in Chennai
working in software and is now back in his village
Ayyanperaiyur, rearing 2000 chickens while earning more
than what he was earning in the city. He also enjoys the
beauty of a 4-acre farm in his village, breathing better
air than in the city. Thus Ashok Kannan, a person who
has never been to school, is now able to provide a better
livelihood for the educated. With just three farmers, the
company is producing 7500 eggs a day, so imagine how
much the farmer is earning—a great example of marrying
traditional wisdom to modern standards and moving from
the old economy to the new economy.

Visiting the Happy Hens farm is one of my favourite
things to do, as I call it the world's best boardroom. We
have our board meetings there, followed by amazing
chicken dishes in his thatched-roof house. It's not just me,
college students who want to learn more about his model
flock to his farm. Also, many entrepreneurs who are facing
challenges visit Ashok for advice as well. It is always
lovely to interact with Ashok, as he is full of ideas and
keeps continuing with his experiments on the farm—with
omega-3 eggs and working on natural immunity booster
eggs with a turmeric-enriched feed. While Ashok continues
to surprise me every time I visit his farm, Manjunath, on the
other hand, takes the post-production processes to world
standards. The eggs come to the Bengaluru warehouse
where they go through a candle test, with each egg being
looked at against the background of light. If they are not
translucent, the egg is rejected. Following that, he prints
the Happy Hens' name and the date on each egg to ensure
there are no counterfeit products, as it's a premium egg.

He arranges stalls at various exhibitions and exposes the eggs to famous chefs of the country as well.

Another jewel they received in their crown is that Humane Farm Animal Care (HFAC) has granted them animal welfare certification according to the Certified Humane Raised and Handled® Programme. Happy Hens is thus India's first company along with one more to receive this certification and the third in all of Asia. HFAC[8] is among the top three internationally recognized certificate agencies. It is based in the US and has a presence across the globe. Also, Happy Hens' operations were certified as Pooled Product Operation (PPO) and therefore are tied to the producers, the farmers. They worked very hard, for more than six months with the agency, passing all the tests to achieve this landmark.

As an investor in Happy Hens, I'm also happy to note that Vital Farms, the first free-range farm in the world to come out with an IPO, is certified by HFAC. With the HFAC certification, Happy Hens is in talks with Google to supply eggs to their employees in India—as Google has a policy to supply HFAC-certified eggs to employees and couldn't find anyone in India so far. When you do so much to ensure quality, you get rewarded as well—the *Economic Times* honoured Happy Hens with the 50 Promising Entrepreneurs of India ranking.

Now that they have reached a peak of 7500 eggs a day, Happy Hens will also be known for its nutritious, exotic eggs from chicken, quail and ducks to Guinea hens. It is also exploring the possibility of taking the franchisee route and engaging women self-help groups to expand operations. They recently launched folate eggs, partnering with a Japanese firm.

As consumers, we can go the extra mile in understanding the value of free-range eggs and give Happy Hens the customers they need to sustain and deliver on their promise of good health.

Tracking Organic Produce: the Case of Jivabhumi

Jivabhumi: know what you are eating

Incubated at NSRCEL, Jivabhumi was started by IIMB alumni Srivatsa Sreenivasarao and Anil Nadig in 2016 to provide consumers affordable and safe organic products. Jivabhumi's USP is using technology to ensure full traceability of their products, allowing consumers to know where and how they were produced and who produced them. Through this traceability, they built customers' trust and foster their enduring loyalty. For me, mentoring them from the pre-idea stage to this achievement was an amazing journey.

Consumers' perception of organic farming and even buying organic food products is affected by the fear or uncertainty that the farmers are only claiming to sell organic food, whereas it is a gimmick to attract a higher price for their produce. I find that scepticism runs high whenever people hear the word 'organic'.

Elsewhere in the world, consumers are now able to track food back to its source. In Italy, a bottle of wine can be traced back not only up to the year of bottling but also as far as the grape, vineyard and the farmer who grew the produce. The same is the case with bread and pasta, as customers have become more discerning about what they choose to buy.

While Jivabhumi tackled Indian consumers' scepticism towards organic produce using technology, promoting organic farming was just one of their initiatives. They consider farmers as their partners and collect product data when working with them. The QR code printed on the product labels enables customers to access this data and trace where and when the production occurred. The farmers can list their products directly on the Jivabhumi platform, which can be accessed either through the website or a mobile app with no charge for registration. The product listing includes details from all production stages, from sowing to harvesting, as well as from the product's journey across the supply chain from the farmer to the market. In many ways, the product label tells the customer a story about the entire history of the product.

Jivabhumi connected the farmer to the consumer directly and enabled the farmers to realize maximum returns for their produce. The data collected from the farmers through their platform also allowed marketing the products effectively and helped them gain better market access, get a fair price for the products and, most importantly, avoid the expense of going through middlemen.

Technology Adoption of Farmers

Another aspect that piqued my interest was the farmers' adoption of the technology offered by Jivabhumi, who were only concerned with ensuring the farmers saw value. If Jivabhumi had approached the farmers and told them that they only sold technology, the farmers may have been against partnering. They established the farmers' trust in the technology platform by elaborating on the value offered in terms of getting them a better price than the market and delivering on this promise. The farmers only wanted two things from Jivabhumi: one, would the company help them

sell all their produce? Second, would it help in getting the
farmers a reasonable, fair price for their products?

This experience made me think more deeply about
determining a reasonable, fair price for organic produce. Is
a fair price fixed solely by asking farmers how much they
spent to produce a particular crop, adding an adequate
mark-up and then selling the produce to customers at the
marked-up price? Does that adequately address the fair
price issue? I also mused whether there was a government
or private agency that had come up with a rating for fair
price and whether a standardized rating exists. Since the
products—and their pricing—are so diverse, each product
is priced differently at different places. For example, one
type of dal or rice may be offered at x price by Jivabhumi,
but the same dal or rice could be priced at y at another
outlet. In such a situation, what should customers choose
and how? My only hope is that the Swaminathan formula
for calculating the cost of production is adopted uniformly
across the country.

Consumer Social Responsibility

The answer to this conundrum is the *sensibility model*
whereby, using technology, Jivabhumi and the farmers
appeal to the customers' sense of fairness. They boldly
mention, as a major part of the information on the
product packaging, that the farmers have been completely
transparent about their production process as well as
about the actions taken to get the produce to the market.
Customers could gauge the production cost incurred by
the farmer as well as the costs borne by the rest of the
ecosystem and, based on that information, make their
decision about buying from Jivabhumi. Through this

initiative, irrespective of their process, farmers were being paid a better price. Although, in theory, buying any product from farmers would benefit them, without the transparency the experience would not be the same. Non-transparent pricing can be quite competitive without telling the customer anything about, for instance, the middlemen involved or the impact on the farmer.

The vision of the Jivabhumi initiative was to create a community-supported agricultural ecosystem that connected the farmers with conscious customers. The aim was to provide healthy, affordable, locally sourced, naturally grown sustainable food without the use of synthetic fertilizers and harmful pesticides that supposedly provide farmers more value for their produce. The Jivabhumi farmers used cow and goat manure and environmentally friendly fertilizers such as panchagavya and neem oil. The technological platform used by Jivabhumi enabled optimizing and scaling up their supply and distribution systems. At the same time, it provided farmers with the information and knowhow necessary to render their farming sustainable. A further advantage was that both the farmer and the consumer were insulated from market price fluctuations. Further, their farming technique was Participatory Guarantee System certified (PGS), which is a globally accepted standard for sustainable agricultural practices meant for small farmers who sold their produce locally and directly.

At Jivabhumi, transparency was their unique selling point that helped them build consumer confidence. Hence, they had what was called the 'Jivabhumi seal of trust', to revolutionize food production by maintaining ethical and sustainable sourcing standards. Their initiative works mostly with small farmers.

TraceX Is Born

Jivabhumi's platform was developed using blockchain technology for in-house use, but they have managed to spin off and sell it to other organizations as well, under the brand name TraceX. Today, TraceX supports major brands like MTR and another dairy brand to provide customers traceability and authenticity. I tell them that they've become Amazon.com, which built a strong web hosting solution for its e-commerce marketplace that has since been sold to other companies through Amazon Web Services. It is personally heartening for me to witness the highly committed journey traversed by the Jivabhumi founders, Srivatsa T.S., Anil Nadig and S.L., whom I have known for over seven years now.

Nine

The Warp and Weft of What We Wear

From the scene in *Swades* (2004) depicting Mohan's visit
to Haridas's house:

Haridas: '*Kheti kisaani karne se pehle mein julaahi karta tha.
Masheenon* [plural for the English 'machine'] *ka badhiya
kapda aane laga toh kaarigar ka muh sookh gaya. Phir maine
hal pakda. Geeta ji se zameen kiraye par li. Socha tha paseena
phasal banke lahrayega toh bacchon ki zindagi sudhar jayegi.
Par sab dharaa ka dharaa reh gaya* [Before I took up farming,
I used to be a weaver. When machine-made cloth became
commonplace, us artisans lost our livelihoods. That's when I
picked up a plough. I rented land from Ms Geeta. I thought if
my sweat would turn a crop, my children would have a better
life. But all was in vain].'

The clothes that Indians wear have a rich history, not
just within the subcontinent but the world over.
Notwithstanding the decline of textile artisanship in India
during the colonial period, India continues to be among the
top exporters of textiles globally. Also, since Independence,
the challenge of clothing a large and growing population
has resulted in traditional handlooms giving way to
cheaper, mass-produced clothing manufactured in mills.

Textiles have a huge potential in India as an item of export and have been ranked the second largest after China. Today, some thirty-five million people work in the textile industry alone, the second-largest employment provider in the country, after agriculture, although the share of textiles in the Indian export basket has declined to around 11 per cent in 2020, from 24 per cent in 2001.[1]

In India, the handloom and handicrafts sectors are governed by the Ministry of Textiles. Together with handicrafts and small-scale power loom units, handlooms account for 75 per cent of India's textile output.[2] The deplorable state of the more than two millennia old handloom tradition in India is a serious cause of concern. The pandemic also made it worse with over nine million weavers and artisans severely impacted due to the shutdown of production activities and sales, resulting in a loss of livelihoods. According to the 2019–20 National Census of Handloom Weavers,[3] there are 31.44 lakh households engaged in weaving and allied activities, out of which 87 per cent are in rural areas. The sector contributes significantly to women's empowerment, with over 70 per cent of all weavers and allied workers being women. This report also underscores the fact that the average household wage of over 66 per cent of the weavers, that is twenty-one lakh weaving families, is less than Rs 5000/month, which, per weaver, is almost at the level of the national minimum individual wage of Rs 4576/month.[4] Around 67 per cent of the weavers are occupied full-time in the profession, making them most vulnerable sections of our population, with no alternative employment as they lack skills necessary to find work in other industries. In fact, around 56 per cent of adult handloom workers have little or no schooling.

If weavers are to survive, they have no option but to migrate to cities to find better employment opportunities, only to end up living in slums, unable to adapt to city life, with no marketable skills and shunned by city dwellers.

Further, the majority of rural handloom workers are women and a loss of occupation adversely influences their children, as a large part of women's income is spent on educating them. In turn, the children's lack of schooling lowers their chances at getting good jobs, even as the one skill they have inherited is rendered obsolete by cheaper, mechanically-produced alternatives. The question to ask is how do we ensure that old economy jobs such as weaving are restored and weavers are motivated to continue living in the rural areas that are home to them, rather than move to the cities?

I felt disheartened discovering on my visit to the Indrayani Handlooms store in Nagpur that there are less than fifty weavers in any given village. The Maharashtra State Handlooms Corporation, which operates the brand Indrayani Handlooms, was started there with the 'socioeconomic objective of helping the handloom weavers of the state'. According to the 4th Handloom Census, there are only 2882 handloom workers in Maharashtra, including weavers and allied workers.[5] Even these workers may soon migrate to other industries. Also, the weavers' children are hired by local textile shops as they are good at handling cloth, but they are only paid a meagre salary.

While the government began marking 7 August as National Handloom Day on the one hand, on the other, the All India Handloom Board founded in 1992 was shut down in July 2020.[6]

A Question of Unique Identity

Apart from being commercially challenged right from the introduction of mill-made products in the nineteenth century, handloom textiles are also threatened by the decreasing availability of natural resources and increasing use of technology. For instance, products made using a power loom and synthetic fibres aim to duplicate the appearance of handloom textiles, but at a far lower price. Such knockoffs are available for almost every type of handloom fabric in India. Likewise, with synthetic dyes being easier to procure and cheaper in cost, the use of natural dyes like indigo or turmeric is declining.

I was visiting Sanganer near Jaipur in Rajasthan, which has a geographical identification (GI) tag for its unique block printing style. It was amazing to see how trained artisans were able to create a flower pattern in multiple colours using various blocks dipped in various dyes. At the reception, they had kept three versions of a fabric, which all looked the same given the similar designs imprinted on them. I asked about the difference and was told that one of the three fabrics was a power loom-spun fabric with screen printing (rather than block printing) and was made for a popular fashion brand selling to the mass market. The second fabric, also power loom-spun but with a block print, was created for a popular brand that claims to be authentic. The last fabric was handloom-spun and block printed, aimed at the export market. As someone who understood little about fabrics, it was tough for me tell the difference just by the look of the fabric, which, precisely, is the enemy of handicrafts in the country. You often hear statements from people such as, 'I can buy the same thing for a cheaper price!' without any reference to the quality of the product.

Some years ago, *Ikat* design (blurry zig-zag patterns) was quite popular. But for an ordinary customer, it would be tough to distinguish the original Ikat from the printed Ikat. Today, sadly, not only specific product identities, but the handloom sector itself is threatened. In the name of economies of scale, centralized mills that control all processes under one roof and are capable of producing in large volumes are preferred. The lower cost of production gives their products a price advantage. Most customers also encourage this trend as they are constantly looking out for cheaper or discounted fabrics. This strains the supply chain for handloom fabrics.

Transitioning from the Old Economy to the New Economy

The example of the Rs 4 lakh Ganesha figurine tells us that there is a way we can make the old economy relevant to the new economy, perhaps by transforming it. Weavers do not want anyone's sympathy but they want people to support growing organic cotton, using vegetable dyes and paying a premium for handloom products. Their doing so ensures that weavers get a better price, are able to preserve the handloom tradition and can maintain their livelihood in the villages they call home. Buying handloom fabrics is not about owning something precious that we can wear alone, it is also about securing the weaver's life and the planet towards a sustainable future.

We need to realize that Indian handlooms have a global, commercial appeal and not just a local, sentimental value. The handloom fabrics produced in India are not made anywhere else but we need to preserve their uniqueness through all possible interventions. To restore India to glorious Bharat, we have to tackle the issues facing not just the weavers but our entire population of approximately 1.35 billion Indians in terms of what we eat, where we live and what we wear. So, what are we wearing?

100 Years of Gandhi Choosing to Wear Just a Loincloth

2021 marked 100 years since Mahatma Gandhi decided to wear only the dhoti, or loincloth and a shawl, while in Madurai.[7] He saw that 'the millions of compulsorily naked men, save for their *langoti* four inches wide and nearly as many feet long, gave through their limbs the naked truth'. He interacted with the poor and the farmers at the Thenur-Cross, where his train had stopped at a signal. After that incident, the next day, 22 September 1921, when he appeared from his room in Madurai, he surprised everyone with this new attire to show solidarity with the poor who couldn't afford full clothes. I had studied by the Nagamalai Hills behind that place and didn't know about this until a few years ago when CCD arranged for me to visit this place. Later, he would even meet the king of the United Kingdom wearing just the loincloth in contravention of accepted court etiquette and he quipped that 'The king had enough on for both of us.'

However, Gandhi did not recommend that everyone wear the loincloth, saying instead, 'I do not want either my co-workers or readers to adopt the loincloth. But I do wish that they should thoroughly realize the meaning of the boycott of foreign cloth and put forth their best effort to get it boycotted and to get *khadi* manufactured. I do wish that they may understand that *swadeshi* means everything.'

Gandhi had been persuading people to adopt khadi, which is a fibre spun and woven by hand, and give up wearing foreign-made fabrics that had been manufactured at the cost of the Indian artisan. So, what we wear makes a significant statement of who we are.

Creative Destruction

Fashion is an endless popularity contest that often defies the logic that clothes should be suited to the local climate, with people left wondering why fashions change over time. For instance, why did bell-bottom jeans fade into the designer jeans and boots look of the 1980s, which then segued into the baggy look of the 1990s? Jeans were functional clothing first designed for mine workers and cattlemen in the West. Today, jeans are ubiquitous—everyone from toddlers to old men and women wear jeans, even in places like Tamil Nadu and Kerala, which are humid and hot almost throughout the year. Further, people wear faded and torn jeans calling them by different names like acid wash, stone wash and distressed. I tell entrepreneurs that if people can sell you torn clothes in the name of fashion, you can sell anything in this world. Torn clothes used to be a sign of poverty or beggary, but the rich are wearing them now.

A movie star wearing torn jeans can get into a five-star hotel, but a beggar wearing torn clothes cannot. The beggar's clothes are torn as he has a few clothes that tore from repeated use, while we waste resources making new clothes and wearing them torn. I once sarcastically asked a person from the fashion industry whether they bet a rupee that many Indians would look like beggars wearing torn clothes. He replied saying it is called 'creative destruction'. If you wear anything that comes with a marketing tag endorsed by a movie star, you are all set, fashion-wise.

Wearing a Three-Piece Suit with the Air Conditioner Running at 17°C

In India, although we have a rich tradition of fabrics and designs, many people prefer to emulate the West. For instance, on a hot summer day in Chennai or Delhi, men dress in thick wool-blended suits as that conforms to the dress code norms for formal meetings. After Rajinikanth wore a three-piece suit (in the movie *Kabali*), people in Chennai— which registers 42 degrees Celsius temperatures—started following that fashion, which invariably meant sweating a lot. The consequence would be that either the deodorant industry would boom, or people would keep the AC at 17 degrees Celsius. Why do people in southern India need a suit which is usually made of cloth good for colder climates and may only be acceptable in the northern Indian winters?

Some of us perhaps feel ashamed, in the wake of colonialism, of wearing clothes that were traditionally designed and are suitable for the local climate. The dhoti, for instance, can seem like an amazing invention. You can fold it up and feel like you are wearing shorts, or you wear it unfolded and your legs are fully covered akin to wearing pants. Whenever I travel anywhere in Tamil Nadu or Kerala, I prefer to wear a dhoti. In many parts of the country, if you wear traditional clothes and speak your language, you cannot get ahead in life, which is a problem requiring rejuvenating people's self-pride.

The Caftans of the Middle East

The sheikhs of the Middle East are among those who have stuck to their traditional attire, continuing to wear caftans—loose white clothes that are the best for their climate. They wear these robes abroad as well, irrespective of the countries to which they travel. These sheikhs probably do not feel ashamed about their clothing, as they are probably richer than many people living in developed countries, whether from Europe or the US. They do not need to show off their wealth as they pride themselves on doing what they do, with aplomb. Somewhat similarly, the only people who wear the dhoti in India without being looked down upon are politicians.

A Salute to Ramraj Cotton

I remember talking to K.R. Nagarajan at a five-star hotel in Coimbatore, who founded Ramraj Cotton of Tamil Nadu, about how he started his company.[8] We both wearing dhotis, wondering whether they would have allowed us here a few years back with this attire. A twenty-something Nagarajan once wore a white dhoti and shirt to a bank, where the security guard refused to let him enter. This experience inspired him to start Ramraj Cotton and change the perception about the dhoti through advertising that highlighted the image of people wearing dhotis. In one television commercial themed 'Salute Ramraj', for instance, a person wearing a dhoti walks into a five-star hotel followed by his assistant wearing a formal business suit and is received with respect by everyone he meets. Ramraj also introduced an easy-to-drape dhoti with Velcro, which would reduce worries about the garment coming loose, a common reason for younger people to avoid wearing it. I was proud to see his name along with mine, among those who received the Vetri Tamilar Award (Successful Tamil Person award) at Sangam4 in 2015. Ramraj Cotton was doing a revenue of Rs 1300 crore in 2020–21 and had just launched stores in Bengaluru and Thiruvananthapuram.

It took the Tamil Nadu government passing a resolution in the state's legislative assembly in 2014 for people wearing a dhoti to be allowed into various colonial-era clubs in Chennai that still followed British rules.[9] Sometime after that, I met a friend of mine in one of those clubs and, as usual, I was wearing a dhoti. He had to come out to receive me as they did not allow me inside. Even seventy-four years after Independence, we are still surrounded by relics of the British Raj.

The Age of Fast Fashion Trends

My father-in-law, who is eighty-five years old, has four or five dhotis and shirts, all of which are white. When I was growing up, the only time anyone got new clothes was for Deepavali, which consequently became a special festival. In those days, we got our clothes stitched by the tailor in our small town, which required anxious daily trips to check if the clothes were ready. Usually, he would only deliver them the night before Deepavali. We used to value that and cherish those clothes. Today, in the name of fast fashion, new clothing designs and patterns are introduced all year round, in every season. For example, the summer 2019 collection is not the same as the summer 2020 collection.

India is a tropical country, with near uniform climatic conditions throughout the year in the southern parts and extreme summers and winters in the northern parts.

However, even in India, the seasonality of fashion is a trend now. A fashion brand that is unable to sell their collection for one year or season discards it entirely. Some luxury brands even burn their inventory because they do not want their clothes to end up in the black market, which I think is a waste of resources. The pandemic has somewhat slowed down this trend, with many fast fashion brands, in fact, struggling to stay in business.

Do I Know What I'm Wearing?

How do we switch from synthetic to organic fabrics? Can we really change customers' thinking across the entire chain of clothing to align with more sustainable values? For instance, people vehemently oppose using plastic grocery bags as they can choke birds and cows. However, they don't realize that the dress they wear is probably made of some form of plastic-based synthetic fibres such as polyester, rayon, chiffon, georgette or satin. Some of these fabrics were originally based on natural fibres—chiffon from silk, for instance. Now, rayon is used to mimic the texture and appearance of a variety of natural fibres like cotton, wool and silk, while chiffon is made from polyester.

However, in the recent past, designers and fashion labels have begun encouraging the use of handloom fabrics like khadi. We also have to view our fabric consumption through the lens of Individual Social Responsibility (ISR). I often say that handloom fabrics and khadi need not be affordable to the middle class, which many find controversial or do not agree with. Khadi, for instance, is offered at discounted prices during Gandhi Jayanti. Similarly, handloom saris are gifted by the government, while the Indian Railways buys handloom bedsheets. None of these are cost-effective and can be replaced by power-loomed fabrics, which are cheaper. Handloom fabrics and garments can then be deemed premium products and sold at a price that can sustain the sector. People, instead of buying ten sarees, buy one handloom saree that has not consumed energy in the making and if that is organic cotton and natural dye, then it hasn't harmed the earth as well. By paying a premium, you are also supporting the weaver as well, thus supporting people and the planet.

As Dastkar Andhra's advocacy coordinator B. Syama Sundari suggests, a 'power loom mark, if strictly implemented, would directly benefit hundreds of low- to medium-skilled handloom weavers producing for the same middle market, which is highly price sensitive'.[10] However, buyers still need to make the effort to research and purchase genuine handloom products at the appropriate prices, which are respectful of the weaving skills handed down across generations of weavers' families. If we continue to consume blindly, without a care for the consequences of where our money goes, we are effectively consigning weavers to unemployment and a life of hardship. Among the actions buyers can take are verifying the marks assigned by the Indian government like Handloom Mark, India Handloom Mark and Silk Mark to confirm that a handloom product is genuine.

Farm to Fashion

When I met Harold Rosen of Grassroots Business Fund (GBF), he spoke very highly of two of their portfolios— Jaipur Rugs and Industree (Mother Earth). Started as an IFC's Grassroots Business Initiative, it was spun off into the Grassroots Business Fund in 2008. Later, GBF mentioned about Apache Cotton support as well in Pollachi. After attending Nativelead's Coimbatore chapter programme, I headed out for a wedding in Pollachi and asked the GBF team to arrange a visit to Apache Cotton as well. We headed to Uthukuli, a place 65 km from Coimbatore. I had heard that Uthukuli was famous for butter, but meeting Viji and listening to what she and Mani have done brought another attraction to Uthukuli—Ethicus. From a textile family of sixty-five years, they wanted to do something unique and eco-friendly. They traced back to the 'Suvin' finest and longest staple cotton in the world known as India Sea Island cotton, which originated in the Caribbean Islands and was brought to the rest of the world by Columbus in 1492. The Eco-Logic project was started in 2004 to bring out organic cotton. With the Pollachi region having a smaller number of cotton growers, they identified and started contract farming with farmers in Kabini of Karnataka, helping them to grow organic cotton with traditional seeds rather than genetically modified ones. The Kabini cotton comes to the Uthukuli ginning facility that we visited, which runs with stringent processes to ensure the bales that are leaving are of a very high quality. Extending that cotton to fashion, the Ethicus was born in 2009, where we saw these cotton yarns being converted by fine handlooms. She was showing the National Institute of Design students a nature-inspired handloom collection—Athangudi tiles designs on the sarees. We bought a saree that has cherry flowers on it, which said that it was made by G. Paramesh and it took seven days to make it. It also has the GOTS (Global Organic Textile Standard) and Textile Exchange certified by Cotton Control Union, the Netherlands. Now, the final touch is the 'Cotton Trail'—one can witness the 300-km story of Farm-to-Fashion starting from the

Elephant Corridor of the Kabini Reservoir to Anamalai Tiger Reserve in Pollachi. Meet the farmers, take some cotton and see how it is transformed into a garment in Uthukuli. That's something on my to-do list.

Sustainable Fibres

When anyone walks into a store, whether in India or abroad, most clothes are made of either cotton or polyester, or a blend of the two fibres. For the most part, we make our clothes out of a few selected materials, which is likely to change sooner than later. There are fascinating discoveries being made in the textile world, with designers and inventors discovering methods for making fabrics that are more sustainable and do not involve vast quantities of water and pesticides (like cotton) or disperse plastic microfibre pollution with every wash (polyester). Recent discoveries have seen microplastics present in placenta and also creating xenoestrogen in women affecting their fertility.

The production of sustainable fibres, for instance, adopts a holistic approach encompassing every aspect of the product lifecycle, even covering recycling. Some examples of sustainable fibres include Piñatex (made from pineapple leaves and resembling leather), MycoTEX (grown using mushrooms and does not require yarning or weaving), Tina Tape Yarn (drawn from the eucalyptus tree, used in knitting), a silky bamboo fibre, banana fibre, coconut coir, cork fibre, hemp, jute, flax linen, lotus flower fabric and peacock feather fabric.

At NSRCEL, we incubated a start-up working on producing banana fibre. I made a trip to Mandapeta, in Andhra Pradesh's Rajahmundry district, to see the weaver who made the fibre. They shredded the stem into the finest strands possible and tied the strands one by one, by hand, to make the longer yarn. At NEDFI Guwahati, Assam, I was able to get a banana fibre fabric that was made by mixing it with cotton. Producing ropes and yarn out of banana fibre increases the revenue streams available to the banana farmer who gets money from selling the leaf and banana as well. The women at home can make banana rope and yarn and sell that also.

When I visited Thapasu Foods in Himachal Pradesh, Amshu showed me how hemp was growing wildly in the vicinity. Since the hemp seeds are considered part of the cannabis plant, they can only be plucked wildly and not cultivated. Uttarakhand and Himachal Pradesh are currently amending laws to legalize cannabis cultivation, which gives entrepreneurs an incentive to develop hemp fibre products. Last year, one of the NSRCEL launch pad start-ups was working on hemp fashion. The start-up by Deepa designed a lovely kurta from hemp fibre and also ensured that the colour was natural and coated using a method called Ayurvastra practised in Kerala.

While considerable work remains to be done on sustainable fibres, it is anyone's guess what kind of clothes we would be wearing even ten years from now.

Ten

Practices for Posterity—Clothing and Home Accessories

> '*The situation the Earth is in today has been created by unmindful production and unmindful consumption. We consume to forget our worries and our anxieties. Tranquillizing ourselves with over-consumption is not the way.*'
> —Thich Nhat Hanh

Sustainable practices require that we simply see the bigger picture. There is no single template for a consumer, farmer, entrepreneur or industrialist to think in sustainable terms. Yet, each one can make a difference by thinking about the larger impact of their individual actions. How will what I do today look like tomorrow, a decade or two decades later? What are the innovations I can bring into present processes that can ease the costs to humans and the environment? How can my business bring prosperity to the larger community? These are questions that may occur often to those who want their decisions and actions to lead to a better present and future.

Answers to these and insights into many of the present dilemmas that face us, both in economic terms and in the face of the frightening effects of climate change, can be glimpsed in the way in which some entrepreneurs have built and carried out their operations.

Some examples of businesses I have collaborated with or mentored bring us insights into practices that can show us a better way forward.

GoCoop: Better Choices in Handlooms

I was attending a conference in 2013 about Impact Investing in India, organized by the Rockefeller Foundation, where Siva Devireddy was also present. At the conference, Siva asked a question about how cooperatives can play a role in social enterprises. I remembered that buying notebooks at the cooperative society in our town and bedsheets from Co-optex of Tamil Nadu had been part of my younger life all along. Siva's question made me think, why not? I pulled him out and said, 'I received your deck through Indian Angel Network. However, your ask was beyond angel round. Let me spend some time with you.'

Siva hailed from a village in Guntur district of Andhra Pradesh, and was working in the IT sector. He would go to his home town every summer and saw the number of weavers were reducing. For example, Mangalagiri of Guntur was once a thriving hub for handloom weavers, but there has been a rapid decline in the number of weavers in the past two decades to under 2000 from about 10,000 handlooms at the turn of the millennium.[1] So, he started to understand their challenges, which eventually made him quit his job to start GoCoop.

Challenges are multifold—on the production side, across the various states in India, there is a huge variety of handlooms and handicrafts produced by rural artisans. Unfortunately, almost all are fragmented and unorganized in their operations, marked by a high intensity of labour and low resources to capital. The products did not have any standardization or quality checks. Supply chains were absent for these products.

On the market side, they were a few self-help groups and cooperatives set up by the weavers in rural areas. However, many weavers were excluded from the benefits of these groups as most of these cooperatives were government-run. Apart from the industry not being supported by finances, the weavers were poor at marketing and depended on the middleman, who exploited them by bargaining hard, where he would buy for Rs 500 and sell at Rs 2000 or so, making huge profits. As the weaver has no connect with consumer, he didn't know what sells and what does not and the likes and dislikes of consumers.

Several small NGOs were marketing handlooms, but the more established players like Fabindia, are from the private sector. Selling products through online or offline channels to consumers to reduce the middlemen has become an attractive business model for several entrepreneurs in recent times. The government supports this industry through trade fairs, exhibitions, emporiums, training programmes and other such interventions.

Weavers also faced another challenge, as the younger generation was leaving the trade and rural areas for better job opportunities. Thus, traditional skills, which were passed on from generation to generation, were now slowly dying.

After understanding all of these, Siva started to look at the cooperative weaver societies that are voluntary organizations, open to all persons to use their services and willing to accept the responsibilities of membership, without gender, social, racial, political or religious discrimination, owned by weavers as members. A total of 44 Apex cooperatives procured from the smaller cooperatives and sold directly to customers. Around 15,926 Primary Weavers Cooperative Societies were set up many years ago but the weaver woes continued![2]

Thus, GoCoop was born to empower rural artisans by integrating them into supply chains, serving domestic and international markets. First, it was a directory listing of artisanal products to domestic and foreign buyers. Then he realized that he needed to change his business model, as both his sellers and buyers had very different sets of problems. The sellers needed to be educated about the market, the various opportunities it offered regarding the quality of production and, most importantly, on how technology could be used for their benefit. In return, they had to be assured of payments in time. The buyers, on the other hand, did not want to work with sellers not known to them, especially those who did not have an establishment. Seeing this, Siva changed it to become a social marketplace.

For large volume transactions, to establish trust between the buyers and sellers, he set up escrow accounts. For those cooperatives that operated on their own, GoCoop provided the marketplace for a commission and did not do any intermediation. For small cooperatives, GoCoop played a major role as they would be intermediaries to procure orders and negotiate with buyers. They worked with suppliers for quality products to deliver to the buyers, obtained payments and paid the suppliers. GoCoop had a margin of 10–20 per cent and ensured transparency. In addition, he ensured complete traceability. If the barcode was scanned, the details of the cooperative, product composition, product specifications and artisan details along with his or her photograph were visible. Siva had a strong ideology of wanting to help artisans earn a better living. In doing this, he had to make sure that he kept pace with the changing styles in the market.

Understanding the depth of what Siva has done, I had told him to reduce the amount he was asking, as it was too much for an angel round back then and also too early for VCs. Today, VCs may even fund ideas but that was not the case in 2013 when Siva needed the funding. So, I worked with him to start with a round of angel funding and Siva accepted. That way, he was open to my mentorship and for angel investors, it is important.

I was further impressed that Siva had employed a finance person, since it was not common for start-ups to focus on finance from the very beginning. GoCoop also earned some revenues through government-funded projects. From the perspective of scaling up, I felt that government projects are not a sustainable business model. Eventually a marketplace model evolved over online and offline. Offline GoSwadeshi exhibitions brought weaver–customer interaction physical, celebrating over seventy of them now. For discerning modern customers, the Good Loom brand was launched to connect modern thoughts to traditional wisdom.

I remember telling Siva that artisans may not have access to resources, but they know what they want. The moment they have more money, they will send their children to a private school, since they know what is best for their children. Hence, my philosophy was that GoCoop should help them sell more products at better margins and put more money in their hands.

His idea evolved from the intersection of the desire to do something socially relevant by using the cooperative form of business organization and applying technology as an enabler. It is great to know that while he is an active marketing intermediary for weavers, he has raised the capacity of the weavers and at the same time, not changed the ethnic character of the products. He has also successfully positioned this as a social impact enterprise. Above all, GoCoop has created a network of stakeholders who are invested in its success and future.

Airbus to Redbus!

When I talk about Siva and his relentless effort to visit weavers first hand in understanding their problems, I used to say he had gone from Airbus to Redbus! This is because when he was employed at Accenture, he used to fly in business class and ever since he started GoCoop, he was ready to travel by state transport bus to meet weavers in the rural areas of India.

Because running a social business is glamorous from the outside and gets a lot of attention from friends, media, etc., as a saviour of weavers, it's hard work and lot of perseverance is required. I joke about it, comparing it with the beauty pageant of the world—after being crowned Miss World or any other title of that sort, you would see people asking her what would she like to do, and you'll get answers such as, 'Saving the world, helping the poor', etc., but you would see them end up as models or actors. This is what being social entrepreneur is—it takes lot of perseverance to stay the course; otherwise, one can easily get discouraged and it would result in mission drift. This is because, many times when they see that someone selling idlis or T-shirts gets big funding, it makes them wonder: Why am I travelling in buses and sitting in 42 degrees hot weather with a weaver in Odisha? It takes years of will to keep the perseverance alive as well. For Damodaran of Gramalaya, it took three decades before the government understood the need for toilets, but at a young age out of college, he had started working on sanitation.

There was enough stigma associated with the profession, but it took sixty-six years after Independence to make manual scavenging illegal in India by the Prohibition of Employment as Manual Scavengers and Rehabilitation Act, 2013, after relentless efforts of the Safai Karamachari Andolan (SKA) by Bezwada Wilson.[3] Thirty years on, SKA is still working to end this practice and rehabilitate the workers. I met Wilson in Dhaka in 2014 at the Change Alliance conference and his focus now is on bringing different livelihoods to them. Social entrepreneurs like these had a strong determination and achieved what they set out to accomplish. They didn't bother how long it took; they stayed on course until they achieved it. The bus is another way I test people wanting to come to the social sector as well. Many of my friends and others call me saying, 'I would like to do what you are doing' or 'I want to support the great cause.' I tell them, 'Can you catch the next bus and go to Hubli?' I will see a hesitancy, saying, 'I'm good in metros where flight connectivity is better.' I've even seen employees working in social business also saying, 'There is nothing in this village.' The funniest of all I heard was, 'There is no McDonald's here!'

Siva's hard work paid off when he received the Government of India's First National Award in 2016 for Entrepreneurship for marketing handlooms. With the e-commerce boom, all the major players started adding handlooms to their offerings, thinking that it was as easy as selling a mobile phone. Soon all of them realized that it was very tough and it was well-proven that when all the major e-commerce players were competing for this award, Siva received it. Now many of them want to partner with Siva. The reason GoCoop received it was because of its strong DNA in understanding and helping the artisans. It's a great lesson to all entrepreneurs that if you are strong in your field, you can even win over big companies and Google's CEO may interview you to understand how you did it. Yes, Siva was among three entrepreneurs in India whom Sundar Pichai chose to interview, to understand how GoCoop is using technology to change the lives of weavers![4] The International Cooperative Alliance (ICA), with cooperative organizations as members across the world, invited Siva to present his paper on GoCoop as a platform for all the cooperatives in the world. He was also part of the United Nations Economic and Social Commission for Asia and the Pacific (ESCAP) Digital Economy Taskforce along with Narayana Murthy, founder of Infosys—the only two people from India. Today, the GoCoop case study done by IIMB Prof. G. Sabarinathan and Prof. S. Ramakrishna Velamuri, China Europe International Business School (CEIBS) is at Harvard Business Publishing (HBP), being studied by students in sixteen countries.[5]

#ilovehandlooms, Do You? Then Flaunt It

How do we change the perception of wearing handlooms? We need to take a cue from how luxury brands get customers to endorse them, simply by making the branding on their products highly visible. GoCoop launched the #ILoveHandlooms campaign in 2014 to popularize handloom among the masses and pledge support for artisans and weavers.[6] Through the campaign, GoCoop invited people to share their love for handloom by posting a photo or writing a story about a favourite handloom product they own. People wearing handlooms can show off, for instance, a photo using #ILoveHandlooms on social media.

As Siva says, 'Many of us love handlooms and each one of us has our own reasons. Handlooms symbolize the rich cultural heritage and tradition of India. They are not only eco-friendly but also make a fashion statement. Our reason for loving handlooms may be unique and very special and that's why we want people to share their love for handlooms with everyone through this campaign. Our main aim is to popularize handloom among the masses and to bring out the uniqueness of handloom products. Even if we wore handloom once a week, it will create work for millions of artisans.'

Investing in GoCoop and working with Siva has taught me quite a lot about this space. First is to change myself from wearing what I used to wear during my corporate time to completely wearing handloom fabrics; Gandhi's 'Be the change' ringing in my head. If I go and speak in various places about the goodness of handlooms but if I myself am not wearing it, my credibility goes for a toss. Moreover, I could experience the product better—calling it 'eat your own dog food' or 'drink your own champagne'.

I buy most of my cloth at GoCoop and my long-time bespoke tailor/designer Muktiar stitches a lovely kurta or pants from it. When I was running a multinational company, I was also into wearing suits. Now I have an opportunity to make a change by, for instance, telling start-up executives coming to pitch to me not to wear jackets. I attend board meetings featuring billion-dollar fund representatives wearing a dhoti as well. In 2013, Prime Minister David Cameron of the UK agreed to meet a few angel investors during his visit to Delhi, with the meeting arranged by IAN. I was the only attendee wearing a kurta and chappals.

I also started adding an embroidered '#ILoveHandlooms'[7] on the back of my kurtas to show that I do practise what I preach and also offer people an avenue to follow. All my kurtas are also monogrammed with my name 'Naga' by an NSRCEL start-up called TechTailor, an online bespoke tailoring venture. At one round table, someone said to me, 'We all know you, Naga. You don't need to put your name.' This person was wearing a branded shirt with the maker's logo on it. I replied sarcastically, 'I asked a brand to pay me money to promote their brand. Since they refused, I ended up putting my name instead. But you are promoting them free of cost.' I've also started a page for '#ILoveHandlooms' on my website showcasing my purchases from various visits to different locations.

Success without Selling Your Soul: Jaipur Rugs

When I met this young girl enthusiastically showing me how to make a rug in her home in Rajasthan's Achrol village, I asked her why she was not in school. She said she could not afford to go to school but was educating herself through a correspondence (distance education) course using her earnings from making rugs. Rug knotting has been a tradition among the people in her community for years. But it was not enough to sustain her family today, forcing her father to double up as a construction worker.

After attending Startup Oasis's Water Accelerator in September 2015, I arranged for a Jaipur Rugs visit through the Grassroots Business Fund (GBF), that is how we headed to Achrol. I met another family of three women knotting a 10'×10' rug together, with 8×8 knots an inch, which makes the design sharper, although it takes a month to make the rug.

University of Hard Rocks of Life

What is common with all these women and Jaipur Rugs is their hard work to revive a fast-disappearing tradition. Nand Kishore Chaudhary (NKC) came up with the idea of Jaipur Rugs (JR) in 1978. He gave up a bank job and borrowed Rs 5000 from his father to start this carpet business. The journey began with two looms, nine weavers and one scooter in Rajasthan. Over the years, his simple idea has grown into a grassroots network of artisans stretching across 600 villages in India with clientele across forty countries worldwide, all of whom subscribe to a common philosophy of responsible manufacturing.

In 1986, NKC connected artisans to global markets through direct exports to cut out the middlemen. Later, in 1999, NKC officially named his business Jaipur Carpets in India while setting up a sister concern in the US called Jaipur Rugs Inc., to ease sales and distribution in North America. The Jaipur Rugs Foundation, which worked for the welfare of weavers, was set up in 2004 and in 2006. The Jaipur Rugs network grew to forty weaver groups across ten Indian states. That same year, Jaipur Rugs brought laurels to India by receiving its first international design award, America's Magnificent Carpet Award.

Crucially, NKC ignored the social stigma of untouchability and hired workers from socially disadvantaged backgrounds. Today, he is the proud owner of a Rs 350-crore company.

Jaipur Rugs' artisan network required logistical support, so the raw material is dropped off at artisans' homes where they work on the product. Once completed, the rug is picked up at the weaver's doorstep and sent on to the next stage of the rugmaking process. Artisans are also supported by supervisors who track their progress and ensure that the products are consistently high quality. The supervisors also make sure that the artisans are not interrupted by the shortage of yarn or other disruptions. Their visits also guarantee that the weavers are paid every month. One of these supervisors took us around to meet the weavers. She was from the same village, which made it easier for her to coordinate with the weavers.

We also spent time at the corporate office where eighteen mind-boggling steps of finishing work are undertaken before the rug is shipped to the customer. I then went to meet NKC for the first time in his office whose entrance welcomed visitors with the unique title 'Director, University of Hard Rocks of Life'. We had a lovely discussion about social business and I discovered the high regard he has for the artisans. He ensured that the looms are located in their homes, allowing them the freedom to work whenever they could. He mentioned installing the loom facing the kitchen where possible so that the weavers can keep an eye on the kitchen as well while knotting. Since then, whenever I visit Jaipur, NKC insists that I stay at their guest house so that we can discuss more about life and business.

In December 2017, I hosted an NSRCEL, IIMB, social event, 'Social and Financial Impact for Start-ups', which focused on social businesses keeping their mission aligned while growing. Who better than NKC to anchor this? I invited NKC as well as Damodaran of Gramalaya and Vijay of Gramvani, one of my investments. It proved to be an amazing session and, after NKC's speech, I told the audience that they'd learnt to manage 'Scale and Soul'.

I also had a candid discussion with NKC over lunch at
the IIMB campus and he gave me very insightful answers
regarding Jaipur Rugs and the progress of his business. I
complimented him on being a great example of a social
business in crafts, as he was keeping Indian culture and
arts alive in the villages of India. His business solved
the universal problem of worrying about the planet and
people. Usually, as companies grow, they lose their DNA
and social element. But NKC had maintained Jaipur Rugs'
DNA, which baffled me as to how he had done it. When I
asked him, he said, 'Business is all about people. The more
you take care of the people working with you and involve
them in the processes like decision-making, the more
efficient and capable it becomes. As a result, the business
will respond effectively to the underserved.'

At Jaipur Rugs, when he received a large number of
orders, they came with huge pressure from the customers
regarding quality and timely delivery. NKC said that this
was when he began developing good relations with his
weavers. He helped them improve their skills through
training programmes, made them aware of the needs of
customers and built a community where everyone came
together as a family. Consequently, the artisans became
more aware of the products they were creating. Most
Jaipur Rugs products have zero defects, are made with zero
wastage and are delivered on time.

By and large, it is the community of village-dwelling
women that weaves for Jaipur Rugs, taking responsibility
for the quality of the product, the timeliness of deliveries
and most other aspects of the business. They are now being
trained in English as well, which would enable them to
represent Jaipur Rugs at the national and international level,
such as at exhibitions, and interact with consumers directly.

BMW vs Rajasthan Artisans

NKC's daughter, Kavita, who takes care of their designs, shared with me how she had once started an experiment and asked the artisans to create their own designs. Usually, the designs are provided to the artisans by the design team (called Pixel) in the form of a huge chart. A 10'x10' rug is typically woven by three women sitting in a row and knotting. When these women thought of their designs, they tried different designs on the same rug, competing with each other, which resulted in various abstract designs. Rather than a precisely ordered pattern, the result is a whole new design borne out of an error.

Jaipur Rugs accordingly called this design collection 'Project Error' and one of the designs, called Anthar (difference), was nominated for the German Design Award 2016,[8] where Jaipur Rugs competed against the likes of BMW, Bentley, Audi and Benz. To quote Jaipur Rugs description, the 'Project Error collection focuses on nature's mistakes', which were seen by Kavi as 'works of art rather than gaffes'.

In a crucial insight into the self-limiting nature of extant ideas about business, NKC told me, 'Business and social are two separate entities. Likewise, the purpose of life and spirituality are considered separate from business and profit. But I believe that just like our body parts cannot operate if you cut them and put them aside, business and society cannot operate separately. If they work in silos, it is a recipe for disaster.'

Buying Blessings

I was also interested in learning from NKC about the sustainability of Jaipur Rugs. I told him that by creating handmade rugs, many of which were coloured using natural dyes, their work was in line with the sustainability agenda. However, the people making this green product—and dependent on it for their livelihoods—were considered to be working in old economy jobs and new economy jobs typically fail to appreciate this kind of labour. How did he position his products and bring in a premium for a sustainable business like this to become viable? As this occupation was traditionally passed down from generation to generation, how did he ensure that the youth from this community got involved in weaving too?

NKC's reply to me was inspiring, to say the least. 'The production process of the artisans is like meditation. It is their passion and it comes from their life. They deserve dignity and respect. At Jaipur Rugs we say, 'You are not buying carpets, you are buying blessings.' It is our tagline. They put in their heart and soul in the production of that rug and you cannot put a price tag on work from the heart and soul. The more we get detached from our human side, the more inhuman and more cunning we become. This type of mindset is leading many corporates and organizations on the path of destruction. Real satisfaction only comes when you are completely involved in something. There is an old saying that your mind should always be calm but your hands should storm (continuously work). But in today's environment, the physical involvement of an individual is far less than the mental involvement. This must be curtailed and one way to do it is to provide equal space, opportunity and dignity to the work done by the artisan. People are very disconnected from themselves and as a result, they are also disconnected from work. We are working to bridge this gap and asking ourselves, how can we bring this connection back? How do we connect to our roots?'

It was clear to me that NKC's drive to ensure the continuity and the dignity of labour in the production of Jaipur Rugs went far deeper than the formulae of modern management.

The Why of Growth

I also spoke to NKC about scaling up, which involves questions that entrepreneurs do not always have answers for, such as, 'Why do I need to grow?' But they still run rapidly to achieve growth. We see many leaders come forth with ideas of giving back to society after spending much time running and scaling up, usually at the fag end of their lifespan. How can one bring up that issue earlier in their lifetime? Nowadays, many youngsters are trying to give back through social enterprises, but they want instant success and immediate scaling up. If we take the example of Jaipur Rugs, creating a base of 40,000 artisans took over thirty years. How does one explain to today's youngsters that building a business that serves people takes a long time and that patience is as necessary as business skills and acumen?

To this query, NKC responded that in his experience, '75 per cent of the efforts that people make are unnecessary' and 'often non-value adding activities'. He elaborated that 'they act on an impulse. They work on autopilot to the extent that they don't know what and why they are doing what they do. Sometimes, they are just rushing without knowing "why". The real struggle is to answer the question of how we bring back the consciousness and mindfulness in people. Constant introspection is very important. The more we work without consciousness, the more we are headed towards destruction. We need to constantly check our activities and motivations to do those activities. At every step we should ask: Do I really need to do this? Will it add value to my life? Will it add value to society or the life of other people? We must bring back that consciousness and alertness in people. It is essential to define the criteria of development: Is it the money? Fame? Scale? What constitutes development is very important. I believe that development cannot be done from outside. It can only be the inner force of an individual that can motivate him for development. The focus of development should be the enhancement of individual consciousness. That individual consciousness will then reflect in each activity that he/she does for society and not the other way round. Today, the impact of the outer environment is far greater than the inner consciousness of an individual.'

Scale and Soul

Musing over what NKC said, I asked him, 'Businesses borrow capital and that brings a constant pressure to scale fast and provide returns. How do you suggest an entrepreneur should manage this?'

He responded: 'We grew but never asked for any investors or grants or anything. We only went to banks to get working capital. This kept the core values of Jaipur Rugs intact. Because we were able to maintain the core values at Jaipur Rugs, today many big names and influential people want to help Jaipur Rugs maintain its soul and core. In the process of expanding the business, it is a constant struggle to keep the values and soul intact and even if at some time we feel we are losing it, we try harder and bring it back. If a business is to scale on monetary considerations alone, then the criteria of growth is wrong. To have your soul and continue the business with the DNA that you want, it is essential that one stays away from accepting anything from external agencies.'

Keeping this DNA while growing the organization is essential, as NKC is relentlessly trying with every new recruit. There is always learning and unlearning at Jaipur Rugs. Every time I visit, NKC ensures I meet some of his key employees. Once, I met a young business graduate who had joined their marketing team. I asked him what should Jaipur Rugs be doing. His answer was, many people don't know about Jaipur Rugs; we need to go viral about our products. In the office, there was a photo of a customer with an artisan, to which I pointed and asked the marketing team member what the customer was wearing on her wrist. It was a Rolex watch. I told him that that's our customer, one who is willing to pay a premium for the quality products. She is not sitting on social media waiting for discounts, she is our customer because of our purpose. You need to figure out a way to tell our story to people like them. This is the unlearning required for keeping the DNA alive. Every employee is required to go on an immersion programme to the villages and understand the artisan and their work. Now, Jaipur Rugs also offers this programme to college students interested in understanding social businesses. As NKC told me once, HR should be renamed 'searching for divine soul'.

In response to the above, I asked him, 'Do you believe that this is the way that every entrepreneur should go—should entrepreneurs look for investors with the right attitude or should they avoid looking for investing agencies completely?'

He said, 'I think the biggest equity is your people. Grow the way you want to grow and not how others want you to grow.'

Future of Development

I was keen to know what he thought of our country's development being driven by models from vastly different countries. 'Where do you think the future of development that originates from western thoughts is going? And do we know if this is right or wrong?'

To which he said, 'In the name of economic growth, that being the crucial criteria for measuring the development of a country as well as individuals, it is leading to madness and makes individuals and countries and society at large very impulsive. This growth can never be sustainable. The growth that brings in value to the lives of individuals can only be sustainable. This kind of approach is detrimental to humankind's existence. There is an organic way of operation which adds value in every step. Humans could extract that from nature but ensure that we give back to nature.'

The goal of poverty alleviation was used to promote the present model of development, which led to my next question: 'How did NKC's model differentiate itself in terms of alleviating the poverty of people?'

NKC said, 'We are living in a highly disconnected world. Dichotomies and compartmentalization are all around us. The differentiation is that there exists in the mindset of people the difference between the rich from the poor and the lack of co-creation. There is a need to bring together the avenues for co-creation in which we have the rich, the poor, the old and the young and all types of people to connect better and in a meaningful way for wealth creation.'

I persisted, 'When we talk of tribal communities, we see they are very accomplished in their environment. But the moment we take them into the so-called mainstream, they are suddenly poor, without resources and become dependent. What is the right way to approach this?'

NKC said, 'Tribal communities are so close to nature that they understand its intricacies. Humans have distanced themselves from nature so much, that it is difficult to find a completely mentally healthy person in this world. Organizations should also follow the tribal ways and systems. The heightened aspirations due to the speed to grow and other developmental mindsets create chaos. It does not allow an individual to relax and disturbs the peace.'

Talking about how the organization is structured, he added, 'There are two entities. One is the company and the other is a foundation called the Jaipur Rugs Foundation. This foundation runs on grants mostly allotted by Jaipur Rugs. The foundation imparts weaving skills and engages in welfare activities like education and health camps for our weavers. It helps weavers get exposed to leadership skills and brings in a mindset change in the community members. It facilitates them to avail of entitlements and benefits provided by the government, like for instance, artisan cards.'

Bringing Pride—Artisans to Artists

In response to my questioning whether the weavers' children were engaged in weaving, NKC offered that 'girls do help their parents on the days when they are not going to school and newlywed brides are also introduced to this art of weaving by the families and communities. But the majority of the people want their children to work at desk jobs and push their children to get educated with a focus on white collar jobs.'

When I visited Aaspura village, also in Rajasthan, in 2018, Kamala—who had created a 9x11 rug in four months and makes around Rs 8000 per month—echoed this as well. She has savings in a bank account and ensures that her three children are studying as she wants them to take up government jobs. The artisans also visit the corporate office on exposure visits to understand the other aspects of making the carpets. She liked visiting the design department and especially seeing people create designs using computers. She wants her daughters to become such designers as she feels knotting is hard work.

This reflects what we are moving towards—the more we study, the more we tend to work with the head rather than the hand. Working with hands then feels inferior. NKC is trying to change this sentiment by introducing the artisans as designers creating their own designs and by bringing them dignity via getting their work recognized at international design competitions. Jaipur Rugs gives them a certificate carrying their photo and a photo of the artwork under their Manchaha initiative.

I met Bugali, a young girl in the village, who has created seven original designs. One of these, which received the prestigious ELLE DECO International Design Award (EDIDA) in 2017, showcases traditional Rajasthani culture, motifs inspired by nature, personal stories and shakkarparas.[9] She brought out all her awards and enthusiastically explained each one of them to me. Bimla Devi from the same village also travelled to Germany, while her father and three brothers are all in construction work. Her brothers are very proud of their sister.

In the same village, I met Suniya who used waste yarn to create her own design. She has been knotting since she was eleven years of age and is now earning Rs 8000 a month and learning English. She is inspired by the other women who received the awards and her husband, Madan Lal, who is learning knotting from her, is encouraging her and has started arranging for her passport. These women, through getting recognized for their work and earning better, usher in gender equality as well. As I noticed, while the wife was working on the loom, the husband brought us tea, which is an unusual sight in rural India. Among the stories of women's empowerment is that of Koushalya, whose husband was not reliably supporting the family, but she is running the household and bringing up four children. Another inspiring story from Aaspura is that of a cancer survivor Sajna Devi. She wove her tumour into a design. After buying it, a European customer flew down and met her, saying he lost his wife to cancer. Sajna's rug now decorates his bedroom. The house she lives in is very inspiring too—in the middle of a farm field with no doors allowing a breeze all around. If we were to calculate the carbon she is saving, I'm sure she would come off better than many of her counterparts in developed countries. Instead of paying a premium on this simplicity, we simply label the likes of Sajna Devi 'poor'. The carbon footprint of rural communities is, in effect, a solution for developing countries which we need to leverage.

From Sustainable Fashion to Sustainable Food

A question that I mull over often is, would organic farming suffice to feed the huge population of our country? NKC had a very encouraging response, 'Many people told me that if I opted for organic farming, the yield will go down and it will not be viable. Last year, we farmed using only organic products like cow dung and other animal wastes. The quality of the yield was fabulous and the quantity was also almost 1.5 times the regular yield. The circle of nature is completed only through organic farming and only the fear accumulated by humankind is stopping us from realizing the benefits of organic farming.'

His thoughts on sustainability also applied to modern, consumption-oriented lifestyles. 'Unless we have a minimalistic way of living and control the urges of material consumerism, we are doomed,' he said. 'It is very difficult to have a sustainable future for humankind. We need to introspect and develop a conscience and not blindly follow the path that is followed by everyone.'

The Secret of Happiness

I also picked NKC's brains about Bhutan's gross happiness index. In his view, 'Sometimes I think that God sent us on earth to appreciate what he has created and that should fill us with gratitude. If we don't have gratitude, it's very difficult to appreciate life. The life we are given is really meant to celebrate our time here and not merely to increase our needs. I think temples were made to convey our gratitude and not ask for petty demands like growth in business and our child's marriage. They were built to say "I am so grateful to you." The more we lose this feeling of gratitude, the more we get disconnected from ourselves and try finding solace in material things. If you ask a flower, why do you bloom and spread fragrance? You don't get anything out of it. It would answer that "this is my nature and if I don't do it, I will die! It is my life."

Similarly, gratitude is an integral part of human nature. I would say it is the lack of gratitude that has really led us to difficult definitions like GDP growth and development and such like.'

I left with a deep respect for NKC and for his ever-smiling explanation of his social business. The respect he has for artisans is propagated across Jaipur Rugs, with every employee required to learn know how to knot—there is even a loom in the corporate office on which they can practise!

I have mentioned to the hundreds of crafts entrepreneurs I've met, during Startup Oasis's Craft Catapult and NSRCEL's women's start-up programmes, that crafts should not be affordable to the middle class. If they are easily affordable, then artisans will have to live in poverty. These middle-class customers end up comparing the products available at multiple outlets but worry only about the price. They are likely to say, 'Crafts are expensive!' or 'I found the same product at a very deep discount/lower price somewhere else.' Such customers don't realize that the cheaper product may not be handmade or even from the claimed place of origin.

We need to take the old economy to the new economy by raising standards and bringing an awareness of India's treasures across the world, as exemplified by Jaipur Rugs. Mostly, we see enthusiasts pick up a craft, come up with a few designs and start promoting these on social media. All their designs look much the same and they mostly attract middle-class working women. The majority of crafts attract women more than men, with the saree still the best crafts product comparatively.

I tell every crafts entrepreneur to ignore India as a market and focus on selling overseas and build a premium brand showing authenticity by using technology. Once you are established overseas, affluent Indians are more likely to buy your products. Jaipur Rugs, after many years of exports and opening outlets in Italy, has now opened a store in Mumbai. There is a market in India for high-end crafts as proven by Lladró or other luxury fashion and car brands. I tell entrepreneurs that people owning a BMW or Audi car are your customers, but I've hardly found any entrepreneurs able to crack this market. Every luxury mall in India is flooded with European luxury brands and we hardly see an Indian brand. Jaipur Rugs proved that such niche success is possible; the country needs more entrepreneurs to follow their example for other products such as Ikat, *Jamdani, Kanjeevaram, Maheshwari, Kandangi*, etc. To do so, however, they need to understand the new narrative!

Cultural Intellectual Property (IP) Rights

I met Monica Boța-Moisin in February 2020 at IIM Ahmedabad, for the Craft Catapult finals and found that the Romanian-born lawyer had some interesting thoughts. She narrated the story of Louis Vuitton's collections being inspired by the traditional designs of Africa's Masai tribes and the legal fight by fashion lawyers to get the tribes their due royalty. Monica started Cultural Intellectual Property Rights Initiative (CIPRI)[10] to take such action worldwide. She works with brands to ensure they duly recognize traditional designs. She highlighted the global popularity of Geographical Identification (GI) tags in the food world compared to the use of GI tags in the crafts sector. For instance, people recognize and reward GI-tagged champagne from France or GI-tagged Italian cheddar cheese but not the GI-tagged Pochampally saree.

Impressed with her thoughts, I agreed to join CIPRI's advisory board. CIPRI has since launched a Cultural Sustainable Academy to train more people in the fashion space. Just as technology companies guarantee their IP rights through registering patents, the thousands of years of traditional designs need to be registered as the IP of the community or place of origin. We see people use prints incorporating 'adulterated' Ikat designs alongside the original Ikat. If fashion houses pay royalties to the Ikat-producing regions, we can preserve the tradition better and provide the artisans with more revenue streams.

IP royalties, carbon credits and a premium price are the three things required to bring crafts into the new economy.

Crafts Carbon Platform

We need to create a crafts carbon platform where everyone involved in, for instance, making a saree, whether producing materials (i.e., organic, cotton, silk), yarn (e.g. hand-spun), fabrics (handwoven), or colours (natural dye) can input their details. Using these details, the effort involved in the processes and the carbon-saving potential of that saree can be calculated. This carbon saving can then be exchanged for credits in carbon markets. As India doesn't yet have a carbon market, the trade can happen in foreign markets.

I have been floating this idea to many international agencies, including the UN, so that global platforms begin to recognize artisans worldwide, whether from India or Indonesia or Laos or Romania. I'm also happy that a start-up called Kosha is developing a product that can be attached to the loom to calculate the number of movements involving in weaving and thus estimate the effort necessary to make the product. One can also enable geolocation or geotagging by taking a picture as proof of where the product was made.

I have been advising Kosha to calculate carbon credits as well, for which they have come up with weaving a QR code into the fabric. This renders the code permanent and accessible at any time, which enables the customer to understand the product's ecological value and brag about their support for sustainable fashion at social gatherings. Usually, this is done using fancy nametags, but these tags serve their purpose only until being sold at a shop and not subsequently. Again, luxury brands primarily provide bragging rights to their customers, such as the prominent Prada branding on spectacles or the large LV on a belt buckle. We need more entrepreneurs to innovate ways of providing bragging rights for people doing the right things. The only solution I have implemented thus far is embroidering #ILoveHandlooms on the back of my kurtas.

Theory of Change

Startup Oasis has put together a nice publication, *Accelerating Indian Craft Businesses: Leveraging Technology and Innovation for Craft Startups*, highlighting the crucial work done by many start-ups in the cohort. When I visited one such start-up, Karomi Crafts and Textiles in Kolkata, I saw the amazing innovations they have brought to *Jamdani* and bought a saree with a unique design. I also challenged them to bring back the famed Indian muslin and the 1000-count products that were once part of Bangla culture. Similarly, Mura Collective has brought the Japanese tie-dye technique called *Shibori* to India, producing exquisitely innovative designs. Another innovator, Cotton Rack, makes 'Indo–Western' wear using handspun fabrics, fighting the stereotype that handspun/ khadi clothing is only suitable for followers of Gandhi or people working in NGOs. These and many other technology start-ups in crafts are featured in Startup Oasis's book, which is essentially about the Theory of Change.

We Need Change

Change is seen as a problem everywhere but, in reality, we need to change—and recognize that change is possible. We need to be authentic, target the right customers, position products accurately and possess strong storytelling skills. Crafts should be a luxury, an aspirational object and not a product subsidized by the artisan. Crafts do not need an empathetic story involving grants, social impact and assistance for the poor artisan; rather, the narrative should be one of pride for an authentic craft.

In Japan, artisans are considered artists and accorded due respect, whereas in India, we consider software engineers more valuable than craftspeople. India has a nearly equal number of software engineers and artisans, approximated at three million households. But the experienced IT engineer earns a salary of over Rs 1 lakh per month while an artisan does not even earn Rs 10,000 a month.

A craftsperson or entrepreneur needs to use blockchain or other technologies to strengthen the supply chain and enhance the traceability of the production process. They also need to develop an innovative yet effective technological platform for retailing their crafts, which allows sharing proofs of authenticity. Essentially, they need to combine their imagination with the right technology to create a captivating story, such as by making wrinkles (of khadi) fashionable, adding a 'wow' factor to the crafts and turning errors into a hallmark of originality and handcrafting, as done by Jaipur Rugs. Doing so successfully can ensure that no discounts are needed, just as is the case for any luxury brand. If the brand value is communicated clearly, viral marketing would not be needed either.

Craft Our Superpower

The crafts sector has the superpower to make both production and consumption sustainable. However, crafts entrepreneurs need to focus more on innovations, need to learn to say no, take hard decisions, build on their unique strengths and discover their true core. They also need to reach the right customers. Some innovations happen through concepts like upcycling and recycling that appear traditional yet are contemporary.

A crafts start-up needs innovation across products, processes and platforms to ensure that the second generation of artisans continues in the crafts sector even through assuming new roles in marketing, design, etc. We cannot wait for a lifetime for artisans to get over the traps of labour migration and concomitant suffering, nor can we wait for entrepreneurs to learn from their mistakes. What we need is an intervention that defines a new theory of change and catalyses the crafts businesses.

Part III

Business Social Responsibility: What Can We Do?

Eleven

Types of Start-ups and Social Responsibility

'The challenge I set before anyone who condemns private-sector business is this: If you are a socially conscious person, why don't you run your business in a way that will help achieve social objectives?'

—Muhammad Yunus

Enterprise has become more feasible for today's generation of Indians who are growing up in an interconnected world, where exploring, executing and sharing ideas has become much easier than at any period in the past. I feel encouraged by the emergence of more entrepreneurship.

How Many Can Sing?

This question was asked by my Prof. Dorothy Brawley, who taught the innovation and creativity part of the MBA that I had pursued at Kennesaw State University, Atlanta. The question asked in class, almost twenty years back has stayed with me forever and I use it in almost all my speeches.

When Prof. Brawley asked our class, 'How many can sing?' one or two raised their hands. She asked again,

'If I had gone to a first standard classroom and asked the same question, what would be the reaction?' The answer was, 'Everyone would raise their hands.' So, what happened to us? When we were in the first standard, all of us would have raised our hands, never doubting our ability to sing.

Now, the moment that question was asked, so much was going on in our heads. 'Is she going to ask me to sing? I'm a horrible singer. Is it a trick question? What would others think if she asked me to sing in front of the class?' This limiting inner voice is called the 'voice of judgement' (VOJ). When we were five years old, we never had a VOJ, we just raised our hands and started singing, 'Twinkle, Twinkle, Little Star'. As adults, we worry about so many things, because every 'yes' and every 'no' we received when we were growing up, defined who we are. We have no idea who we are any more, someone has to tell us, 'You are a good singer', 'Your hair is nice', and so on. But aren't we all good bathroom singers? Even though I did not ask that question for an audition with A.R. Rahman, the VOJ still stops people from replying. The few people who do raise their hands when I ask, are those who have gone through proper singing lessons, or picked up singing and were recognized by someone as a singer. So, what does singing a song have to do with entrepreneurship?

What's Entrepreneurship?

When everyone sees a problem, an entrepreneur sees an opportunity. If someone sees a problem and complains about it and blames it on someone else like the government, politicians, the system—then she is an ordinary citizen. If someone sees a problem and sees an opportunity to solve that problem, she is an entrepreneur. You identified the problem, then you find a solution. Once you provide the solution to the person who has the problem and if she pays you because your solution solved her problem and she is happy—that's it, you've become an entrepreneur. The important thing to remember is her happiness. If a person is happy, she would tell a few people; if she is not happy, then she would tell the whole world about it, thanks to social media.

So, an important aspect of a business is 'customer delight'. If the customer is happy and tells a few people and those few people tell a few more, then, the 'product–market' fit is proven, enabling you to scale. Once you've done business with a growing number of customers, then the investor would be happy to invest in you. Today, I see more entrepreneurs spending time thinking about what the investor wants, instead of what the customer wants. Instead, 'problem-solution-happy customer' is a basic principle that can be understood as a formula for any business, whether you are selling idlis, rockets or AI.

There is pull and push in marketing. Pull means the customer is pulling a product from you. Push means you are pushing a product to them. Example of push would be the touch smartphone. If someone asked you fifteen years ago whether you would like a phone without a keyboard, we would have said, 'Are you crazy?' but someone created one and gave it to us and we liked it. In my experience, in India, we hardly have push products; most of the products are pull, which means that you are solving a customer problem. So what problem you are solving is important!

If more people tell you your idea is wrong, then you are on the right track.

You found a problem and called it an opportunity, when most of them were calling it a problem. This means that if everyone is calling something 'x', you are calling it 'y', so what will the world call you then? I sometimes get answers such as, 'Innovative, creative, out-of-the-box thinker, etc.' People are not that polite. They are likely to call you 'mad'. That's why the 'singing' question comes into play. When the whole world is calling you mad, you should be like a five-year-old who can start singing, not bothering what any one would think about their singing ability.

This is the quality of an entrepreneur—boldly look at solving tough problems! Also, when you talk about a problem you are solving and find many people saying you are mad, or saying things like, 'This is how India is, you cannot change. He tried and failed. These problems are there since my grandfather's time . . .' The more people talk like this, the more you are likely to be on the right track. This is because they are speaking from a place where they have not even thought about the problem. When people see a long-existing problem, they often become 'numb' or indifferent to the problem. They settle any inner disquiet they may have by saying this is how it is, nothing can be done. That's where the entrepreneur comes in and questions the status quo.

Can You Hear the Sun Rise?

The second question I used to ask in my speeches is, 'Can you hear the sun rise?' I get many 'nos', then suddenly someone says, 'Yes, through birds chirping.' In the place where I was growing up, we used to get the water in the morning and people used to fight at the pipe for it, so you would know the sun is up. So, there are other senses that are telling us the sun is up. That means, if we wait for the one sense (vision) to tell us something is happening, then we miss out on what the other senses are telling us.

What does this have to do with entrepreneurship? First, you need to find a problem in order to solve it. The more sensitive you are, the more you can notice problems and perceive their probable causes. Give a toy to a three-year-old child and observe what she does with that toy. She plays with it, she tries to dismantle it, she breaks it, she also puts it in her mouth and hears her mother telling her not to do that. So, isn't she applying all her senses to understand what the toy is? This is what *childlike curiosity* is. We all had it and lost it as we grew up. Studies have shown that when a child reaches early adolescence, that ability starts to go away.

Food Courts and Platform Shops

There are problems you can see every day if you look around you with your eyes and senses open. Let me speak from my own experience. I have travelled on a particular road for the past three years and the road is fantastic. On one side of this beautiful road, there are about twenty-odd small shops. These have come up primarily because there are many who work in a corporate office that is on the opposite side of the road. Many who work in the office cannot afford the food available in the building, so they end up eating on the opposite side of the road, where the small shops serve reasonably priced food. The small shops are always bustling with activity. At midnight, the place is bustling even more, as there are several BPO companies in the building and people who work in nightshifts eat at the roadside shops. These small shops, their need for hygiene and proper waste disposal, the contrast they present against the gleaming corporate building opposite, all this is seen and generally ignored. That's the reality in India. People pass such roads every single day and hope that the problem is not there. But that's where the future is, so it will continue and thrive. There are at least a billion people that need help, there are millions who go to bed without food and millions who do not have electricity in India. So, these are all amazing problems to solve.

That's why Prof. Dorothy Brawley would remind us, don't let your brain fatigue. Don't even take the same route to your office every day, then you will fall in a rut. The more sensitive we are, the more the problems around us will start bothering us. When they start bothering us, we will tend to look for ways to solve them. Look at what we wear, how we live, what we eat, how we travel. Does the waste lying around bother us? Or do we just keep our house clean, dump waste on the streets and say now it's the government's problem to figure out what to do? If we start looking at every small thing around us with childlike curiosity, we can keep our sensitivity sharp and will notice problems around. Otherwise, we search on the Internet, find problems of some other countries and tend to solve those. To become an entrepreneur, only two qualities are required: 'Sing a song and hear the sun rise!'

Now, based on the entrepreneurs I've met over the decades, I categorize the Indian start-ups into three types, as follows.

Category I: Copycats

There is a group of entrepreneurs who believe that success is easily achieved. Most of them read magazines like *TechCrunch*, look around at what's happening in the Silicon Valley of the US and immediately start writing a business plan. I call them 'Copycats'.

Now joining the US as a template to copy from are China and Israel (the agri-start-ups tend to copy from Israel). Let's look at e-commerce. It took fifteen years to copy an Amazon that had started during the dotcom boom. In the early 2000s, the non-tangible e-commerce sites for ticket booking worked okay, but the ones to buy tangible things online took longer to establish. Why did it take fifteen years? Are we bad at copying? There are many reasons I have been offered at various places—infrastructure like Internet availability, supply chain problems and the arrival of smart phones.

But in my opinion, the major reason is—trust. I ask this question every time I speak to a live audience and it usually takes a few minutes before I get the answer, 'Trust', from someone in the audience. I call that person as a true Indian, as he understands India better. To do business successfully in India, you need to understand India.

Yes, we are a trust-deficit society. We don't trust siblings, neighbours—look at sibling rivalries in public, whether there is money involved, like the Ambanis, or not. So, the problem was always, who is this person who is going to take my money and run away if I buy online? How did they solve the trust problem? The e-commerce trust problem was solved with the introduction of cash on delivery (COD). You don't have to pay up front; you order and upon receiving the product only, you would pay the person who brings that product. If you don't like the product, you can reject it.

But COD is not new to India, it has always been one of the reliable and time-tested features of India Post. I usually ask the audience what that is and most of the time, I get the answer, 'money order'. If there are people from an older generation present, I may get the answer correctly. It's VPP—value payable post. As India Post explains on its website:

> 'The value payable system is designed to meet the requirements of persons who wish to pay for articles sent to them at the time of receipt of the articles and also to meet the requirements of traders and others who wish to recover, through the agency of the Post Office the value of article supplied by them.'

I remember seeing advertisements in the paper while growing up, saying you could order this or that product through VPP. It just took someone to copy an Amazon and India Post, then the entire e-commerce industry took off. What does this teach us? Just merely copying the technology that worked elsewhere alone won't work, we need to understand the psychology of the people to whom we are selling.

The tendency of Indians to be sceptical and wary of people whom they suspect will fleece them of their money had to be overcome. It was important to be aware of this Indian-customer psychology and only then 'copy' the technology. Marrying the technology with psychology is important to have success. Without doing that, making Amazon work in India ended up being a struggle and a challenge. This, however, slowly changed. When it came to consumer products, faith slowly began to build, though it took us fifteen years, and many e-commerce companies shut down during that time and people lost money.

The Dotcom Era

As e-commerce picked up, the whole world was caught up in the Alibaba syndrome by 2015. In 2000, the Japan-based SoftBank Group Corp., one of the world's largest VC funds worth $100 billion, made its most successful investment—$20 million in a then-fledgling Chinese Internet venture called Alibaba.[1] This investment turned into $50 billion when Alibaba went public in September 2014. If a China-based company could bring this much fortune to an investor, next to China in terms of growth was India, as so many e-commerce companies were founded in India. In those days, I used to joke that if you can spell the word e-commerce, you'll get funded.

Over eighty-five e-commerce companies were founded in India. In that period, it was tough to see the news in the newspapers, as the first few pages were of full-page advertisements; TV channels were filled with Bollywood stars endorsing many e-commerce sites. It was a great time to be a consumer, as people were able to buy lots of things with heavy discounts. There were jokes about people applying for leave for the 'Internet Shopping Festival'. It was amazing to see the frenzy and my blog in January 2015 with the title '.Com Era' captured this.

'After a long time, I watched TV and was overwhelmed by the number of ads by e-commerce companies. From Bengaluru guys selling Adidas T shirts and Samsung gadgets to Dindigul Thalappakati Biriyani getting online. These number of e-commerce ads bring the feeling of the .com era of US. Interesting that it took 14 years to arrive in India. Reiterates the fact that just copying US idea won't work—product-market (readiness) fit is important—tech is just an enabler.'

Did all these e-commerce companies survive? If money is the only thing, which makes many entrepreneurs think that by raising the money alone they would be successful, then all of those eighty-five e-commerce companies should have survived. Why did so many of them not succeed? We have to thank Walmart, which did a strategic investment in Flipkart, the number one e-commerce company of India. If that had not happened, we would have handed over the e-com key of India to Amazon India.

Understanding India

So why is it that some things work and some things don't in India? For that, we need to understand India better. What is India's GDP (gross domestic product is a monetary measure of the market value of all the final goods and services produced in a specific time period in the country)?[2] I've asked this question in all my speeches and hardly anyone is able to get the answer correctly. Usually, people confuse it with the GDP growth rate which is often discussed in the media. People hardly know the absolute numbers.

India's GDP was at $3.1 trillion in 2021 as per the World Bank,[3] while China was at $17.7 trillion,[4] that is 5.7 times more! The *Wall Street Journal* predicted on 13 March 2015 that it would take seventy-eight years for India to catch up with China, with China growing at 7 per cent and India growing at 8.5 per cent.[5] That's almost three generations; I would be gone by then. We know the turtle–rabbit story; if China slows down, then we could do it in twenty-three years, where India is growing at 10 per cent and China at 5 per cent. This was, of course, before the pandemic. China was a $10 trillion economy in 2015. Since then, China went up to $17.7 trillion, while India is still a little over $3.1 trillion only, as of 2021. Imagine now, post-pandemic, how these numbers would be! I would encourage entrepreneurs to listen to Budget speeches to understand these numbers. If you are doing business in India, you need to know where India stands economically.

India's geographical size is often blamed for its slow growth rate. But then, is it not more important to check why China, which is equally big, is already ahead of us? We will 'arrive', no doubt, but it is going to take us time and we need to break the glass ceiling. Of course, people argue that GDP (nominal) per capita does not reflect differences in the cost of living and the inflation rates of the countries; therefore, using a basis of GDP per capita at purchasing power parity (PPP) may be more useful when comparing living standards between nations. Nominal GDP is more useful in comparing national economies on the international market. But whatever the terms we use, the problems are visible on our streets, that data we cannot deny.

So-called Lakhpatis

What's our per capita income? This, of course, is the average income earned per person in a given country in a specified year. Calculated by dividing the area's total income which could be GDP by its total population, India's per capita income as per the World Bank was $2256 in 2021. This means, if you make more than Rs 1,57,920 (at Rs 70 to the dollar) in India in a year, you could consider yourself rich in this country. Is it possible to survive on such an amount for any one person for a whole year? It's pretty bad, isn't it? This calculation includes the billionaires of India.[6] If you exclude them, what would this number be? The inequality we have in India is clearly visible from these figures. As of 2021 data, we are a low-income country, with even Bangladesh doing better than us at $2457;[7] and China is an upper middle-income country with a per capita income of $12,556.[8]

Internet Everywhere?

I have often been in arguments with entrepreneurs over the years about the low Internet penetration in India. I always get the answer that everyone around me has it; every place I go, I've seen people with phones and the Internet. I have seen an entrepreneur presenting his idea where he wanted to target 640 million Internet users in India. I asked him, with 21 per cent[9] of India in extreme poverty and only 24 per cent of households having Internet access,[10] how is such a target possible? He said he had taken the number from Google and I said, fine, the number may be right.

But the problem is how many unique users are there in that number? When I asked him how many Google accounts he had, that entrepreneur himself had fourteen. Like him, there are many users with multiple accounts and that pushes up the number of Internet users. Similarly, when I get asked how is it that we have one billion mobile connections, it's the same answer—we have people carrying multiple phones. I used to say we have a culture where we haven't learnt how to say 'no'. If a person keeps calling someone, if the person called doesn't pick up, then the answer is 'no'. But it is tough to understand that in a country where people carry multiple phones, with each phone having a number given to a certain set of people.

I remember Rajesh Agarwal of Micromax once telling me that when he introduced the dual SIM phone, everyone was kind of looking at him saying what, why would you need that? He told me, 'I know Indian culture, I'm actually helping them so that they need not carry multiple phones.' Today, I can see phones with five SIM cards and honestly, I can't figure out why someone would need five SIMs. That's the reason we have one billion mobile connections, but the real answer lies in how many unique subscribers we have. Like this, entrepreneurs get carried away by numbers without understanding India well.

Ignoring the Billion

How the pandemic made every small crack wider, is something we are able to understand more in recent months. In August 2020, UNICEF released the *Remote Learning Reachability* report[11] highlighting how just 24 per cent of Indian households have Internet facility to access e-education[12] and there is a large rural–urban and gender divide that is likely to widen the learning gap across high-, middle- and low-income families. The report further said that students, especially girls, from most marginalized communities do not have easy access to smartphones and even if they do, Internet connectivity is poor and quality education content is often not available in vernacular languages.

So only around 300 million would have proper Internet access. Every one of those eighty-five e-commerce companies was targeting the people who have Internet access, saying it's a big enough market for more people and offering discounts to lure them. Also, wait, they were calculating that 300 million is almost equal to the population of the US. That's where the speculation started coming from. Wow! So, can we say that there is a USA in India? Not yet. Right now, there is a very tiny bit of it only. There are a few who speak English and have Internet access, but the according to the World Bank for 2021,[13] the US is a $23.3 trillion economy and India is just $3.1 trillion. The 325 million people of the US make 7.5 times more than 1.3 billion people. We are not China, we are not the US, we are not India, we are Bharat (Bhindia)—the one billion people are the market. That's why at many of my sessions I call this 'Ignoring the Billion'. More and more start-ups are targeting the same people who have Internet access and are thus bound to fail, as within this bandwidth, there may be room for only one or two players.

Developed–Developing–Under-Developed?

Which is the answer for India? I usually get 'Developing', but India is all the above. On one hand, someone is living in a billion-dollar house overlooking a slum, where in a 10x10 single room, a family of husband, wife and children live. If they have cows, the cow also lives there as they cannot let it out because of the mosquito problem. There is a middle class in between trying to figure out, where do I belong? We have a Germany on one side and an Africa on the other side and there may be a Malaysia in between. If we know this, then entrepreneurs can target the customer segment accordingly.

Open the Door of Your House from Office

These days, the Internet of Things (IoT) is a popular topic. Internet services have advanced to such a stage that with a mobile phone, it has become possible to operate facilities in your home. Fantastic, isn't it? IoT is often shown in the popular imagination as a person putting on the lights, geyser, music and TV in their home while they are still in the car, a few minutes' drive away. Apps based on this are available in the market for you to choose. However, what if the power fails? How will the app work then? That's India for you. When we lack even appropriate and continuous power supply in most places, how can one expect IoT to work? Let's look at this critically—what needs to be done? If one can find the answer for this, then they are winners and one can say there is potential in IoT working in India. We need to localize innovations accordingly.

Shared Economy

We have a huge, aspirational middle class. Let me give you an example. When I ran my IT company, one of my employees bought a Honda City and each month he spent nearly 80 per cent of his salary on EMIs. But he would not share his car to work by paying Rs 100 for a car pool. How many people do you think have cars in India? And, in comparison, how many people have cars in the US? As of 2018, there were 980 cars for every 1000 people in the US and the comparable number for India in the same period was 22 cars per 1000 people.[14] Do we see evidence of a shared economy in India? The carpooling culture has never really taken off. On another note, there is also the tendency for us to make many assumptions. Because we see traffic in Bengaluru is messed up, we assume that the whole of India has traffic problems. This is India's reality and entrepreneurs need to understand it—when they understand more about how Indians think, they can build successful companies.

Uber of . . .

The model for Uber in the US is that you can share your car with another and make some money. When Uber was launched in India, it changed the model to book a cab operated by some operator, as only yellow board vehicles can charge customers. Uber solved the problem in India of booking a cab. Earlier versions of these apps would show cabs for you to pick. If you wanted to go from Koramangala to M.G. Road, you would get ten different options for the same Indica car with different prices. Why different prices?

Earlier, we had the garage-to-garage model. You booked a cab, the meter started running from his garage, he came to pick you up, then once your work was done, he had to go back to his garage and wait for the next customer. Along with this, you had to pay the driver a daily charge, evening charge, etc. So, renting a cab was a tedious task, as you had to find a friend's friend to find a known travel company. Also, you wouldn't know the final bill until he gave you one.

Uber has just made that easy, to travel point-to-point, with all the calculations up front without any surprises. Based on your budget, you pick a car segment that you want, you need not know what car, who is the driver, etc. If you have a problem, you just call Uber and get it resolved. They needed to change the model to solve an Indian problem, and then Ola and other Indian versions of the service copied that. When you copy someone, you need to do what they do. When Uber started selling food, Ola also started selling food.

There are many successful copycat stories. Many people declare they are the Uber of this or that, but at the same time, there are many failures as well. When thousands of people copy the same idea, there are one too many companies that spring up with the same idea. I was in Hyderabad the other day and I was told that there are approximately 1000 to 3000 start-up companies in Hyderabad. But hardly 2000[15] companies got funded in 2022 in the whole country, while Startup India has 93,435 start-ups registered with them as of April 2023. It's an investor's market with more start-ups than money available in the market. As we talk only about successes, we hardly know the failures that exist alongside them, so more and more people want to copy those successful ideas that have worked elsewhere. Hence, the copycat category of entrepreneurship might not work for everyone. It's a tiger—if you can ride it, you could be that one successful one.

Bermuda Triangle—Starting from Failures

To bring out entrepreneurs by talking about failures, I advised the Entrepreneurship and Innovation (EnI) cell of IIMB students to organize this session as part of their annual Eximius event. The first edition streamed virtually in 2020[16] amid the pandemic with two entrepreneurs, one who raised money and another who had failed two or three times. They came forward and discussed the pressure on them from family and friends, how they handled failure and both of them also candidly talked about coming out of it.

We need more experienced entrepreneurs like these to come forward and talk, so other entrepreneurs know how to handle failure and figure out what not to do. As entrepreneurship is an art, even though there are many tools available, finally it's an art and one has to go through it to understand it and it may not be for everyone. For the second edition in 2021, we struggled to find entrepreneurs who wanted to share their experiences. I had reached out to a few funds and entrepreneurs directly, but they were not keen to come forward to talk. Finally, we found two entrepreneurs just a day before the event, who came forward, through one of the NSRCEL-incubated companies, ReCharge, that tries to find jobs for former entrepreneurs. We need to remove the stigma around failed businesses—I tell them, don't call yourself failed entrepreneurs, call yourself a 'serial entrepreneur'.

Category II: Playing to India's Strengths

Now let's look at India's strengths—what has India got? Probably, 'a population of 1.3 billion people' is the first answer that would occur to us. This brings to mind our management guru C.K. Prahalad.[17] We must thank him for describing through his book, *Fortune at the Bottom of the Pyramid*, how the large population (of India) means more opportunities and over time, with the merging of the people at the top of the 'triangle' and those at the bottom, there would be no more triangle. (There is a thought now that 'bottom of the pyramid' [BOP] seems a bit harsh and people have started using the term 'bottom of the economic pyramid').

Do we have any other strengths? Yes, the fantastic youth of India! We are also a fast-growing economy. From $441[18] per capita income in 2000 to $2256 in 2021, we have been able to accelerate our growth and this acceleration will continue as we gain momentum. The 'train' is running. It does not seem to matter who runs the train, but the train is running—and that's what matters. Look at the many states in India that seem to have growth side by side with terrible local governance issues—it is amazing!

People, Problems, Technology (PPT)

What about opportunity? There are so many, many problems to solve in India. From dawn to dusk, there are zillions of problems. Energy, garbage, water and whatnot. All those complaints we have, each one is a business idea, that's the strength of India—the thousands of problems around us. Unfortunately, when a problem is discussed, the normal and common attitude of people is to blame the government. 'Someone else will/has to take care of it' is the majority view. While such a majority is good at finding problems, only an entrepreneur can 'find' a business opportunity in each problem.

By now, some elements of technology can also be thrown in to solve problems. In Bengaluru, the definition of technology has become just 'another app'. Even the Supreme Court warned the government, citing the digital divide when they asked people to book for vaccines on the CoWin app. But real problem-solving does not happen just by 'writing apps'. Look deeper and we can find that there are an amazing number of problems that can be solved in creative and innovative ways that involve and empower the community. Technology could be anything that applies what our engineering, medical, Ayurveda, science and arts students study—apply physics, math, mechanical, civil, even from literature that can bring a lot of ancient wisdom. If you don't know coding or tech, no problem, tech is just the enabler. What's important is what problem you solve and how you solve it. You can get lots of technical people to help you in solving that. Just consider so many of the people I have spoken of in this book—Damodaran of Gramalaya studied social work and figured out a solution using anaerobic bacteria for his toilets; one company in my portfolio, Freshworld, founded by Rajiv Rao, found technical people to develop electric vehicles to carry vegetables; Wilma, a literature graduate, is today using robots to segregate waste; Ashok Kannan never went to school but uses technology to print on eggs.

On the other hand, we have lots of technical people innovating for tech's sake and trying to figure out how to force-fit that solution. I have seen entrepreneurs who say, 'I have an app that I'm giving away free and I would need money to market that app.' If someone is offering something free, why is that not going viral, as people would love free stuff, isn't it? That only means the solution is not solving something that people really wanted to be solved. That's what I mean when I say that India's strength is PPT—People, Problems and Technology. Pick the problems you would like to solve, through 'hearing the sun rise' and pick a tough problem to solve. If it's easy to solve, then it's easy to solve for a hundred more people. If it's tough to solve for you, then it's tough to copy as well. Also, when you look at the problem, look at the root cause of the problem, not just the surface; then the problem doesn't get solved completely. If you've picked such a problem and every Indian pays you a rupee, you are a billion-rupee company. Thus, India's strength is PPT—People, Problems and Tech!

When I talk of the second category of start-ups or entrepreneurs to you, these are the people who play on India's strengths. I will do this with a few examples.

Gaining in Translation—My Million Dollar Story

I met a young man, Umesh Sachdev, in late 2013, who had co-founded Uniphore along with his college friend Ravi Saraogi. He was working on technology for voice recognition. According to People Archives of Rural India (PARI),[19] as per the People's Linguistic Survey of India, the country as a whole speaks some 780 languages and uses eighty-six different scripts. Many of them don't have scripts and hardly 246 million Indians speak English, so one billion people are not part of the digital revolution, as it's all in English.

India is a unique country; you travel 50 km in any direction, and you have a chance of eating different food, seeing different attire and hearing a different dialect or language. That's the extent of our diversity and the unity in that is what makes India unique and has kept it going. As we celebrate the centenary of Subramania Bharathi,[20] the famous Tamil poet born in 1921, what he said around seventy years back is still valid! 'முப்பது கோடி முகமுடையாள் - உயிர் மொய்ம்புற வொன்றுடையாள் - இவள் செப்பு மொழி பதினெட்டுடையாள் - எனிற் சிந்தனை ஒன்றுடையாள்— *Mutpathu kodi mugamudayal yuir moimbura onrudaiyal, seppumozhli pathinetudaiyal enir sinthani ondrudiyal* (While describing India's diversity—30 crore faces, still the spirit is one, she speaks eighteen languages, still the thoughts are the same).

This is the problem Uniphore was solving. They found that many languages are passed on through voice even though they may not have a script. They decided to understand many of these languages and translate them into English so the computers could understand. They approached IIT Chennai and Prof. Ashok Jhunjhunwala, a Padma Shri awardee of the country who pioneered academy–industry partnerships forty years ago. He started IITM Research Park in 2010 and guided them to build voice recognition technology with the support of IITM. They also realized that as with the human iris and fingerprints, everyone has a unique voice as well. Mimicry artists can make us believe they are celebrity voices, but they cannot do so with computers. Applying voice biometrics that recognize more than fourteen Indian languages in hundreds of dialects, with many patents with IITM, Uniphore built a system with 98 per cent accuracy. A tribal woman could buy a feature phone and do an entire bank transaction using voice, as her voice was her password as well.

Uniphore—*Intha Naal Iniya Naal* (Today is a Good Day)! is the slogan with which Umesh demonstrated the technology that they had developed being used by a microfinance organization. When a beneficiary applied for a microfinance loan, the system recorded her/his voice, and that would become their password. For further transactions like reviewing or repaying money, the system would ask them to repeat a phrase—in this case, it was 'இந்த நாள் இனிய நாள்'—their slogan in Tamil. The person repeating this in their own Tamil dialect enabled the system to recognize them and help her/his microfinance agent to complete the transaction. When I was learning more about Uniphore as part of my due diligence before investing, I remember talking to Suresh Krishna of Grameen Koota, a microfinance organization that was using Uniphore technology. It was important for me to understand how customers felt about the product.

Believe in Your Vision!

Almost twenty investors had rejected Uniphore's proposal. Umesh was not disappointed and neither did he turn towards other trending e-commerce businesses. That's the perseverance I liked so much in them. I use their example to tell entrepreneurs, 'If the problem statement is valid and the solution is original, never give up.' After around 200 years of being a British colony, only 246 million in India speak English[21] and one billion do not—that's the problem statement. This is not going to change overnight. The solution they developed for this problem is their own, by painstakingly developing the system to recognize the fourteen-plus Indian languages. However, if you copy someone, then you have to keep doing what they are doing, like Ola starting to sell food when Uber started selling, even though there is no real link between the cab business and the food business.

When you are original, you chart your own path. When twenty people told them they were wrong, they never gave up. They continued to work on their product. When I met them at the IITM incubator in 2008, they were already a five-year-old company. They would not even have fallen in the start-up definition for angel investment. What made me invest in them are these two reasons—believing in their vision and solving an important problem.

Later, Uniphore technology was used by farmers of Tamil Nadu. Forty lakh voice calls were made informing the farmers about the weather forecast in Tamil. The system translates the English information into Tamil and explains it to farmers. If farmers ask a question such as, 'What should I do if I grow chillies?' in Tamil, the system does audio mining and gets them the information they would need. In a complicated situation, it connects them with the call centre. What Umesh did was not just solving the problem of people in rural and semi-urban areas, but his company brought one billion people to the digital revolution. The founders of Uniphore believed in themselves and were not ready to compromise.

Adaptability

When I was investing in Uniphore, I remember what Prof. Jhunjhunwala told me, that the team would need more mentoring than money right now. I saw that the company was doing mobile development as well, for survival. I told them, let's stop that and focus only on the voice recognition, and we should be a product company in that space. Umesh is amazing in the way he adapts to a need. Before the planned date, he had moved the entire company towards only products.

This turnaround was described by *Forbes* when they did a story around my work 'How Nagaraja Prakasam is Engineering Social Change' in late 2016.[22]

> 'Sachdev admits that, five years later, the story of Uniphore "was not sellable". The start-up was doing "bits and pieces of many things", he says, as it had started to digress from voice recognition and created "non-core" verticals such as mobile apps. More so, Uniphore had modelled its voice recognition business as a service rather than a product . . . Uniphore has raised two more rounds of funding and counts Infosys co-founder Kris Gopalakrishnan as an investor. Prakasam's advice for the company to ditch the "non-core" mobile app business and start selling the core voice recognition business as a product, not a service, has helped Uniphore clock revenue growth of 250 to 300 per cent over the last two years. Moreover, the start-up has taken its business global to the Philippines and the UAE and has banks, telcos and airlines as clients. "After Naga came, our story has crystallised and has been fine-tuned to such an extent that of the same 20 VCs who had rejected us earlier, three have come back and invested in us," says Umesh Sachdev.'

With Uniphore's innovative products, Umesh was recognized by *TIME* as one of the Next Generation Leaders in 2016[23]—one of the millennials changing the world. Umesh was the only entrepreneur on the list from India![24] Later, he was on the cover of *Forbes* along with Carbon Master's Som Narayan.[25] It was indeed a proud moment, as entrepreneurs who are choosing uncharted paths are being recognized and it is a good motivation for more entrepreneurs to follow suit.

Another quality of Umesh that I truly appreciate and would like all entrepreneurs to know is how passionately he talks about his product. He provides details on how his product could help a customer's concerns, doing a lot of homework before reaching out to anyone. So, he is thus able to convert every connection I've made for him. One interesting example was while we were doing the Series A round, I had connected him with Kris Gopalakrishnan of Infosys and arranged a call with him after briefing him about the company. After one call with Umesh, Kris sent me a message that he is investing.

Similarly, I remember a story Umesh told us of how, after winning the India Edition of MIT Technology Review's 'Innovators Under 35',[26] he had an opportunity to have a mentoring time with John Chambers, chairman emeritus of CISCO. When John asked him what questions he had, Umesh replied, 'I have this customer, CISCO, and don't know how to sell to them.' John liked this question so much that he offered to spend more time with him. This relationship went on to John becoming a chief guru of Uniphore and taking a 10 per cent stake later. *Fortune*'s story on Uniphore called 'Gaining in Translation',[27] narrated this:

> 'In 2014, Uniphore caught the attention of leading angel investors including Nagaraja Prakasam, partner, Acumen, a non-profit global impact investment fund. In the following year, Infosys co-founder Kris Gopalakrishnan invested too. Later, in 2017, the founders impressed former Cisco CEO John Chambers who put in, in his personal capacity, an undisclosed amount in the Chennai-headquartered company. This was his first investment in an Indian start-up.'

I can write a whole book on the Uniphore story with Umesh and Ravi at some point. I spoke for an hour and half at an IITM Incubator event on 'Uniphore Story:

The Angel Touch'. Umesh has another habit that I always feel is a must for entrepreneurs—taking notes. This means he will come back with closure on every suggestion he gets, saying I've tried, this worked and this didn't work, or this I don't want to do. It shows he is keeping his entrepreneurial spirit alive. I don't like an entrepreneur saying 'yes' to everything, because not everything is feasible and just offering a 'yes' to every suggestion suggests an employee not an entrepreneurial spirit. An entrepreneur is a free spirit, that is what makes them what they are. Working with Umesh is always enjoyable.

Interestingly, when the problem of a billion people is solved, one will find that there are four billion more with the same problem, as only two billion people in the world speak English. Today, Uniphore is a global leader in conversational AI (artificial intelligence). While he was waiting for the first five years, he was strengthening the technology, listening to 25,000 hours of Indian voices in many Indian languages and dialects at 98 per cent accuracy. This made the system more intelligent and today, it is one of the best machine learning (ML) engines in the world for voice. Today, in speech recognition, Uniphore competes with all the technology giants of the world that have billions of dollars of R&D budget, proving again that money is just one component of a growth trajectory, operating in multiple countries and employing hundreds of employees. Thus, solving an important Indian problem, Uniphore can take on the world. During the pandemic as well, Uniphore technology helped the Aarogya Setu app of the Tamil Nadu Government with voice support.[28] The technology he developed for tribals and farmers of India is helping corporates worldwide. As of 2022, the company has achieved $2.5 billion valuation[29] and my investment in the company is worth a few million dollars, even after I've taken out around a million dollars in the past.

The Trusted Co-founder

Uniphore also brings out another great example of co-founders working well together. Ravi Saraogi always stood behind Umesh as a rock-solid pillar as he faced the outside world. He was always ready to pick up anything the company needed so that Umesh was freed up. While Umesh sells, Ravi delivers the product. He was always in the background, ensuring the customers are happy and the products are working well at the customer's site. When we were scaling, we hired our first salesperson in Singapore, who came with a decorated past and signed up for a huge revenue from there. As a start-up, we went beyond our budget to accommodate his remuneration. That person couldn't deliver and the company couldn't afford to have another employee there. We all looked at Ravi, as, over a dinner, Ravi, Umesh and I discussed the problem.

The next morning, Ravi said, 'I'll go to Singapore and build the company there from scratch.' He went off and within a year, that region overtook India's revenues and helped the company to go to the next level. Umesh ensures he communicates with Ravi often and they are always there for each other while the company scales new heights.

As a mentor, I spend quite a lot of time in handling co-founder issues and there were many even before the company had revenues. But I have always shared the Uniphore example of how co-founders should work. Even though they are classmates, they never take each other for granted. They are good friends outside and in the boardroom, they treat each other with respect.

Breakthrough Business—Paramedics and Diagnostics

The tremendous significance a social business can assume can be illustrated by a significant enterprise like Sameer Sawarkar and Rajeev Kumar's Neurosynaptic. I had met Sameer Sawarkar at the Ashoka[30] fellows' induction programme in 2014, where I had been invited as a mentor for the fellows. Over forty years, Ashoka has been identifying and supporting the world's leading social entrepreneurs, learning from the patterns in their innovations and mobilizing a global community that embraces these new frameworks to build an 'everyone a changemaker world'. It was very interesting to hear about his venture around telemedicine.

As only 40 per cent doctors are in rural areas where 70 per cent of India lives, the medical expenses for them are triple-fold.[31] For you and me in the city, in a few hours, we can visit a doctor. But people in rural areas have to travel to a nearby town, so they lose a day's wage. If they are going to a nearby town, they take someone with them, so they bear the expenses of the person accompanying them and his wage loss too. This makes them not seek healthcare until it's very late. Once it's late, when they get admitted to a city hospital, the expenses would be very high, and if they survive and come back, they fall in debt for life. If they pass away, their family is put in debt for life—thus healthcare expenses are one of the top reasons for the poor not to be able to come out of poverty or get pushed back into poverty. Sameer wanted to address this problem and started Neurosynaptic Communications Pvt. Ltd (NSCPL) with Rajeev Kumar, both of whom had studied at the Indian Institute of Science (IISc). With its patented ReMeDi® digital telehealth solutions aiming to improve this situation,

Neurosynaptic has successfully demonstrated scale on the ground. Later, he approached me looking for investments, so I had visited their centre in Madurai in December 2015.

After attending an Internal Quality Assurance Cell (IQAC) Board meeting at Lady Doak College (LDC), Madurai,[32] I left the next morning for Meenakshi Mission Hospital and Research Centre (MMHRC) to pick up Rosemary, the telemedicine project coordinator at MMHRC and we drove 44 km to Thonugal village, near Kariapatti. We reached the centre named Meenakshi Mission Telecare Centre and interestingly, there was PURA library in that centre as well. PURA (Provision of Urban Amenities to Rural Areas) had been the dream of Dr Abdul Kalam, the then President of India. I was glad someone had implemented a part of that in this centre.

Viji, Our Doctor

Viji welcomed us to the centre. A Class 12 graduate from the same village, her house is just opposite the centre, so there is no commute to work. This is a great way to get more women into the workforce by bringing work to their home. Viji grew up in this village and married a man from the same village as well. As I am a board member of the Lady Doak College IQAC board, I visit them twice a year. This all-women college was started seventy-three years ago. During one of the convocations, I handed over 900 diplomas to girls and a few came with their babies to receive their certificates. 30 per cent of them were first-generation graduates. The convocation went on for hours and the principal asked me, aren't you tired? I said not at all, as I know the value of this degree. After all, I'm a first-generation graduate as well.

But sadly, I had found out from our board meetings, that only around 20 per cent of the young women preferred to take up jobs; the rest of the girls were not allowed to, as they were all from nearby villages and their parents were not keen. I have narrated the example of Viji to our students many times, to see how they can pursue work that need not require leaving their village. That's what I liked a lot about ReMeDi; like Viji, there are around 8000-plus Vijis across the country enabled to become caregivers in their own villages.

We met Ponram who had come to the centre for a regular check-up. He was narrating his experience of visiting the telemedicine centre earlier to get treatment for a pain he was suffering from. He thought that it was some minor medical issue and to his surprise, he was immediately requested to visit the hospital in Madurai (one hour's drive away) where he had to undergo a surgery that saved his life. This centre is enabled by ReMeDi, with over thirty-two diagnostics tests. Now with advances in wireless technologies, the entire ReMeDi can be placed in a bag and a person like Viji can start a mobile diagnostic centre. Viji was trained by the hospital and runs this centre all by herself. She was demonstrating the system and called the Madurai hospital to inform them about Ponram's visit. Once the registration formalities were done, she had enabled the videoconferencing.

Reverse-engineered for Bharat

This is one of the key innovations by NSCPL partnering with IIT Madras.[33] While we talk about 5G these days in the metros, we also know many parts of the country don't have Internet. However, there is always a BSNL landline available in most of these places. NSCPL relies on these landlines and can work with even the smallest bandwidth possible, as low as 64 KBps (kilo bytes per second). 1 MB is 1024 KB and currently, you can expect more than 200 MBps in 5G available in cities.

That's what made for India means. Once you understand the current status, you would be able to innovate accordingly. That's why it's important for entrepreneurs to understand India better, if they want to solve her problems. The videoconferencing is a must, as the patients would like to see the doctor and he should move around, so they know there is a real person on the other side. Again, understanding psychology is more important than the technology. Viji then inserted the thermometer in Ponram's mouth, and the doctor on the other side enabled that thermometer. Here is a control to ensure Viji doesn't operate any of these without the doctor enabling it, thus reducing errors. It also enables a person without much skills to operate the system. That's how 8000-plus Vijis were possible. Once the doctor finished his diagnostics, including checking Ponram's ECG remotely, he typed the prescription in Madurai that got printed out here in Thonugal. Now, Ponram could buy these medicines at any shop and the centre also keeps some emergency medicines. In some of the villages, people want injections. Without injections, they don't feel the treatment is good. In such villages, nurses are employed at the centres. This is a classic example of how technology can address problems, especially in the rural parts of India.

Viji took us around the village, talking to people about their health and why they've not come for a check-up, etc. As she wore a blue coat and walked around, it was great to see her relatives proudly calling out that our Viji is a doctor! Viji also made us aware of the local practice—she sent a child to a shop in the village for a health tablet for Rs 5. Before the centre came into the village, that tablet was the first cure for the villagers—the tablet was given for any ailment, making things worse. That shopkeeper is now scared of Viji as she had warned him not to sell this cure-all any more!

No Landline, Go Satellite

On our way back, we learnt from Rosemary that the hospital runs fifteen telemedicine centres using ReMeDi technology, as far off as in Rameswaram, which is 150 km from the hospital. She was explaining that if there is a serious ailment diagnosed for any patient, they can catch the next train and come to Madurai for further treatment. They were also planning to start a telemedicine centre in Sri Lanka to be supported by the doctors from Madurai. We reached the Madurai hospital where we met the doctor who singlehandedly managed those fifteen telemedicine centres sitting in Madurai, making his time very productive. I was also shown the satellite Internet connection with ISRO available to them as a backup. In case they face Internet issues, they use the satellite Internet. That showed me that we have the technology; we only need to find ways to use it appropriately.

Salem to Sirumalai

As we started to look at investing, Payal Shah of Axilor, a VC fund, and I drove to Sharon Hospital in Salem in April 2016 from Bengaluru. They had just bought ReMeDi and the telemedicine doctor there showed us how he was supporting two centres, one near Salem at Chetti Chavadi and one in Sirumalai, a tribal hill around 210 km from there. After seeing the doctor's side, we wanted to see the patient's side as well and visited Chetti Chavadi village, about 10 km from this hospital. This is managed by Nithya, who has done a diploma in nursing, along with Mani Nandan, who has done a BSc in microbiology, supporting over 1000 people visiting them in a month.

Later that month, after a GUARDIAN board meeting in Trichy, I travelled to Dindigul, as Nativelead member Sugumar Nagarajan of Anil Foods was interested in this as well. After having the popular Dindigul Thalappakatti Biriyani, we headed out to climb the Sirumalai hills, reaching the Sharon Sirumalai telemedicine centre managed by a nurse, after an hour's drive. Since the hills are a part of reserved forest, the people living there drive for over an hour to reach the nearest hospital. With only the telemedicine centre in the hills, today people can use this centre. Sirumalai is famous for its tiny version of bananas and they tasted particularly good to me on that visit, as I considered how we could use technology to help the poor.

Believe In Your Vision

Guess what? This start-up was also rejected by eighty-five investors,[34] but the team did not give up hope. They knew that their vision was clear and that their mission was very important. I was impressed with what I saw and invested in NSCPL along with two other VC funds. The potential for such a service across the country is huge and success always demands time. Sameer and Rajeev are the examples that I give to entrepreneurs on resilience. They had a setback earlier, when their growth was stalled, when an investment supposed to come through was pulled back at the last minute. They hit rock bottom and rebuilt the company again, with the sincere hope of making a mark. All their hard work is paying off now as the pandemic made their vision clear to everyone and what they started a long time ago, everyone wants today!

1B to 4B

This is why I reiterate that if you solve problems of one billion in India, there are four billion with similar problems. ReMeDi has gone global and is implemented in Africa. The World Health Organization (WHO) listed ReMeDi Solution (e-health with medical devices) in the WHO Compendium 2016–17,[35] with a note that access to essential medicines and health technologies is one of the cornerstones of the Universal Health Coverage (UHC) initiative. Medical devices, assistive devices and e-health solutions are important components of health technology, which have the potential to save lives and improve the quality of life and well-being. However, too many people worldwide suffer because they don't have access to high quality, affordable health technology with the problem being more acute in low- and middle-income countries.

The pandemic in 2020–21 has demonstrated convincingly how the poor are losing their lives due to the lack of access to healthcare. According to the WHO survey in India, we have one doctor for 10,189 people, with Bihar at 1:28,391, Karnataka at 1:13,556 and UP at 1:19,962, while WHO recommends 1:1000 as the doctor:people ratio, where Delhi is at 1:2203. According to Rural Health Statistics, if Ayush doctors and specialists are included, it comes to around 1.4 per 10,000 people. The estimated population considered is around 136.7 crore.[36] But, even before Covid-19, most villagers would have been daunted by the thought of having to consult a 'big doctor' in a 'big city'. Considering the expense of travel, boarding and hospital costs, many choose to have even serious health conditions remain untreated in villages, or managed with palliative care from primary health centres (PHCs) and local doctors. By bringing more qualified and experienced professionals within reach of the rural population, NSCPL has released thousands from fear and suffering, besides unleashing their productive energy. This pandemic made most stay at home, and telemedicine became a must. The changes that Sameer has been asking from the government finally happened through telemedicine regulations being relaxed, thus making NSCPL a visionary in foreseeing these problems almost twenty years ago. Today, they are the leaders in this space and during the pandemic, they enabled telemedicine in two aspirational districts of India, with a model of CSR funding the initiative, a local NGO partner training paramedics on the ground and enabling the government PHCs with telemedicine capabilities.

HCL Samuday

In December 2021, it was heart-warming to see this press release by the HCL Foundation:

> Transforming the rural healthcare ecosystem by bringing the community closer to affordable and quality healthcare services through teleconsultation, we at HCL Samuday are happy to announce the launch of 10 new telemedicine centres in Uttar Pradesh by Ms. Roshni Nadar Malhotra, Chairperson, HCL Technologies and Chairperson, HCL CSR Board Committee.

Expanding the initiative to 8 new blocks of Hardoi district to benefit over 1 lakh people, it is another step forward to mitigate the impact of pandemic with technology and innovation. Operational for 6 days a week and supported to run on renewable energy harnessed by state-of-the-art rooftop solar PV systems, these centres offer free services that include an initial examination, consultation with a medical officer through video conferencing, diagnostic tests and report/data generation, real-time data sharing with doctors, authorized prescription, medicine dispensation and explanation of medicines along with precautionary measures. We are hopeful that these facilities will help the community to access quality healthcare and lead a healthy life. HCL Samuday has partnered with Neurosynaptic Communications Private Limited to deliver and implement the project on ground.

Category III: Disruptive Innovators?

The third category of start-ups is made up of entrepreneurs who aim for disruptive innovation. We in India are zero at it. I heard someone remark that India is not zero in its innovations. Look at OYO Rooms, they are innovative and amazingly disruptive! If OYO Rooms are considered disruptive innovation, can we imagine the standards we set for ourselves?

Someone asked me, what is your definition of disruptive innovations? What I am looking for are amazing innovators. We need an Edison who invented the lightbulb and had an angel investor like J.P. Morgan and started General Electric (GE).[37] Even today, GE is one of the world's most valuable companies. Today, the *light* invented by Edison defines the GDP of countries. Economists look at the night-time view of the world from the sky and based on the light they see, they predict the growth level. Obviously, the brightest part from the sky at night is Las Vegas, where all the money is floating in gambling and the darkest part is Africa.

Where are our Edisons in India? Missing because people are not willing to spend at least five to ten years going deep into research and making developments in their area to make a difference to the world. Also, we tend to settle down in life with trending sectors. A person working in metallurgy in the US may be working on the next version of gorilla glass (the strong glass that is used on smartphones), but the person studying metallurgy in India wants to write an algorithm to find the cheapest gorilla glass phone on the Internet. In that sense, we have zero disruptive innovations in spite of having amazing potential. However, even though there are no great models or frameworks for entrepreneurs to emulate or replicate as yet, as a country we could become role models with our innovations, especially in the social sphere. I say so primarily because there are four billion with just about the same number of problems as India. Disruptions need not be technology-based alone, it could be social as well, such as Prof. Mohammad Yunus's simple idea that has transformed the lives of billions of poor in the world.

The Western world is not a place that can be copied by us. The US has problems with equality that can be summed up as the 1 per cent versus the 99 per cent. Poverty in the US has different causes, which are very different from our country. People may fall into poverty there because of cancer and its long treatment. But their lifestyles are also likely to cause cancer, with microwave ovens, processed foods and chemicals being an ordinary part of life. So many instances of these harmful effects reach us through the news—the 'bread basket' states of the American Midwest contaminate a river that flows into the Gulf of Mexico where the fish are dying. That's the reality of the US. Definitely not a model one can follow. India is not far behind; we started seeing cancer stories around us—even after practising sustainable living, I lost my wife to cancer.

This is the departure point from which flows the major potential for us to find problems and solve them. Bear in mind that start-up companies might not get funding as early as they wish to, but that does not matter as money is just one part of it. In 2022, $24 billion came into the system as equity investment.[38] We are a $3+ trillion economy and within that, $24 billion is a small percentage. The country is running with traditional businesses, of which there are many amazing people who do not want equity funding and yet they are building amazing companies. It would be better if entrepreneurs looked at them and didn't get disillusioned by the fact that this tiny portion of the $24 billion is too small for our needs and that's what we've got.

Customer Should Buy, Customer Should Not Be Bought

In a way, doing business is simple. All you need to do is to find a problem, then the solution, and you will definitely find someone who will pay for your solution because it is so awesome that it solves the problem. That's the basic principle of any business. Besides, 'free' is not something that is going to work. There are only two things that have worked on the principle of free—one is Google and the other is Facebook. I joke about it; in India we have a saying that if we give anything free and even if it is phenyl, people will drink it. But then the apps available are becoming worse than phenyl. Even if they are free, no one wants to use them because there are eight billion downloads and 99 per cent free apps. So don't look at any shortcuts or quick ways to get rich, but instead focus deeper into problems.

I am saying this for budding entrepreneurs to get a better insight into what being a disruptive innovator means. Only hard work pays off in the long run. People spend years to develop that one solution that disrupts the entire market. Nothing comes easy, but most of us think that it is the other way round. I feel we are zero when it comes to disrupting the market and I do not come across such disruptive solutions very often.

What Can I Solve?

Where are such innovators? We have enough problems in our daily lives waiting to be solved. Two-thirds of the world is water, but we have a water problem. All the energy sources known to humans cannot solve the energy needs of the 7.5 billion people of the world.

What is the future of mobility? With twenty-two cars per 1000 people,[39] we have traffic problems. What am I eating, what am I wearing? Where am I living—all require disruption, as that's not sustainable. It is quite sad, but the fact remains that a part of our population goes to bed without having enough food to eat. Millions in India do not have access to electricity. Where do they belong? What were their predecessors doing? What keeps them away from development and basic standards of living? Attempts to answer these questions will help entrepreneurs identify a billion-dollar business plan as per their answer. Such solutions will obviously lead the country to further development. The gap between the haves and have-nots in India is not negligible. It is pertinent to reduce this gap for any country to progress. No one else other than entrepreneurs can make this happen. The power of marketing makes people opt for things that they really don't need. For someone to understand this, they have to walk out of their comfort zones and meet the real customer. Siva of GoCoop did this and he ended up adding value to the lives of 5000 weavers while making authentic handloom available online for patrons. This did not happen overnight.

Our entrepreneurs need to explore the real-life situations around them. Technology is an enabler, not the final solution for our people who are still way behind. There is zero competition for hard work. The mantra for success is perseverance, constant innovation and a determination to solve genuine problems.

Student Entrepreneurship

MyCaptain

Over the past decade, my NSRCEL journey has been quite inspiring. I met Mohammad Zeeshan and his friend for a mentoring session in October 2014. He felt that today's youth are unable to connect with—and find relevance in—the magazines meant for a teenage audience, which are also largely written by older adults. They started a magazine for Classes 11 and 12 students, but with first- and second-year college students as the writers. Since these writers would have recently completed their schooling, they would be able to write more relevant content. Mohammad Zeeshan and his friend were then second-year college students studying in Chennai.

I agreed that their idea was brilliant but wondered why they needed to come to Bengaluru for mentoring, to which they said that since they were not creating a technology start-up, support was hard to find. Prof. Suresh Bhagavatula of IIMB had visited their college and directed them to NSRCEL. Since then, they have been diligently working on their venture, even pivoting from publishing the magazine to teaching topics of interest to the students in the same manner, that is first- and second-year college students— called captains—teaching students of Classes 11 and 12. I remember speaking at their massive event, 'I-Seize the Day' in August 2015 in Chennai, where students arrived in three buses and learnt from people who had followed their passion.

By the time they graduated, Mohammed Zeeshan and his friend had Rs 8 lakh in the bank as well. But then a problem arose as their parents only thought of their magazine project as a college-time extracurricular activity and expected them to take up full-time jobs thereafter. I spoke to their parents and told them that their children, who may not even have helped them with household chores, had developed into good entrepreneurs and were running a company in which CEO meant Chief Everything Officer.

They won a competition at IIMB and got incubated at NSRCEL. When they graduated from the incubation, I inaugurated their first office with thirty employees in October 2017. Their parents attended the inauguration and I could see them feeling proud about their children's success. Their idea was good enough for their venture, MyCaptain, to succeed, but even if they had failed, their entrepreneurship would be equivalent to ten years of professional experience. Of the five MyCaptain founders, four continued with the venture while one went on for further education.

Their success motivated many other students from their college to work at MyCaptain, making it one of the largest employers. Today, with 300 employees, Zeeshan, Sameer

Ramesh and Ruhan Naqash have received the Forbes 30 under 30 special recognition for running one of the most successful companies in the edtech space. MyCaptain boasts an average employee age of twenty-seven and its founders have been recognized by the UN for their futuristic way of educating a younger generation to find their passion. They bootstrapped their business all these years and as of January 2022, they have bypassed angel investing and raised $3 million in Series A funding.

Let's Be the Change

I met Anirudh S. Dutt in November 2017 while conducting a session on entrepreneurship at his college and learnt about his efforts towards making Bengaluru cleaner. By then, he had already been awarded the Rising Star of the Year Award in 2015 by the Namma Bengaluru Awards initiative. Even as a second-year college student, he wasn't satisfied with this recognition as he really wanted to ensure a clean Bengaluru. Being a true entrepreneur, he didn't blame anyone but instead took up the broom and began cleaning places that had become dumping sites and toilets—and painted them with nice earthen colours too.

He often visited NSRCEL for mentoring and he continued on his mission and got incubated at NSRCEL Social after graduating from college. Meanwhile, many of his friends who had supported him during his college days ended up working full-time jobs. In 2018, he also received a Guinness World Record for collecting 33.5 tonnes of plastic bottles in twelve hours. During the pandemic, Anirudh's team managed to mobilize 700 volunteers and started mapping Bengaluru to understand who might need help and who could provide the necessary resources, thus offering valuable assistance to the Bruhat Bengaluru Mahanagara Palike (BBMP) officials. Having appropriately named his non-profit organization 'Let's be the Change', Anirudh's relentless mission to clean Bengaluru continues even as he helps channel youthful energy towards positive change.

Broken Crayons Still Colour

Alina Alam, a young dynamic woman full of energy who participated in NSRCEL Social's first launch pad, had the aim of running an organic café fully staffed by persons with disabilities (PWD), called Mitti Café. I advised her to solve one problem rather than two. While she didn't make it to the incubation, her determination grew stronger. As I always tell any entrepreneurship jury of which I am a member, 'No one can judge an entrepreneur; it is purely an academic exercise to rank a few.'

However, Alina persevered with her dream of starting a PWD-staffed café and found a unique way of setting up the café in IT companies' offices, supported by their CSR. It turned out to be an instant hit despite the multiple outlets present in the food court. Mitti Café stood out as a result of the staff also handling the entire interior decoration. Alina came back to us and got incubated in a later cohort at NSRCEL Social, along with Suicide Prevention India Foundation (SPIF), Rural Caravan (promoting rural tourism), Blink (helping dyslexic children learn), Thinkzone (starting schools in rural areas), Econut (the first FPO to be incubated), Taxshe (women-driven taxis), Inqilab (inculcating innovation among government schools), Saurav Mandala, Let's be the Change and The Apprentice Project (TAP—delivering twenty-first century skills to government school students).

Mitti Café was soft-launched at IIMB in June 2017, with food prepared and served by disabled workers. The following year, she joined me on a panel at the NSCEL Social Incubator Conference at IIMB, by which time she was running a few cafés. I visited her café on the Infosys campus in January 2020 and was blown away by the determination of the nine staff members, each of whom faced various challenges ranging from the physical to the intellectual. The love they poured into their work made us proud and we saw how Alina had brought in dignity to people facing such challenges, who were otherwise often considered a burden to the family and some of them may have ended up on the streets. I saw a poster in the café saying, *Broken crayons still colour*—which Alina made possible. She invited me to inaugurate their Wipro campus café the following month where I also heard a great story about two of their employees getting married. When the cafés had to close during the pandemic-related lockdown, Alina quickly pivoted using the kitchens to make meals for the needy in the city. She shared with me a photo showing one of their staff members handing over a meal to a daily wage worker. They have served over five million meals through sixteen cafés employing hundreds of disabled staff members. Alina was also recognized by Forbes 30 under 30 Asia and became a Commonwealth Youth Award winner at the age of twenty-seven.

As exemplified by Alina, Anirudh and Zeeshan, student entrepreneurship definitely paves the way for creating more job creators than job seekers and thus enables us to build India entrepreneurially. I was impressed that the last India Innovation Challenge Design Competition (IICDC)—organized by NSRCEL in partnership with the Department of Science and Technology (DST) and Texas

Instruments (TI)—received applications from one lakh students. We have incubated over thirty to forty student ventures from across the country, working on various ideas like ten-minute NPK soil tests, vomit analysis using sensors to support Ayurveda, etc., and many of the entrepreneurs were running their ventures while studying.

Twelve

Inclusion in Practice

*'Corporate social responsibility is measured in terms of
businesses improving conditions for their employees,
shareholders, communities and environment. But moral
responsibility goes further, reflecting the need for corporations
to address fundamental ethical issues such as inclusion, dignity
and equality.'*
—Klaus Schwab, founder and executive chairman,
World Economic Forum

Social Entrepreneurs

Outside-in

I've seen two kinds of social entrepreneurs: one is the
highly educated, seen the city life or life abroad and
suddenly a bulb goes off in their head saying, what am
I doing with life and they start looking at the purpose of
life and then at giving back. I am of this kind, that too I
find quite of lot of people from the IT industry falling for
it. I'm not sure why, but my theory is we are all middle
class, worked hard and saw success in that process, and
after some time, our conscience wakes up. But why not
the other industry? I feel industries have been there for a
long time, so growing and achieving success in those areas

seems a relatively slow process. The IT industry grew
pretty fast from 1988 onwards. I was right there to take
a ride on that—while I was in Class 12, the government
introduced math, physics, chemistry (MPC) or MPB
(math, physics, biology). I went into MPC and started
learning statistics. In engineering, we already saw in 1992
that computer science was part of the offering. I had no
clue about this and opted for mechanical engineering. I
studied in Kalloorani and when I ranked first in school, I
had no idea about IITs and there was only one engineer
in my home town. He said that my marks were very good,
don't worry, apply for engineering. This is what I tell every
student I meet, now the horizon is wider—expand the
horizon further and get exposed to as many opportunities
as are available. Any area you pick, you could be the
best in that. Otherwise, the education process is getting
skewed to a few areas such as engineering. With over 500
engineering colleges in Tamil Nadu, many students are
still not able to get a job and end up doing odd jobs. With
the focus on computers in 1988–92 because the Y2K
problem was around the corner, there was a sudden need
for computer programmers across the country. My first
job was at Aptech as I had learnt computer aided design/
manufacturing in college. I was given an opportunity to
use AutoCAD in 1993. With more opportunities opening
up, I left for the US in 1996. In sixteen years, I grew from an
engineer to president. Like mine, around five million jobs
were created over the period, resulting in a $250 billion
Indian IT industry now. Interestingly, many of them who
benefited started giving back. I always say that people in
the IT industry's behaviour follows the standards set by
N.R. Narayana Murthy, founder of Infosys. He stayed
very humble, not wearing his success on his sleeve all the

time. I've seen this with another co-founder of Infosys, Kris Gopalakrishnan, as well, as he supported many of the social businesses I've supported as well. This created a pretty good culture in Bengaluru, as all the successful IT folks are relatively humble and approachable, as they know the pain of first-generation entrepreneurs. Thus today, Bengaluru is the start-up capital of the country. I'm a first-generation graduate; I've seen that education has helped me, and many people have supported me in reaching this level. This is further fuelled by the example of Bill Gates, another successful IT person, who started giving away his wealth and bringing more people along with him for his Giving Pledge. This led to more people from the IT industry coming into the social sector for enabling the ecosystem and also as entrepreneurs.

While slighter older people have been coming into the system, the younger ones are coming in through the various fellowship programmes. I see the Prime Minister's fellowship programme started to bring young ones to work in rural areas—such as i-Saksham. Three co-founders went to Jamui, Bihar seven years ago, never left the place and are running a successful non-profit there. I see Teach For India (TFI) that brings young ones into government schools as teachers, which created a big pool of talent. With education being the number one focus for non-profits, these young fellows are coming forward to further strengthen the initiative with new ideas. At NSRCEL Social programmes, I see many of the TFI fellows getting incubated for their ideas, such as Inqui-Lab Foundation, The Apprentice Project and Mantra4Change. Acumen India fellowship, a one-year programme offered now to government officials and working professionals along with social entrepreneurs, also brings this talent into the social sector.

NSRCEL Social

The experience of working with social businesses has brought out the importance of grants as they help in working out tough experiments. With this I realized that grants cannot be totally and completely done away with, hence my recent article in *Forbes*—'Social Businesses Must Receive Risk Capital from the Government and CSR'. Further, there are a few problems that cannot be solved by the market alone and need to necessarily depend on charity. I was further convinced when Prof. Sabarinathan enlightened me on the non-profit incubator thought at NSRCEL. At our first advisory council meeting, Michael & Susan Dell Foundation (MSDF) stated that 'for non-profits, don't change any process that you do for for-profit incubation'. Non-profit businesses are similar to for-profit businesses except that in the case of non-profits, there are two types of customers: one is the beneficiary and the other is the donor. If both customers are satisfied with the outcomes, they would be able to scale.

With a combination of these insights, we were able to set the following broad guidelines:

- Bring in systems and processes that enable efficiency improvements
- Look at the depth of a business to help it become the category leader in problem-solving
- Increase collaborations to bring in more partners to help solve various problems
- In mature markets that are ready for solutions, try being a hybrid organization

On setting these guidelines, the aim was to attract one-year-old non-profit organizations to mentor. With their

DNA being to solve social problems if they could articulate their business approach and succeed in their ventures, they could possibly become the next Ela Bhatt of SEWA, M.P. Vasimalai of Dhan Foundation or Harish Hande of SELCO.

With Sattva's help, over 160 applications were received. The shortlisted candidates were met by mentors and twenty-five of them were selected to go through a three-month pre-incubation process. Out of these, eight non-profits were selected for a grant of Rs 18 lakh each, along with eighteen months of incubation. I was truly impressed with the younger generation for having given up great jobs to work in the space of solving serious social problems. Thus, India's first non-profit incubator at NSRCEL Social took off in September 2017. These non-profits are doing excellent work, redefining non-profits in India. Time flies; the fourth cohort is running now, touching over sixty-five non-profits and incubating nineteen of them. I visited a few organizations and was very excited to see the way they were solving problems. I'm writing about the organizations I visited. I hope to visit others soon.

No Danda

In the start-up capital of India, two million people live in slums. In the labyrinth of Fraser Town, I visited this affordable English medium school in March 2017, where Mantra4change had been working for two years and it was time to exit. Khushboo and Santosh started Mantra4Change through an intensive two-year partnership with schools, with an aim to transform aspects of instructional leadership, teaching–learning processes and the school culture. That's what I liked about Mantra—they would work with schools and exit after they enabled the school to operate on its own. I asked the principal, 'What impact have you seen?'

The answer was, 'No more danda (stick) in the school.' 'What challenges did you face?' The answer was, 'I can't understand why the teachers are not applying what they learnt from Mantra.' On hearing this, I asked Mantra to stay on for some more time until I was able to figure it out. Mantra, too, was unable to answer the question and hence, intended to organize an offsite workshop for the teachers to be able to analyse the problem.

My School May Not Exist

During our mentoring sessions, I used to ask Mantra how they would replicate this. The answer came as a total surprise, when Anthill invited me on 2 January 2018 to inaugurate their twenty-fifth playground in Bommasandra School, not too far from Bengaluru.

I was surprised to see the collaboration between Mantra and Anthill. Mantra had selected the Bommasandra government school cluster to transform and had created an Anthill playground in the school. I will dwell more on Anthill later. I attended the cluster's Jeevadhare committee meeting, represented by the headmaster, parents and government officers. They enabled Mantra to transform the cluster. The committee proposed to Wells Fargo CSR a list of their needs and based on their request, they were soon given the required support.

I asked the headmaster, 'You have a government job, why do you want to do this?' The answer was, 'In my fifteen years here, the number of students went down significantly and we fear that this school may not exist if this continues.' The committee discussed conducting an admission drive to increase the strength. They revived the midday meal process. I also partook in the meal along with the children. It was not at all bad, especially when I compared it to the midday meal that I ate during my school days in Tamil Nadu. What struck me here was that the local stakeholders were empowered to solve their problems on their own.

Edumentum

Mantra4Change invited me to address their cohort. Yes, it was very interesting how they were able to document the entire process of the School Transformation and Empowerment Project (STEP) programme, and now they are training other non-profit organizations in the education space using the same method. One of the social cohorts, i-Saksham, was already a part of this and taking this model to Bihar, while another non-profit organization, Vidhya Vidhai, had taken it to Chennai. I was so glad to see this great role model, as collaboration is needed for scale otherwise, in India we have around three million NGOs of a very small size who are not able to replicate their success elsewhere. With this initial DNA in place today, they've scaled to help many state education systems and have incubated over forty non-profits from twenty states. They are one of the true successes of NSRCEL Social vision.

Calvin Becoming Ram

The new-age development at Gurugram on the outskirts of Delhi has produced tall buildings housing offices and residences. Behind a cluster of such buildings is a small village, Silokhra, with an even smaller affordable school, Sahpathi Shiksha Kendra, for migrant workers' children.

I visited them on 27 October 2017 when I had come to attend an event at International Management Institute, Delhi. While the migrant workers work on various jobs at building sites, their children attend the school.

Tarkeybein Education Foundation (TEF), founded by Akanksha, develops English language learning tools and training programmes for students and teachers. Learning tools are being co-created with children from low-income groups. The core focus is on children building skills of observation, interpretation and expression, and acquiring English language skills in this learning process. I attended an English class where the children were doing creative work. They were given a Calvin and Hobbes cartoon without any storyline and the students had to imagine the story. It was interesting to hear multiple versions of the cartoon substituted with names like Ram, Rahul, etc. The school administrator claimed that now there were more conversations in the classrooms instead of the monologue of the teachers. The children come from various regions and hence, speak different regional languages. Owing to this, they do not fit into regular schools in the area. This school mainly focuses on such children and keeps growing as more construction workers are added. The school also moves when the construction site changes.

I Want to Be an IAS Officer

The next day, 28 October 2017, Seemant Dadwal (an IIMB alumnus) of Meraki asked me to come to Navyug School in Sarojini Nagar, Delhi to see his work. When I arrived, I was wondering what an NGO was doing in this beautiful private school. Later, I learnt it was one of the few well-run government schools. The parents were sitting in a circle and the team was explaining the importance of their involvement in their children's education. It was for the parents of Class 1 students, so parents could be involved from a young age with their children. Seemant, with Ghajal Gulati, started Meraki to offer solutions for intergenerational burdens that disadvantaged families carry, by equipping parents with knowledge skills and mindsets to be able to transform their children's lives. After the session, I was talking to a child, who was accompanied by his parents. I asked him, 'What do you want to become when you finish school?' Pat came his reply, 'I want to be an IAS officer.' I asked him, 'Why?' and he said, 'My father is a security guard at an IAS officer's house.' He explained the work that the IAS officer did and told me the officer kept motivating him to be one.

Tyres into Playgrounds

I visited IIT Kharagpur in June 2017 to be a part of the Hult Prize competition jury. In this competition, Pooja Rai, who had earlier been the Hult Prize regional winner, was part of the jury. Pooja is an alumna of IITK with an architecture background, who co-founded Anthill Creations along with her classmate Nancy Charaya. They are determined to bring back play for kids by building sustainable playscapes using recyclable material.

She took me to visit the first playground they built when they were students, at the campus school for workers. After three years, it was still in great condition considering the children played there frequently. Anthill builds playgrounds in government schools up-cycling used tyres.

Anthill's sofa chairs made of tyres were so good, that I had donated a few to The Valley School. During the pandemic, when children could not step out to play, Anthill quickly pivoted to bring the play to their home by creating play objects and activities that they could do at home and shipped them home. By 2022, upcycling over 210 tonnes of waste, they have built over 300 playgrounds across the country and featured on National Geographic's OneForChange programme.

i-Saksham, Jamui, Bihar

Incubated at NSRCEL Social, i-Saksham was founded in 2015 by ex-Prime Minister's rural development fellows Ravi Dhanuka, Aditya Tyagi and Shravan Jha. It aims to enhance learning outcomes by training community youth educators using technology as the main facilitator. It enables these educators to run their own learning centres and meaningfully engage in various other educational activities. As fellows they worked together in Jamui, Bihar in 2013, and since then they never left that place. As it's a place of extremists, Shravan told me how they were captured by them once, as they were mistaken for government representatives. After a lot of explanation, having understood that these young boys had come to help develop the region, the extremists let them go. Even after that incident, their conviction has grown only stronger.

This is the great thing I see with people who have created a bond with the place they come from, or have decided to work in. They started working on solving the gap in teachers' availability in the area by training men and women who were mostly from the village itself and having the locals solve local problems.

In August 2018, after visiting Nagpur for the Raisoni College Ignite event, I took a flight to Kolkata and then a train from Howrah to Jamui, arriving there early the next morning.

We headed to the i-Saksham centre. On the way, there were lots of students walking on the road. When I said that it was good that education was being given priority,

Shravan told me that they were all going towards tuition centres and i-Saksham was trying to solve the very problem of proliferating private coaching centres. At their centre, I learnt more about their work.

Thanuj completed his BBA and was doing his masters in social work. He had been with i-Saksham since the beginning. His father is a government lawyer and also does farming on a 7-acre plot in the village.

Aman, Bablu Katlona, Golden Ahravan Sharma, Shweta Sinha, Nikhita and Divya also came with bachelor's degrees in various disciplines from different parts of the state, as well as other towns, like Dehradun.

Coming from relatively humble backgrounds with parents in the old economy, the children have studied and have degrees, but there are no opportunities in their fields. So, they end up migrating to cities, where they still may not get jobs appropriate to their subjects.

That's what i-Saksham is trying to solve, using these educated youth to educate others to bridge the gap. Also, to encourage these youth to study further and get them jobs in schools and other places as well.

Loco Pilot Aspiration

After the interaction at the i-Saksham centre, we proceeded to visit a training centre in Mallehpur that was 8 km away.

It was raining and green paddy fields could be seen everywhere as we passed the Kiul River that was full of water. I have seen this in Bihar going from Patna to Jamui and Vaishali—there is water everywhere. Getting borewell water at 60 feet is a dream in Bengaluru, as we generally have to drill to 900+ feet to get water. In spite of good natural resources, people are poor. When i-Saksham did a survey on the youth, they found that government jobs are sought after and farming is the least sought after, as government jobs are seen to be very safe, that too mostly in railways as technicians and loco-pilots as they see trains passing through Jamui a lot.

I saw many of them carrying Staff Selection Commission (SSC) and Railway Recruitment Board (RRB) books and forms. Still, hardly a few from that village are able to get those jobs. Yet, there is hope and they are studying for it and all the tuition centres make use of that demand. When I asked if there were no other opportunities, they mentioned about a rich doctor and a contractor, and there are no major businesses around.

Exposure to the larger world is key for them to understand opportunities beyond government jobs. This was very common in the early days, as government jobs are considered safe havens. Even I remember, when I visited one of my aunts after a long time, she asked whether I was in a government job. When I told the youth about various other opportunities such as the twelfth-passed Viji running a telemedicine centre, and Class 8 students studying robotics and doing computer-related work, I could see their amazed expressions. They couldn't believe that was possible. The more exposure we can give to our youth, if we expand their horizons. More importantly, we need to inculcate in them the confidence that they can do it. I have often told Nativelead not to use Steve Jobs's picture. Then people would think, I need to go to Harvard and drop out to be Jobs! We need to provide examples that our people can relate to.

The College Acts as a Remote Centre

On the way, we visited the Kumar Kalika Memorial (KKM) College, established in 1955, where everyone I've

met seems to have studied. It was very heartening to see
that a college was established here that early, but today,
it looked in very bad condition. The entire compound
wall of the college is filled with posters of tuitions and
coaching centres. We went inside to see many students
thronging the office, but the classrooms were collecting
dust. The students use the IGNOU centre to pay fees and
study on their own, and visit the college to write exams,
that's about it. Even though everyone aspires to study,
no guidance is available. I saw the IGNOU poster there
offering new economy courses like cyber law, computer
applications, etc., but still people here all seemed to be
studying rural development and political science as that's
what their peers were opting for. IGNOU is popular, since
colleges are not reliable—there are only three colleges
but hundreds of tuition centres charging Rs 5000 for
bachelor's, Rs 10,000 for master's, Rs 25,000–50,000 for
BBA and Rs 5000 for Hindi qualifications. There are ten
providing training as technicians.

We went to visit another i-Saksham centre run by
i-Saksham fellow Mamta in Devachak. She teaches thirty
children, from nursery to Class 8 making Rs 5000 a month,
charging children in Class 1 to 5 Rs 100 and those in Class
5 to 8 Rs 200. She's doing all this from her house, equipped
with i-Saksham's training and material. I also saw that she
had a hanging library on the wall with Pratham books.
Here I met eleven-year-old Sharma who spoke to me in
English and said he loves cricket.

We met Praveen ji at his centre—aged twenty-two, a
BSc graduate who is teaching 125 children and receiving
Rs 75 per child. It's about 13 km from the Jamui centre.
Like him, there are fifty fellows who, after three months
of training, run centres teaching 1500 children, charging

around Rs 50 a month. A whopping 80 per cent are not able to collect the fees.

Then we proceeded to the i-Saksham work at KGBV where 1500 girls are staying/studying, and we met another fellow named Mamta who has been teaching there for three years. It was a very nicely maintained facility. We headed out to the railway station to catch my train to Patna. On the way, the whole gang was explaining their other centres in Mungai. They were talking about becoming police, block development officers, lawyers. They have three programmes; the first programme is the NSDC fellowship with Rs 1000 for three months—around 120 youth have gone through that. The second programme is converting forty of them into micro entrepreneurs and the third is school intervention, supporting three KGBVs and six government schools.

During the pandemic lockdown, they made more resources for children, involving the parents working with them, using household items. Once the lockdown was over, the local youth were able to resume activities, with a smaller number of children. They also became a part of Bihar Development Collective (BDC) during the pandemic with all the social entrepreneurs working in and for Bihar, collectively solving the state's problems. I had a virtual meeting with all of them in August 2021 and saw the impressive work, sharing each other's strengths. That's what I would like to achieve at NSRCEL Social to bring more collaboration among social entrepreneurs.

Inside-out

There are many non-profits in the country started by a visionary entrepreneur who either saw the problem for themselves or got affected by seeing the problem happening to someone in front of them and started working towards that. Asif of Jan Sahas who worked against manual scavenging, Kamleshwar working for tribals in his region with Desert Greens, CCD Muthu Velayutham, Ganshyam of Samvad, etc. They understand the problem very well, they understand the system and they are able to effectively bring the change. We were exposed to these kinds of entrepreneurs during my AID times. Now, I got an amazing opportunity to work with them through Change Alliance (CA). Belinda Bennet, South Asia head of CA, was on a panel with me arranged by CA and Partners in Change (PIC) in Delhi in 2013. She was very happy to hear about social business thought and also has read *The Blue Sweater*. She requested me to advise CA in their Poorest Areas Civil Society (PACS) project.[1] Development Finance for International Development (DFID—it has now been transformed into the Foreign, Commonwealth and Development Office [FCDO], UK Government) initiated the PACS programme in 2001 to support and strengthen civil society and help poor people claim their rights and entitlements more effectively. There are eight million socially excluded people in ninety PACS targeted districts, in 516 blocks and 22,404 villages in seven states—Bihar, Chhattisgarh, Jharkhand, Madhya Pradesh, Orissa, Uttar Pradesh and West Bengal. This provided me a great opportunity to look at many of the humble and committed people on the ground working for decades on various issues. I had met quite few of them and looked at their livelihood initiatives and how to transform some of them into a hybrid structure as well, so they could be a social business. A few of them have done quite well, such as CCD, Jan Sahas and Desert Greens. But still there is quite a lot of wisdom in those hundreds of organizations that are on the ground. More work needs to be done to have them move into social business as they have the heart, and if they can marry it with good business thoughts, they can make the world better—I've travelled extensively in those seven low-income states and gained quite a lot of understanding of the problems first-hand.

Thirteen

Equity Models and Their Limitations

'. . . *we must have the audacity to imagine a different future*
. . . we must have the kind of audacity that drove a new
generation to build technologies that changed the way humans
interacted across the globe. And we must balance that audacity
with a new humility that considers and is accountable for the
unintended consequences of our actions.'
—Jacqueline Novogratz, *Manifesto for a*
Moral Revolution (Macmillan, 2021)

Capitalism, which involves privatizing the ownership of commercial enterprises, is the go-to economic model the world over for the development of countries. Its core principles include survival of the fittest, for instance, in a competitive, 'free' market and the capital is provided by private individuals rather than governments. The US is considered a champion of capitalism, as many of the most profitable industries and companies are driven by private entrepreneurs. These include facilities like railroads, mines and public utilities such as electricity and gas. However, the US government does intervene from time to time to prevent excessive monopolizing of profits.

Arguably, capitalism has delivered economic prosperity for the US, as measured through the country's GDP, which amounted to approximately $21 trillion in 2020,[1] or $63,416 per person living in the country. Almost every developing country wanted to emulate the US in terms of achieving similar levels of material prosperity. The US has long been seen as a land of opportunities and many people from other parts of the world have aspired to claim those chances for themselves. I, too, was among these aspirants, who went there for work and become an overseas citizen of India.

The Dotcom Boom

I moved to the US in 1996 and was introduced to the stock market there by a colleague at my first job, who bought me a book about it. He said I must invest in the stock market, which provides a thriving capital source for companies to raise money by listing their shares. I found investing in the stock market to be an amazing experience and put my money in companies like Dell, Sun Microsystems, etc., which performed well, as also a few no-name companies.

As Internet businesses became ever more lucrative, I saw the capital market go wild, creating what was dubbed the dotcom boom. Theoretically, given the US's market-driven economy, even if there was a boom or a bubble, the market was expected to correct itself. You could start a dotcom or Internet-based business one day and list it (make it available for public investment) on the NASDAQ market—traditionally preferred by technology companies—a few days later and see the stock price escalate significantly in no time. I recall seeing the NASDAQ index jump from 1800 in 1996 to over 7500 in February 2000.[2]

Alan Greenspan, then the board chairman of the US Federal Reserve (which is the country's central bank and equivalent to India's Reserve Bank of India) warned about the dotcom boom and bust as early as 1996, calling it an 'irrational exuberance'.[3] Despite his warning and the consequent slight dip in the market, the dotcom stocks continued to remain the focus of major speculation whose outcome was the dizzying rise of stock valuations that continued until early 2000, as noted above, before plummeting. Many people, including me, lost their investment, with the percentage of Americans who directly invested in the stock market plunging from a high of 67 per cent in 2002 to 15 per cent in 2019. However, many Americans indirectly invest through mutual funds or retirement funds, which has also been my preference thereafter. While many may have figured out and profited from the stock market, I decided that it was not my cup of tea.

Housing Bubble

In 2003, I bought my house in Atlanta, just when real estate prices were rising. A neighbour of mine would buy a house, own it for a while and then sell it. One day, I received a seminar invite, which was about how people were overpaying on their mortgage or home loan and how they could reduce this by half. I asked them to provide more details as I was puzzled. I had bought a house at 4.9 per cent rate of interest—could a mortgage get cheaper than that?

The company that conducted the seminar sent across a book with the financial details—it was about just paying interest payments only. I then asked them, since I anyway owed the principal amount to the bank that I would have to repay at some point, how I could save on the repayment. Their answer was that I should postpone the repayment as much as possible, sell my current home when the prices went up suitably and then repay the mortgage. I could then go on to buy another bigger house, since I might have some amount left over from selling my home. Something about this did not add up for me and I decided I would not fall for it as I had already burnt my fingers during the dotcom bubble.

But the vast majority of the American people did fall for it. Many people ended up buying houses with loans they could not afford to repay. The banks that provided the loans bundled the good loans with the bad loans and sold them to another financial services company. Over time, this practice resulted in many bad loans accumulating and, eventually, crashing the whole economy. The further consequence was the subprime mortgage crisis, so called because of the historically high number of loans given to borrowers whom lenders knew may face difficulties repaying the mortgage. This crisis, in turn, triggered the 2007–08 global financial crisis.

The Global Financial Crisis

Owning a house is considered a cornerstone of the American dream. The housing bubble saw homeownership in the US increase to an all-time high, only to sharply decline when the bubble burst. For many people, unmanageable home loans meant squeezing their household budgets. They began buying less and investing lesser, also as a result of decreased confidence in financial institutions. All of this snowballed into the Global Financial Crisis (GFC), which saw a number of businesses the world over shut down, causing large-scale unemployment. In the US, the unemployment rate shot up to 10 per cent (October 2009).[4]

To rectify this situation, many governments were forced to bail out some of the larger banks and lending institutions to the tune of trillions of dollars, which took several years to recover. Ironically, many of these institutions were supposedly 'too big to fail'[5] as depicted by the movie of the same name, but had to be rescued using taxpayer funds.

We Are the 99 Per Cent

An idea suggested by the Canadian anti-capitalist, pro-environment organization Adbusters resulted in the Occupy Wall Street (OWS)[6] protest at the New York Stock Exchange (NYSE), as well as similar Occupy movements across the world. This protest highlighted issues such as social and economic inequality, greed, corruption and the undue influence of corporations on the government, particularly from the financial services sector. The OWS slogan, 'We are the 99 per cent', referred to the stark wealth disparity in the US between the wealthiest 1 per cent and the rest of the population. While many of the Occupy movements were themed 'occupy everything, demand nothing', the original demand behind the idea was 'to separate money from politics'.

Chasing the Top Line

While it is common for companies to expect profits from their operations, people were building companies in the 2000s that were extremely growth-hungry. Why were people and organizations focusing on growing in size and in profits? Why was generating revenue suddenly so important for most organizations?

Typically, any company's financial performance is assessed using three documents—the income (or profit and loss or P&L) statement, the balance sheet (describing assets and liabilities) and the cash flow statement (summarizing the cash available based on the net profit or loss). The first line of the income statement shows the revenue (also called sales or turnover in India), which is why the revenue is sometimes called the business's top line. The company's expenses are then listed below the revenue. If the difference between the revenues and the expenses is positive, the company is said to be profitable but if the expenses exceed the revenue, the company has made a loss. The last line of the P&L statement shows this profit or loss, often called the bottom line. A company's success is usually determined on the basis of either the top line or the bottom line.

If a company chases top line growth rapidly, it can be forgiven if it misses out on a profitable bottom line. Also, a company's numbers are usually measured on a quarterly basis. If companies' financial results miss their quarterly projections, their stock price will likely go down. In our company, after a great quarter, we used to get a pat on the back and were told to do even better in the next quarter. Invariably, every company has to project continued growth and strive to achieve as much.

The 1 Per Cent

The economic growth of countries worldwide has not created the expected outcome of equity across society. According to a Credit Suisse report,[7] the world's total wealth amounts to over $400 trillion, but half this wealth is owned by just 1 per cent of the world's population. This stark discrepancy is the root cause of inequality, which will continue to remain a prominent issue. There are more than fifty-six million millionaires in the world (as of June

2021) and their numbers are expected to grow to eighty-four million in the next five years. It is sad that out of 7.7 billion people in the world, there are just fifty-six million millionaires.

Unfortunately, businesses tend to focus on ensuring that their owners and top-tier executives gain most from their profits, which only serves to widen the gap between the ultra-rich and the extremely poor. The vast majority of the world's population lives in low-income countries and struggles daily to make a dignified living. One aspect of this struggle is hunger. In 2020, between 720 and 811 million people faced hunger.[8] Our economic models need to grapple with this reality rather than continue the enrichment of relatively fewer people.

According to the same Credit Suisse report, 6,49,000 Indians feature in the global top 1 per cent, in terms of their wealth, of whom 4316 are worth more than $50 million (approximately Rs 367 crore) each, while 1695 have wealth in excess of $100 million (approximately Rs 734 crore). Since 2000, the wealth per Indian adult has grown by 8.8 per cent annually, faster than the global average of 4.8 per cent.

The Ponzi Scheme Approach to Business

The equity model of investments is one of the reasons how companies grow big in my opinion. This model has prevailed for many decades and I call it the Ponzi scheme.

When a start-up needs investment, there are three possible sources: debt, grant and equity. These have typically been the only sources for the last hundred-odd years, with one new addition—crowdfunding. It's just the advance payment for products/service. The start-up, using available money, works on creating the product or service and delivers it when it is ready to market. Debt can be money the start-up founders borrow from close associates who may be friends or family, with or without collateral and with or without interest. The founders are obliged to return the money to the lenders. In many cases, banks play a major role in providing debts to ventures.

Grants are another form of funding wherein a start-up receives money to fulfil its objectives, but is not bound by repayment conditions. The start-up may choose to offer something else in exchange. The most common examples of grants are governments giving universities money for conducting research, which may solve social or technological problems, or find a cure for a disease. A non-profit organization could get a grant from a donor, aid agency or government to support a cause, such as providing free education, food or skills to the poor.

The third form of funding is equity, which is today the most common model and is synonymous with funding itself in many contexts. Equity investing usually comprises private equity. For example, a start-up requires an investment of Rs 10 lakh, which I agree to give in exchange for 10 per cent equity in the enterprise. Effectively, my valuation of the start-up is Rs 1 crore, of which 10 per cent amounts to Rs 10 lakh. There are several other models available for estimating a start-up's valuation, such as discounted cash flow. However, most of these models rely on the enterprise's financial data, which may not be available for a start-up. An investor who decides to invest in an early-stage venture looks at various parameters such as innovation, the strength of an entrepreneur, the market potential and the growth potential.

Continuing with my example, I now have 10 per cent equity in the company, but how do I make money as a PE investor? As the start-up is still in its early days, it may not become profitable immediately and I cannot expect instant dividends. Besides, an equity investor does not usually invest for dividends, but for creating value. You may well ask, how does this value get created? Let's say this start-up in which I invested Rs 10 lakh is growing well and needs more capital for further growth. Given its growth, the founder manages to clinch an investment of Rs 1 crore from an angel investor, who estimates the start-up's value at around Rs 5 crore. On paper, the start-up's value has gone up five times since I valued it at Rs 1 crore. The angel investor too is going to make money by value creation, which may happen when a venture capitalist (VC), optimistic about the start-up's growth, agrees to invest a further Rs 5 crore, raising the valuation to Rs 25 crore. With this investment, the value of the start-up has multiplied twenty-five times.

With this latest spurt of growth, the VC offers to buy my shares, giving me an opportunity to realize twenty-five times the amount I invested. However, if the VC does not offer to buy my shares, I'm stuck with the investment until someone else makes an offer. Again, how will the VC get their returns on the substantial investment of Rs 5 crore? As the company continues to grow, it may attract more VC funds and/or list itself on the stock market through an initial public offering (IPO). When that happens, any investor can buy the company's shares, while I can start selling the equity I own.

You may ask, what is the problem with this model? To continue attracting investors, the company needs to keep growing. Unless the next level of funding is secured, the earlier investors have no way to cash in on their investment. They may start pressuring the start-up to deliver growth, which can result in the venture moving away from its original vision, in turn causing mission drift. Effectively, the company's growth is only meant to attract the next round of investment rather than meet any of its original objectives. Ultimately, such growth can become a vicious cycle that caters solely to the next investor's needs, regardless of the company's original mission.

A Level Playing Field

One way to solve this inequality would be to allow smaller businesses to grow alongside larger organizations that are racing to grow further. In September 2012, I received an email from Saurabh Srivastava, founder of Indian Angel Network (IAN), which I am a part of for ten years now, with the subject 'Planning Commission Report on Creating a Vibrant Entrepreneurial Eco System'.[9] It recommended to create 2500 new, successful ventures; thereby repeating the success of the IT/BPO industry in three or four other industries, with a combined revenue of over Rs 10 lakh crore ($200 billion), generating ten million direct and twenty to thirty million indirect jobs across sectors and regions, consequently, powering India's economic progress with inclusive economic development; innovative products/ services for India's young population; India as a hub for frugal innovation; attracting investment flows and creating substantial wealth.

This recommendation came out from the research by the committee that found that:

'Large Indian businesses—both in the public and private sector—have not generated significant employment in the past few decades and are unlikely to do so in the coming decade or two. Public sector and government employment has declined in the last few years and is expected to grow very slowly in the coming years. Large private sector firms have also been slow in generating employment, which is unlikely to change due to increasing automation, digitization and productivity gains. For example, the banking sector in India has recorded almost no employment growth in the last two decades despite manifold growth in its revenue and assets. Agriculture employs nearly a half of India's work force but employment is likely to decline in this sector, due to improvements in productivity.'

With this as a precursor, the Start-up Policy was defined and today, with many start-ups registered with Startup India. However, all of them fall into the trap of growing big, but as of 2022, India had over 7.9 million registered Micro, Small and Medium Enterprises (MSMEs) that contribute 33 per cent of the country's GDP and generate over 120 million jobs across industries and regions in the country, leading to wealth creation at the grassroots level.[10] So, more small companies would help in reducing the divide between the rich and the poor and to some extent, help address the economic inequality at a macro level.

Risk Capital

I define social business as either procuring a product or service from low-income families (GoCoop with weavers, Farmers Fresh Zone with farmers) or providing a product or service to low-income families (Telemedicine by Neurosynaptic) while keeping the planet in mind (People, Planet, Profit—triple bottom line). Thus, a social business is designed for low-income sections or people who don't have access to essential services.

I live in Bengaluru. Until about a year ago, the only broadband Internet service provider in my locality was the state-owned Bharat Sanchar Nigam Ltd (BSNL). Only when the people residing in our area increased, did a private company enter the market.

Bengaluru-based Neurosynaptic Communications, one of my investments, has been supporting over 1500 telemedicine centres in the country. Again, BSNL is its choice for Internet services as other players do not have a presence in the remote areas the start-up caters to.

Many innovations have been created on the Internet and multibillion dollar companies are riding on it. This speaks volumes for the nature of market forces—the government must first set up the infrastructure and lay the roadmap so that the market can innovate around it.

India has numerous problems that need urgent resolution. But many subtle minds are applying their skills to solve the relatively trivial problems of the well-to-do as that is where the market-oriented investors put their money. To encourage more people to look at the country's more pressing problems, we need to attract more risk capital into the system. There might be failures initially, but each one will add to our collective wisdom and a winner will eventually emerge. (This is also true for today's hot sectors. India took fifteen years to successfully replicate the business of online retailing giant Amazon as we were late to enter the dotcom era. In these fifteen years, many companies went bust trying to do it.)

So where will the risk capital come from? Two sources—philanthropy and the government.

Risk Capital—Philanthropy—Giving Pledge

The Giving Pledge[11] is a unique philanthropic partnership that changed the dynamics of philanthropy. Initiated by forty American billionaires, including Bill and Melinda Gates and Berkshire Hathaway chairman Warren Buffett, the Giving Pledge requires wealthy individuals to commit to giving away the bulk of their wealth to philanthropic causes. The Pledge has since been signed by over 200 global billionaires and is open to anyone with 'at least US$ 1 billion in personal net worth, ready to make a public pledge to donate the majority of their personal wealth to philanthropy'.

Many foundations, like Tata Trusts, have been doing wonderful work in philanthropy. These foundations should also try various models of investing, apart from giving grants. There is an increasing discussion around creating dignity within charity by transforming the beneficiaries of social work into customers. Social business thoughts have also emerged based on the idea of marrying the heart of a non-profit with the efficiency of corporate management. Many foundations have started investing using the equity and debt models as well.

Risk Capital—Government

The second source of risk capital is the government. The India Inclusive Innovation Fund (IIIF),[12] which had an initial target of raising Rs 5000 crore, was jointly announced by the National Innovation Council and the Ministry of Micro, Small and Medium Enterprises (MSME) in early 2014 under UPA-II. The current government has also approved a Rs 10,000-crore Fund of Funds for Start-ups (FFS).[13]

These are wonderful ideas but FFS money seems to be going only to market-driven funds that are supporting the app-based economy where the government need not play a role. We need a balance. Funds should also be targeted towards disruptive innovations (let's help the Edisons out there), where the government has to lay the road as it is riskier. But once the early stages are taken care of and scale is proven, the market-oriented investors will start investing. Until then, the government has to help those entrepreneurs.

Risk Capital—CSR

Another. resource that can be tapped to fund social businesses is corporate social responsibility. The new Companies Act-mandated CSR rules are one of the best changes that have happened in India in recent times. Around Rs 25,714 crore were funnelled into the system in FY 20–21. India is proudly saying at world forums that we have learnt to solve our own problems.

Provisions in CSR rules allow corporate entities to support government-recognized incubators. It would be great if that support is extended to social businesses that are solving serious problems. It was brought to my attention that policymakers could not do so as they cannot define what a social business is. I hear similar questions from my friends as well, 'What do you mean by social business, does that mean other businesses are anti-social?' and 'Why is Airtel not a social business even though many people in the bottom of economic pyramid are using its services?'

My answer to the latter is: Airtel's business plans were not written with low-income families in mind. The use of the company's services by the poor is just a collateral outcome. A social business, on the other hand, is designed for low-income sections or people living in remote areas who can't access essential services.

There are still many people in India who don't have electricity. We see more and more people in the hinterland losing their livelihood and ending up in the slums of cities. The city exploits them with low wages. So, it is necessary to start social businesses that tackle these problems, for which some portion of CSR funds must go into social businesses.

Risk Capital—Social Stock Exchange

When it comes to investment and growth, many want to ride on the road but very few want to help lay the road, because there isn't sufficient risk capital. Again, why does the onus of investing risk capital lie only with the government and not with the market? Can economies depend on the market to solve their problems and if not, how should they address this issue? One way would be to create investment models that disrupt passing the buck, such as developing platforms that can help start-ups raise anywhere from Rs 50 lakh to Rs 50 crore. Similar to the IPO market, allowing more investors can spread the risks out across many people.

Encouraging entrepreneurs to invest in issues typically the focus of governments, such as the well-being of society, can be a first step. Equally, we could ensure that investors are aware of the companies that are working on solving longer-term problems. In 2021, the Securities and Exchange Board of India (SEBI) announced a framework for a Social Stock Exchange (SSE)[14]—something I wished for in 2016[15]. However, we need to ensure that social investors come on board with a full understanding of what they are getting into. Recently, I realized some capital gains but was surprised to see that the only tax-saving option involved meant investing in a house. Why not allow investing in social businesses, which would ensure that the investors get the due tax benefits without worrying about exiting the investment? Making more tax and social benefits available to investors, consumers and entrepreneurs can encourage them to do further good.

There should be an emphasis on defining the social investor as well. When impact investment picked up in India twenty years ago, many funds and individuals started jumping in. But the impact wasn't clear as they followed a Ponzi model of growth and, as a result, many social businesses were unable to raise the next level of funding or came under pressure for drifting from their original vision. Today, many impact funds claim they want to focus on the next 500 million of the population, while mainstream funds that have exhausted the top 250 million also talk about the next 500 million. This results in a marriage between the mainstream and impact funds at the middle 500 million level, emptying the bottom and providing a fantastic opportunity for actual impact investors. Strict guidelines should be established for both the social businesses and the social investors joining the SSE to ensure that the SSE's objective is truly realized.

Growing further and larger alone cannot be the motive and we need an equal opportunity for the many to grow and to flourish as well so that competition and wealth are not restricted to just the few. Although this may seem utopian, it can be an ideal approach for emerging economies. After all, isn't this utopianism what we believe India's golden era was all about?

The mysteries of India have proved alluring to both Indians and outsiders for centuries. The country boasts a fascinating diversity, with several languages, food, culture, attire, practices, architecture and varied geography. Unfortunately, from being looked at with awe and wonder, India's hitherto healthy diversity has slowly given way to sharp contrasts. There are now steep, clearly visible divides in health, wealth, amenities, basic living and human rights, which is dangerously seeping into our very DNA. Simplistically, it is a divide between those who have wealth and opportunities and those who cannot afford either.

The 'haves' design systems and policies for themselves that by and large exclude those who cannot afford to have. We need to rise beyond these divides and carry out our social responsibility.

If there is to be any enduring approach to both, business and collective well-being for the future, it could well be— slow down. Build businesses that work for us and become role models for the rest of the emerging nations.

Fourteen

Models of Conscious Capitalism

'On the one hand, markets, the part of the economy that fulfils the needs of customers with products and services provided by businesses, have a fundamental role to play in healthy societies . . . On the other hand, if markets enable individual freedom, they also create inequality. Unchecked, capitalism overlooks or exploits those who cannot afford to pay; insufficiently considers the well-being of employees; and does not integrate on to balance sheets the cost of poorly utilizing earth's precious resources.'
—Jacqueline Novogratz, *Manifesto for a Moral Revolution* (Macmillan, 2021)

Growing levels of inequality are forcing us to reconsider many of the ways of doing business that we have taken for granted for decades. There is an increasing awareness that we must choose to adopt different approaches to people, products, selling and markets. A friend of mine told me that, when it comes to his business, he is absolutely cut-throat and cold-hearted. My question to him in return was, 'Why does business really need to be cut-throat?' Many people have perpetuated this version that capitalism is lacking a conscience, is the domain of heartless, soulless people, and the need of the hour is true stakeholder integration. Not only does it not have to be this way; frankly, it cannot continue this way. Without a change, we are marching into deep disaster. However, fortunately, there is the solution of a more evolved path that is emerging. This has taken shape with many models evolving like Conscious Capitalism, B-Corp, Business Call to Action by UNDP, Yunus Social Business, etc. Let's look at some of this and see what the country should do moving forward!

Capitalism

Capitalism is defined as an economic system based on the private ownership of the means of production and their operation for profit.[1] The word 'profit' alone in this definition needed to be relooked at. Harvard Kennedy School economist Dani Rodrik distinguishes between three historical variants of capitalism:[2]

> Capitalism 1.0 during the 19th century entailed largely unregulated markets with a minimal role for the state (aside from national defence, and protecting property rights).
> Capitalism 2.0 during the post-World War II years entailed Keynesianism, a substantial role for the state in regulating markets, and strong welfare states.
> Capitalism 2.1 entailed a combination of unregulated markets, globalization, and various national obligations by states.
> Capitalism 2.1 or 3.0 has been up to 2008 crisis. In his book *Capitalism 4.0: The Birth of a New Economy in the Aftermath of Crisis*, Anatole Kaletsky suggests that capitalism is 'not a static set of institutions but an evolutionary system that reinvents and reinvigorates

itself through crisis'. This reinvention is required and few models have been developed by various organizations and many entrepreneurs align with those models follow certain guidelines of those models.

For example, Business Call to Action (BCtA) by UNDP recognizes and advances inclusive businesses with a clear commitment to benefit people in low- and middle-income markets to help achieve the Sustainable Development Goals. Saahas Zero Waste is a member of BCtA.

Another model, Conscious Capitalism[3] uses four specific tenets—higher purpose, stakeholder integration, conscious leadership and conscious culture and management—to build strong businesses and help advance capitalism further toward realizing its highest potential. Aspiring leaders and business builders need to continue on this path of transformation—for the good of both business and society as a whole. We need to build a defence and reimagine capitalism. This cannot be less than a blueprint for a new system for doing business that is grounded in a more evolved ethical consciousness, a new lens for individuals and companies who are looking to build a more cooperative, humane and positive future.

The truth is that all businesses have begun to recognize that the landscape is changing. The world has shifted from where it was twenty years ago, with evolving value systems and rising intelligence. Businesses have to adapt and every major company is moving along one or more directions towards being more responsible. Once the transformation is initiated, it implicitly encourages another kind of behaviour. However, clarity and commitment are necessary, an understanding of the higher purpose of business with a win-win proposition for stakeholders.

A certain leadership culture and organizational values can, over time, result in superior performance. Many large-scale cultural transformations are now headed in this direction, with the result that conscious capitalism is seen as the next evolution of social media, social business and social impact and even the next phase of the new interconnectedness of the world.

We are at a moment in time wherein technology, opportunity and understanding coalesce into a major leap forward for human history. We have seen the construct of capitalism gain power over the last 500 years, to the point where it holds an extraordinarily high place in modern society—above lifestyle, health, family, happiness—and at times, above humanity itself. This crisis has manifested as drastic levels of decay in the current global, socio-political and economic environment, as evidenced by some amazing statistics.

Forty-two people hold the same amount of wealth as 3.7 billion of the world's poorest, while 50 per cent of the world's population has seen no increase in wealth.[4] In 2017, 82 per cent of the wealth generated globally went into the pockets of the wealthiest 1 per cent. As many as 192 million people are unemployed or underemployed but 85 per cent of employed people hate their jobs. An estimated 1.6 billion people are homeless worldwide and over a tenth—815 million people—are malnourished. Yet, 1.3 billion tonnes, comprising 30 per cent of the food produced globally (40 per cent in the richest countries) is lost or wasted. One in nine people lack access to clean water and one in three people lack access to a toilet. This scenario is evidently unsustainable. Why on earth do we want to keep going down this path? Or, to rephrase: who wants to maintain the status quo?

On the flip side, we have seen that several entrepreneurs, especially the new wave of millennials, lead their companies with passion, purpose and conviction, delivering increased profitability.

Patagonia, the designer of outdoor clothing and gear for silent sports, is a company that is well-known for donating millions of dollars to grassroots non-profits, building global supply chains around better-quality raw ingredients such as organic cotton, traceable down and sustainably grazed wool; and providing on-site childcare at its offices. Patagonia is not an anomaly. When I first spoke to potential entrepreneurs about the need to create 'values-based businesses', I met with some resistance. Now, however, I have a full roster of ethical, responsible, values-based entrepreneurs dedicated to creating companies that benefit all stakeholders. The tide has turned and I have had the privilege to witness personally the consequences of leaders and teams discovering their inner light and greater purpose and infusing that into their work.

When values are at the heart of a business, capitalism suddenly acts and feels completely different. It feeds our starving souls and makes us realize we want and deserve something more. When we bring purpose, passion and presence into our work, when we commit to tiny acts of doing-it-differently and when we intend to create companies, leaders and teams that are integrated on a human level, we create conscious companies. Companies that matter—and will continue to matter for the next thirty years in the future. You need to lead your business consciously; you can then watch as growth in profitability follows.

Another example is of Anita Roddick, who pioneered the conscious business movement with her company, The Body Shop, in 1976. The company has been an environmental leader and worked to support various activist causes, including putting an end to animal testing and defending human rights. Several conscious businesses can be found in the health food industry as well as the Lifestyles of Health and Sustainability (LOHAS) market. However, conscious businesses are now emerging across the business world. I also find that several companies catalogue the social and environmental practices of businesses for use by consumers, while other companies consult with businesses on increasing their awareness and globally beneficial practices. After all, conscious business is about people who are aware of the impact their actions have on the environment—both people and the planet. It is about people who live their lives based on knowing that everything is interconnected.

Given my curiosity about this topic, I trawled the Internet for interesting articles, which I have tried to encapsulate here. The first article was about the Coalition for Conscious Capitalism's Embankment Project for Inclusive Capitalism[5] (EPIC) which began in 2017 and involved eighteen months of workshops and discussions featuring, apart from the Coalition, thirty-one corporate entities as well as the professional services network Ernst & Young. EPIC had a single-point agenda 'to identify and create new metrics to measure and demonstrate the long-term value of inclusive capitalism to financial markets'. The framework proposed as EPIC's outcome gave companies a more accurate reading of their long-term success, in terms of the value created for not just their investors or stakeholders but for society as a whole.

While social entrepreneurship may still comprise a fraction of the syllabus in management institutions, more countries, governments and corporations today recognize the long-term value of inclusion at every level of decision-making. In March 2023, I was invited by IIMB Prof. Dahlia Mani to address her class as she was teaching the SZW case study. Wilma and I had a very engaging conversation with this top B-school of India, introducing them to a triple bottom line company. I am certain that we can take concrete steps to make capitalism more inclusive[6] and more ethical, capable of spreading its success further out to the largest number of people.

Huber Social—Social Well-Being

While businesses are reinventing themselves, countries are asking, 'Is GDP growth alone sufficient?' If yes, why aren't people in rich countries not happy? At a broader level, countries now seek to define their economic growth with greater nuance, beyond simply calculating their GDP. Hence, addressing the credibility and accountability of social impact is crucial and just as important as the financial well-being. According to OECD's How's Life? 2020 report, they are using over eighty indicators covering current well-being, inequalities in well-being outcomes and resources for future well-being.[7]

Similarly, measuring an organization's social impact involves identifying the framework and/or method most suitable for it. For instance, the UN's Sustainable Development Goals (SDGs) may be used as a framework if useful for the organization along with the relevant methodology. However, there is as yet no universal standard for measuring social impact. Through my contacts, I got connected with Georgina Camp from Huber Social,[8] who gave me insights into how they measure social impact. Some insights from our discussion are given below:

Moving away from using financial measures like GDP, individual wealth and cost-benefit ratios as metrics of success is not a new argument. Developing a more holistic measurement methodology has been gaining momentum over the past few decades. Starting at the top, the UN has accounted for other indicators of progress through the International Human Development Index (HDI) and the SDGs. These frameworks, along with others explored below, all provide potential methods to build a picture of humanity's progress and measure social value consistently. However, even if every organization were to map their impact to the SDGs, this would still not quantify each organization's contribution nor does it demonstrate how effectively the organization achieves the goals and finally, it would not deliver us actionable results to demonstrate where resources should be directed to have the greatest impact.

To provide a universal measure of social value akin to financial value, Huber Social identified the following design principles as the criteria for a suitable measurement framework:

1. Outcome-focused: Beyond tracking inputs and outputs, does the design focus on measuring their effect to achieve the outcome? Prescriptive frameworks do not allow the flexibility required in a dynamic environment and thus prevent innovation.
2. Empirical: Quantifying how much was achieved as opposed to defining or classifying what was done.
3. Contextual: Determining the worth of something relative to its context.
4. Comparable: Consistently enabling comparisons between programmes.
5. Actionable: Identifying what works to direct resources and achieve the greatest impact.

6. Universal: Ensuring applicability at all levels, whether individual, organizational, community, or country and collectively for the world.

When Georgina goes to a corporation to explain social impact, she's often asked how measuring social impact can make them money, which indicates that the company is still measuring success in terms of financial growth. The main challenge is thus not understanding the benefits of measuring social impact. When people realize that financial growth and social impact drive each other and are both necessary, they understand the value of measuring the social impact.

But well-being cannot stand alone and has to be included among or merged with financial measures. The things that matter most to us have everything to do with well-being rather than wealthiness, which only suggests that any evaluation of well-being cannot be about money alone. We need to separate the two to measure the value of things accurately but we also need a holistic measure to understand the organization's overall well-being and what is necessary to maintain it. Huber Social collects data at every level within the organization to enable informed decision-making. They also credit people for creating data locally.

After hearing Georgina, I felt that as we are in a state of building India entrepreneurially, upcoming start-ups can look to embed the DNA of social business within their operational structures. Just as we are creating an SSE for raising funds, we need to define and model a social business. In my attempts to define a social business, I have compared many different frameworks and techniques, such as ESG norms and the triple-bottom-line approach. However, given the role that such measurements play in a company's well-being, none really encapsulate the actual impact on the organization.

There is much noise about what social impact is and the things we should consider when measuring it. But how do we standardize it? Adding to confusion is the climate. Many entrepreneurs in waste management and clean tech think they are social ventures too, but we need to realize it's only the 'Planet' or 'Earth', while the 'People' or 'Social' part is missing in many. So social impact also involves being transparent about where you fit along the scientific process and the need for social value. We also need a measure of overall progress to achieve a genuinely positive outcome, possibly via minimizing the negative points. I think that's an important characteristic.

Fifteen

Future Safe

'We owe it to ourselves and to the next generation to conserve the environment so that we can bequeath our children a sustainable world that benefits all.'
—Wangari Maathai

I have worked with and mentored all types of start-ups since I became an investor focused on social businesses. It brings me great satisfaction when I feel that I have supported initiatives to address the two threats to our existence I have mentioned at the start of this book—growing inequality and climate change.

While inclusion has been an important part of the profiles of many enterprises we have discussed thus far, those companies and entrepreneurs who are fulfilling responsibilities towards our environment are vital for safeguarding our future. The key to building a social business is thinking long-term, with a sense of responsibility. If this goes against the textbook definitions of profits and volumes, it is something social entrepreneurs have to take in their stride.

Defining a Social Business

Social businesses in India have seen rapid expansion since the last decade. However, there has been no formal or legal body that has defined what a social business is. With the lack of a definition, we fall back on the UK government's definition that 'A social enterprise is a business with primarily social objectives whose surpluses are principally reinvested for that purpose in the business or in the community, rather than being driven by the need to maximize profit for shareholders and owner.'[1] These businesses have also grown in India with little or no governmental involvement.

SEBI defines a 'social venture', for purposes of its Alternate Investment Funds Regulation, as 'a trust, society or company or venture capital undertaking or limited liability partnership formed with the purpose of promoting social welfare or solving social problems or providing social benefits'.[2] Even so, many associate it with NGO activity or government activity, while others classify it as any business working with poor customers, producers or suppliers as a social enterprise.

There is also confusion between non-profit and for-profit social enterprises. It's good to see in the SEBI framework for SSE, it has started calling Non-Profit Enterprises (NPE) and For-Profit Enterprises (FPE). This should reduce the confusion, however still there is a need to define 'FPE'. Let's see what else happening in this space across the world.

Resilient Bangladesh

While writing this book, I realized how much I had been impacted by my trip to Bangladesh in 2014. I got an invite from Change Alliance (CA) to speak at the Regional

Consultation on Pro-Poor Market Development and Inclusive Growth in Dhaka. That Bangladesh trip ended up as very good first-hand understanding of the impact of both environment and inequality, and was one of my longest trips on the road for sixteen days. Bangladesh being at the receiving end of climate change, there is no better place for us to witness and understand that, than with our neighbour. I reached Dhaka on 22 September and left only on 4 October to India, continuing for another few days in Jharkhand, on another CA project. I travelled extensively in those few weeks and managed a short vacation in the Sundarbans with a night stay on a boat.

Billion-Dollar Non-profits of Bangladesh

The meeting was at BRAC Inn. I was asking about the place and I was told that BRAC is one of the largest non-profits in the world. I was going, 'What?' Today, they are employing around 97,000-plus employees. Ventured into various areas like dairy, handlooms, telecom, banking, micro finance, education—all are as a non-profit. Later during the trip, I visited Aarong, the handloom and crafts brand of BRAC. I was really impressed and I've not seen such a well-equipped shop with handlooms and crafts with a nice display, arrangements and very knowledgeable staff explaining the crafts. I couldn't believe that this shop was run by a non-profit. I've been to many shops by khadi co-operatives of many states in India, but I haven't seen much vibration and energy there. I bought nice Jamdani sarees and few kurtas from Aarong. In 2013, Jamdani was declared a UNESCO Intangible Cultural Heritage of Humanity and Bangladesh holds the GI tag for it as well. As per the BRAC 2020 Annual Report,[3] the annual budget is $1.89 billion for the year 2020 with only 16.6 per cent coming in as development grant. This is also another form of social business, where the wealth is distributed across and not accumulated to few people. After the conference, with two CA partners, I proceeded to Manikganj, a few hours of drive from Dhaka.

Making the Market Work for the Poor

This was the topic I spoke on in Dhaka, about the impact of investments and how civil society can look at the business side for an organization's sustainability, for bringing people into entrepreneurial thinking and for talking about Aid vs Market. If a benefit has been provided to a beneficiary, they are at the receiving end and cannot question the donor. However, if the same services are provided to them at an affordable price, we are moving them from being a beneficiary to being a customer. The customer tag brings them dignity as well as the power to question the vendor if they are not happy about the services. Thus, it automatically brings the opportunity to demand accountability.

I have seen how this operates at GUARDIAN, when people asked us about the impact we are making and how to ensure that the people who are taking the loans were actually using the toilets. We had people willing to donate sensors, to put it in the toilet to see the utilization. To them, we would say, we are recovering the loan that people have taken to build a toilet at 98.9 per cent. This shows that they already understand the need for the toilet; that's the proof of the social business's impact.

The Nobel Cause

I was back in Dhaka in March 2016 for a CA programme on South Asia Regional Conference on Social Inclusion and Dalit Women's Concerns. After a session on affirmative action and diversity measures in the government and private sector, Belinda and I went to meet Prof. Muhammad Yunus. It was truly an honour spending time with Nobel laureate Prof. Yunus on the sixteenth floor at Yunus Centre, Dhaka. Our discussion covered various topics. I was struck by his humility and the curiosity he showed in listening and learning about various issues. After having set off a revolution in micro-financing, it was amazing how he has kept coming up with new ideas and models. At the time, he was seventy-six years old and had just brought out his new book, *Super Happiness*. He defines super happiness in simple terms as making other people happy. The book is a good collection of his speeches and thoughts. He emphasizes how a social business has great potential to lift people out of poverty. 'Over time, starting a business became a habit with me. Every time I confronted a problem, I created a business to solve it. Soon I had created many companies and company-like independent projects, providing goods and services for poor people that included housing, sanitary facilities, affordable health care, renewable energy, improved nutrition, clean drinking water, nursing education and many more.' He calls it 'social business' and defines it as a 'non-dividend company dedicated to solving human problems'.

Prof. Yunus continues his work through the Social Business Fund. Yunus Social Business (YSB) provides financing to the most promising social businesses. It's an equity model without exit pressure, where the SB buys back the investor equity. He has also set up a Social Business Design Lab at the Yunus Centre—a meeting place for people of diverse backgrounds having a single common goal: developing social business for the betterment of society.

Social Business with Yunus

Meeting Prof. Yunus and understanding better how he defined social business brought me a lot of clarity as well. The term social business, once loosely used, was first defined by Prof. Muhammad Yunus in his books *Creating a World Without Poverty: Social Business and the Future of Capitalism*[4] and *Building Social Business: The New Kind of Capitalism that Serves Humanity's Most Pressing Needs*.

> 'Social business offers advantages that are available neither to profit-maximizing companies nor to traditional charities. The freedom from profit pressures and from the demands of profit-seeking investors help make social businesses viable even in circumstances where current capitalist markers fail—where the rate of return on an investment is near zero. But where social return is very high. And because a social business is designed to generate revenues and thereby become self-sustaining, it is free from the need to constantly attract new streams of donor funding to stay afloat, which drains the time and energy of so many people in the non-profit area.'

I have been struck by Prof. Yunus's statement that, 'A charity dollar has only one life; a social business dollar can be invested over and over again.'

In discussing a safer and more sustainable future, I have included more insights from my meeting with him and from my first-hand observation of how such strategies have worked in Bangladesh. As he says, '2008 will go down in history as the year of a rude awakening about the gross weaknesses in our capitalist system. It was the year of the food price crisis, the oil price crisis, the financial crisis and the ever-worsening environmental crisis. In combination, these crises caused a profound loss of faith among people who thought they had full understanding of and control over the global system. They also prevented the fulfilment of the hopeful promise represented by the Millennium Development Goals (MDGs) now called as Sustainability Development Goals (SDG).'

Billion-Dollar Non-profits, Not Billionaires!

While there are billion-dollar non-profits in Bangladesh, why is this not happening in India? When I was inviting Prof. Yunus to IIMB for a speech in January 2017, I was telling people, if he had not registered his entity as a non-profit, he could have been a billionaire, sitting in a twenty-four-floor building in Dhaka at Grameen Bank—the bank for the poor—having multiple operations across the world with $2.8 billion in assets as of 2016 in Bangladesh alone.[5] It's quite possible, however, here is the man who is talking about 'Super Happiness' and giving to others. Can India look at this model as well, enable non-profits to hold shares, invest in companies and start for-profit ventures? Tata Sons comes closer to this model and I always say they are one of best social businesses in the country, as 60 per cent of Tata Sons is owned by Tata Trusts, which supports various social programmes across the country.

Indian Corporation Action Tank

After that visit, I was very intrigued by his social business thought and started working with Aarti Wig, who is helping corporates adapt to social business with the Indian Corporate Action Tank (ICAT) initiative. ICAT was trying to make few corporates start looking at solving problems of the poor with their expertise, how YSB has done this with Dannon in Bangladesh. Dannon co-created business units and started a yogurt product for the poor with nutrients that followed YSB principles. It was great attending and speaking to those corporates on that in August 2017. I met the professor again at Social Business Day in Bengaluru in June 2018, where I learnt more about the Nobin Programme (New Entrepreneurs) and spoke about the Nativelead model. The conference was aptly named after his latest book—*A World of Three Zeros: The New Economics of Zero Poverty, Zero Unemployment and Zero Net Carbon Emissions.*

JLG in Social Business

JLG—Joint Liability Group—this one idea of Prof. Yunus's, transformed billions of poor across the world into credit worthy. When the poor weren't able to access banks, he provided money to a group of people and collected money from all of them at the same time in instalments. When they go to collect their instalments, even if there is one woman who cannot repay, they will not collect. It makes other women come forward and pay for their friend this time and she repeats the favour the next time. So together (jointly), they are liable for the loan they borrowed. This one idea won the professor the Nobel Prize. I've asked him what would be the equivalent of JLG for small businesses as start-ups struggle to raise debt. He said it has to be to known people. Grameen is providing loans to businesses, usually that are the children of the borrowers of Grameen Bank, so there is a long history and they know the person and their intent to pay. Also, Suresh Krishna of Grameen Koota started the Yunus Social Business, Bengaluru, where I am working with him and still exploring bringing the Joint Liability Group that Prof. Yunus invented into businesses.

Debt Syndicate

In angel investing, each angel investor puts an amount and shares the risk among themselves and they invest in equity. It's called a syndicate. Each person gets their share and as the company grows, there is an opportunity to exit or if the company doesn't do well, they'll lose. How about bringing this similar concept into debt? Taking Prof. Yunus's thought around known people, we are thinking of Nativelead start-ups to explore this. Many scalable start-ups can be given equity investment by our angels. Similarly, can we all syndicate small amounts to give a start-up a loan? At Startup Tamil Nadu 2020, we've started a programme Aiyram Pookal Pookattum (Let 1000 flowers bloom) to be conducted over ten years with 100 each year. In 2020, we shortlisted 100 start-ups from small towns all over Tamil Nadu. Twenty of them were shortlisted to pitch to our angels and four of them received a commitment for investments. So, eighty of them may not be scalable today, and they may not be eligible for equity today. So, how can we make the debt available for them today? This is what we would like to explore, where we would like to identify 100 start-ups wherever they are not scale-ready, do a debt syndicate with our angels and invest in them. As I write this, I've spoken with Ram at Rang De—a peer-to-peer (P2P) platform on using that platform so individual angels could invest in the start-ups. We already saw green financing through a debt syndicate by two Nativelead investors providing debt to Carbon Masters.

Social Business in Israel

Concerned about this state of affairs, I decided to work on the issue in depth when I chanced upon Jackie Goren, the director of the Israel Venture Network (IVN), who had been working on a legal definition of social businesses for the past few years in Israel. I had a long discussion with her over a lunch, as she had visited IIMB for teaching a course that was part of the Israel Centre that was launched in 2017[6],[7] at IIMB to strengthen India's academic collaborations with the Middle-Eastern nation.

On social business, the basic premise that Jackie worked with was that when a corporation was to be formed, it had to choose between being a not-for-profit to which a specific law system, a regulation and regulator applied, or become a regular company that came under a different law, regulations and regulator. However, both of these structures did not fit the concept of a social business. The main reason was that social businesses needed to be able to get money from both investors and philanthropists or donors. The catch here was that if a corporation was a not-for-profit outfit, money could not be raised from investors as dividends would not be distributed and on the other hand, if the corporation was for profit, donations could not be taken nor could they attract tax incentives; they needed to pay GST and all the other taxes associated with a commercial enterprise. And from the donor's side, they would hesitate to donate to the enterprise as they were firstly not incentivized to do so.

This dichotomy led to social businesses having no structure and hence, no definition. There was also a current need for a clear definition as many social businesses had started to evolve in the recent past. In addition, regular businesses would pay taxes to the government and the government was meant to use the taxpayer's money for improving social issues plaguing the country. Over time, the government realized that taxes were not being paid and businesses were reluctant to pay taxes, so the government fell short of money without the taxes and inevitably, social problems began to grow. Besides, there was no incentive to start a social enterprise. This was a dilemma that had to be addressed.

This made Israel look at England. Sometime in 2000, England created a special task force under the government with people from the business world, NGOs and other sections of society, to think on how to create an ecosystem that would incentivize money to route into solving social problems. They developed different solutions, one being the setting up of a bank to give loans to social ventures and for those who wanted to start a social business.

In following England's model, Israel realized that the social sector was not growing. Part of the reason was that there were not adequate funds and no legal structure for the incorporation of these businesses. Hence, IVN thought it was important to develop a structure. It began by creating a definition that initially was not legally binding. It was a forum called the Round Table Forum. Those involved in the forum were IVN, some members from the office of the prime minister of Israel, from NGOs, people from the finance department, people from the business world—a wide cross section of people. Discussions on social businesses were conducted frequently and at the end of a year and a half, an initial definition was decided upon: 'Social business is a business that is for making money but not for maximizing profit. It has a social goal and if it is a company it is registered with an article of association and can distribute and give dividends to its shareholders but it cannot distribute more than 50 per cent of its net income. The remaining 50 per cent is to be reallocated for the social side of the business.' That was a soft definition and not yet the legal definition.

With this definition, the forum again had a discussion with the prime minister's office and specifically with the government's finance department. They managed to convince the government for a tri-sectorial fund that would invest only in social businesses. The fund was to raise money from three sources; firstly, the government invested and the terms of the government were that they would fund the basic money and two-thirds needed to be from other sources. The funds would have to be invested in social businesses that had as their agenda the aim of solving some specific social problem that the government was interested in. This was in 2014. The fund was made up of a third of the money from philanthropists and one-third from the government. The last third of the loan was taken from investors on available market terms, but not with very high returns. It was easy to raise this money as the government was associated with them and safety was assured. With this fund, it was the first time that the soft definition of social businesses got a life in Israel.

In 2015, IVN[8] started with two funds of $10 million each. Though it did not solve much of the problems, it was a beginning. The fund was to be disbursed to social businesses that dealt with employment problems associated with people such as the mentally challenged, ex-prisoners, physically disabled, drug addicts and so on. IVN has since been getting the fund invested in sixteen or seventeen social businesses by giving them loans and some of them equity.

After a one-year break, all the loans were to be returned. They have touched approximately 35,000 lives so far.

The loan on being returned is given back to the bank or organization that invested in IVN with interest, but the remaining money received from the government and the philanthropists is rotated to other social businesses that are set up.

The process involved a vote at the Knesset—the Parliament of Israel. A presentation was made of a proposal to introduce the law in the first round, then after a few iterations, two more rounds of meetings had to go on before the final sign off was done. The people involved in clearing the law were from different walks of life, such as people from the prime minister's office, the justice department, the finance department of the government and some others. However, as the law would come from the government, it was almost 100 per cent guaranteed that it would have the majority in the vote and the law would be passed.

An interesting aspect of the proposed law was that, though in the beginning prior to the law, social businesses used to work without any incentives, the law proposed that incentive should be given to business investors so they would be willing to invest in a social business. For instance, if an entrepreneur of a commercial business has a lot of money, but during one particular year that entrepreneur has lost money at the stock market, he or she would still need to pay taxes. The law proposes that you could offset your tax and instead invest in a social business and that year, you don't need to pay tax because you have translated your tax into paying money to a social business. In case in the future if the social business is profitable and they pay dividends, the commercial organization will pay tax on the dividend. So, this acts as a social incentive as the corporation is doing well. In the future, with the hope that the business does well, the corporation might get the investment back to then pay tax. This was a way in which modified taxation was used to give incentives for early-stage start-ups.

Sixteen

The Way Ahead

'If you measure the wrong thing, you will do the wrong thing.'
—Professor Joseph Stiglitz

In looking for countries who have set standards for health and well-being, I heard Prof. Joseph Stiglitz, the Nobel laureate at the Social Outcomes Conference (SOC) 2021, organized by the Government Outcomes Lab[1] at Oxford University in September 2021, in which he talked about a dashboard required for measuring countries' progress. 'We don't measure the performance of a car by just the speed alone; similarly, we can't measure the country's progress just by GDP alone,' he explained, speaking about the Organization for Economic Co-operation and Development (OECD) dashboard of various indicators to assess a country's well-being.

How does a country fare in building back from Covid-19 a stronger and more inclusive, green and resilient economy and society? 'In our world of enormous inequality, GDP could be going up and yet most people could be experiencing a lower standard of living,' he said, and this can ultimately undermine trust in government.

As an alternative, he argued for adopting a broader set of metrics to judge the well-being of society and find ways to reflect these metrics in the way institutions operate, both at the macro level and at the level of service delivery. As we get the social business to adhere to well-being standards, as a country we may have to redefine how we measure as well. At the conference, Dr Rodney Scott, Kaitohutohu Mātāmua/chief policy adviser, spoke about New Zealand's efforts on those lines and he shared a very comprehensive framework that they have built. After the conference, he gave details on their progress.

Ngā Tūtohu Aotearoa—Indicators Aotearoa New Zealand[2] presents the big picture of lives of New Zealanders. More than 100 indicators have been chosen to go beyond economic measures, such as GDP, to include well-being and sustainable development and to help monitor progress around social, cultural, economic and environmental well-being.

The indicators support the government's well-being vision to provide a more holistic view of well-being and sustainable development than a purely economic measure does.

These measures cover:

- New Zealand's current well-being
- Future well-being (what we are leaving behind for future generations)
- The impact New Zealand is having on the rest of the world (international impacts)

In addition, contextual indicators are included that provide valuable context to the well-being indicators.

Setting Standards for India

Why have we been unable to set such standards and execute them in India? Three prime reasons present themselves. One, India is basically a rural nation; there are no effectively funded centralized plans and the existence of huge regional variations. For instance, in 1951, India had only five cities with a population of not more than ten lakh and only forty-one cities with more than one lakh people in each city. However, in 2016–17, more than 65 per cent of our people lived in rural areas and there were forty cities with more than a million people, 397 cities have between one lakh and one million people, and 2500 cities have between 10,000 and one lakh people.[3]

With economic liberalization, Indian cities grew substantially, both economically and spatially, which in turn has led to tremendous pressure on infrastructure and resources such as water, energy, public transport and sanitation. Mohammed Yunus, in his book *A World of Three Zeros*, writes of the lack of the services that the poor suffer: 'lack of institutional services, lack of clean drinking water and sanitary facilities, lack of health care, inadequate education, substandard housing, no access to energy, neglect in old age and many more.' He goes on to say that the poor suffer the same problems even in rich nations. He quotes the economist Angus Deaton, 'If you had to choose between living in a poor village in India and living in the Mississippi Delta or in a suburb of Milwaukee in a trailer park, I am not sure who would have the better life.'

As of 2015, 15.6 million people born in India were living in other countries. India has been among the world's top origin countries of migrants since the UN started tracking migrant origins in 1990.[4] As of 2015, about 5.2 million immigrants live in India, making it the twelfth-largest immigrant population in the world. The overwhelming majority of India's immigrants are from neighbouring countries such as Bangladesh (3.2 million), Pakistan (1.1 million), Nepal (5,40,000) and Sri Lanka (1,60,000).

Sikkim—Well-Being of Generations

In India, states have been thinking about this already. I heard Assam mentioning about SDGs and Kerala adopting it seriously and become number one in achieving India's SDG goals. Sikkim is thinking way ahead with well-being. As this state had led the way in organic practices, I was happy to see their efforts towards more SDG thoughts. The Ministry of Statistics and Programme Implementation (MoSPI) has been entrusted with the responsibility of evolving India-specific indicators for the seventeen goals. In the spirit of cooperative federalism, each of India's twenty-nine states is to begin planning within the SDG framework and report to the NITI Aayog periodically.

Sikkim, one of the smallest states of the country with a population density of eighty-six persons per square km, in response, is attempting to create a guideline-based, empowering law (currently named the Sikkim Well-Being of Generations Bill 2017) that will incentivize development planning of the state in line with the SDG goals.[5]

The proposed act will be grounded within a few guiding principles such as those of shared responsibility, precaution, transparency and participation, rights of citizens, integration between economic, social and ecological needs and thresholds, inter and intra-generational equity, strengthening of local economies and valuation of social and natural capital. These principles are expected to drive the planning and functioning of various departments under the state as well as consumer/citizen behaviour. Similar to the Wales government's the Well-being of Future Generations Act, with seven connected well-being goals for Wales[6]— prosperous, resilient, healthier, more equal, more cohesive communities, vibrant culture and thriving Welsh language, and globally responsible Wales. Sikkim has shown the way for a climate resilient and equal, happy earth and people! Others should follow as well.

Rebuilding the Trust—G-Biz

For farmers and the people to start trusting corporations, businesses should be measured on a triple bottom line of people, profit and the planet.

It's Pongal day in January 2021.[7] Every year, I put out Pongal wishes as it is celebrated as a harvest festival in the south, especially in Tamil Nadu. The previous day is celebrated as Bhogi, where people discard old and derelict things and concentrate on new things, causing change or transformation. On Pongal day, you thank the sun by offering it Pongal made with freshly harvested grain outside the house to offer to the sun. The following day is Maatu (cattle) Pongal—to thank the cattle that helped farmers in agriculture.

During my Bharat Darshan, visiting around twenty-eight states/union territories, I've met many farmers that I used to thank for our food on this day. At this harvest festival, thanks to Kalimuthu—Valasu, Ramu—Amle, Mahadeva—Hunsur, Ranjit—Mala and many other farmers for making food for us! Happy Pongal, Lohri,

Utharayan, Makara Sankranthi. Thank you Muralidhar (Rajasthan), Hari Lal, Chaveram (Himachal), Kathirappan, Baiju, Kanchana (TN), Balu (Kerala), Khoveio (Manipur), Vilas (Maharashtra), Sathya Sai FPO, BCT KVK (AP), Sai Krishna (Telangana) whom I met in 2019 and many other farmers for our food—Happy Pongal (farmers day)! For some reason, this year I was not in a state of mind to put out that message, as I was feeling uncomfortable that a section of the farmers was braving the cold weather and didn't want something that the government feels is good for them. If it's good, then why is there a reluctance and over fifty days of struggle?

One of the underlying understandings is that, there seems to be a trust deficit among them. I always say to start-ups working in agriculture—farmers don't trust anyone and we need to earn their trust. The current situation is proving that point again. Trust deficit seems to be not only with the government, but more with the corporates.

We can see these days that in Indian movies, the roles of bad politicians, bad cops, a rogue person as a villain are reducing and they are being replaced by corporate honchos—in medicine, agriculture, land-grabbing of the poor, tribals, etc. It's worse with corporate hospitals now; even I had an experience recently with my relative in the hospital ICU. Some of my relatives didn't trust the doctor's advice at all, and I kept hearing that they asked us to do this procedure to extract money from us. This is pretty bad as people may not be heeding the right advice and putting their life at risk. On the other hand, I didn't see the hospitals trying to dispel this fear.

The country is finally coming out of the fears of the East India Company, a corporate that ended up ruling the country, and is celebrating entrepreneurs. So, at this time, this is not a good trend as today's start-up is tomorrow's corporate.

This trust deficit with corporations seems to be trending across the world right now. Recent WhatsApp policy changes seem to have created a lot of questions in its users' minds.[8] Some seem to be opting for a non-profit and open-source alternative like Signal, moving away from a corporate.

Silicon Valley, over the last few years, has been blamed for many things, where its business models have been questioned. Across the world, there seems to be an ongoing dialogue about corporate intentions, which is why the field ESG has come into action to measure corporates in terms of their impact on Environmental, Social and Governance (ESG).

Compared to the rest of the world, India is a pioneer in making CSR a law, mandating corporations to spend 2 per cent of their profits for the good. This has done good to the country and according to India Data Insights, an initiative of Sattva, a portfolio of mine, Rs 71,909 crore was spent by 29,655 companies during the period 2014–19 in ten sectors (education, healthcare, livelihood, rural development projects and more), trying to get people out of poverty.[9] Many corporates have solid CSR teams in place. Then why is there still a trust deficit among farmers with respect to corporates? I used to say that the 2 per cent (kept aside for CSR) is like a holy dip in the Ganga. What about the other 98 per cent where I can do anything?

In the 2017 article I had written for *Forbes India*, titled 'Social Businesses Must Receive Risk Capital from the Government and CSR',[10] I've put forth a point about having the government define social businesses so CSR funds could go to businesses that are doing good for people.

I focused on start-ups at the time, in the way of bringing more patient capital into helping those entrepreneurs solving serious problems. I suggested creating a section in the Indian

Company Law for social businesses that would be measured on triple bottom line—people, planet and profit. Looking at profits alone would make companies lose focus on long-term impacts and they would live on a very myopic quarter-by-quarter basis. This way, India can lead the way in building an equitable country, taking everyone along!

With the current scenario, I feel the time has come to define social businesses for the country so that many corporations follow those guidelines and reduce the trust deficit people have today with the corporates. This might even accelerate achieving the SDGs the government has set out to do by 2030.

Corporates that farmers are afraid of can take the lead and announce their SDG goals and ESG standing today. If the Indian government comes up with its own definition of social businesses, including SDG and ESG, there could be one rating system to assess the corporates on.

Could publicly-listed big corporates do this? Yes. In 2018, I heard Emmanuel Faber (CEO of Danone) speak at the Yunus Social Business Day in Bengaluru. He depicted how a multinational can turn its path around and initiate change. The Grameen Danone social business example has not only helped thousands of undernourished children, but at the same time, the relationship Danone has with its employees and themselves. Most of their employees have now invested in social businesses, demonstrating that social cause and business can act as one.

He was alluding to taking the €25 billion company towards that vision and today, I see that Danone has become the first listed company to adopt the 'Entreprise à Mission' model created by French law in 2019.[11]

An Entreprise à Mission[12] is defined as a company where social and environmental objectives are aligned with its purpose and set out in its articles of association. Unilever has been working on its sustainability living plan (USLP) since 2010,[13] with a bold ambition to achieve change within the company, saying, 'We believe that business growth should not be at the expense of people and the planet. That's why we're changing the way we do business and why we want to change the way business is done.' Ben and Jerry's say, 'We believe it's an important aspect of our business to share with you, both the highs and lows. As a part of our Social and Environmental Assessment Report (SEAR),[14] we have a third-party review of our Company priorities for that year.' They've done SEAR for thirty-one years.

It is also heartening to see efforts of the Cultural Intellectual Property Rights Initiative® (CIPRI) that I've joined as an advisory board member, which was spawned from incidents of design plagiarism where fashion brands like Louis Vuitton, Nike and Max Mara had some of their designs replicating traditional designs of the Maasai tribe of Kenya, Africa, the Guna culture of Panama and Colombia, and the Oma ethnic group of Laos. The organization is helping brands recognize and reward these tribes—because of their cultural IP.

Similarly, the World Fair Trade Organization (WFTO)[15] is a global association of 401 organizations committed to improving the livelihoods of economically marginalized producers. WFTO has members in seventy-six countries and their members use commercial activity to achieve a social mission. They have been referred to as Fair Trade Social Enterprises. WFTO's stated mission is 'to enable producers to improve their livelihoods and communities through fair trade'. But these are on a volunteer basis or after an incident.

In 2016, in an exclusive interview with *Forbes India* headlined 'Needed: Entrepreneurial Models That Work for

"Bharat"',[16] I suggested SEBI's attempt at an alternative investment model—through an online exchange—as an option for somewhat mitigating the problem of inflated valuations. For instance, making it easy to raise between Rs 50 lakh and Rs 100 crore on this platform can help people exchange or sell the shares in a promising business which they already own, without waiting to complete the investment's valuation cycle. What I recommended in 2016 as a way to raise money for a social business start-up eventually happened in 2020 when SEBI came up with a paper on a Social Stock Exchange (SSE). In February 2023, the National Stock Exchange received a nod from SEBI to start an SSE for both For-Profit Enterprises (FPE) and Non-Profit Enterprises (NPE) can start listing.[17] It's an amazing start and India has indeed paved the way to disrupt capital markets. In a similar vein, my recommendation in 2017 on the definition of social businesses may come to fruition soon.

We have a golden opportunity to get Indian corporates to adapt to measuring their triple bottom line in terms of the people, planet and profit, but the government needs to set up guidelines for social businesses. Once that becomes a reality, everyone in the country can feel good about opportunities to enjoy and participate in the available growth. Otherwise, India may end up facing the problems that the US is facing today—the 1 per cent scenario that has created more disturbance in the world's oldest democracy as described in *Saving Capitalism: For the Many, Not the Few*. In that book, the author, Robert Reich, recalls similar issues that happened in 1880–90, resulting in the antitrust legislation—which seems an apt name![18]

The year 2021 also has significance as we entered the 100th year of Mahatma Gandhi changing his attire to a simple loincloth. So, we might even call India's definition of social business 'Gandhian Business', or G-Biz, as a tribute to this incident and resolve to change the farmers' situation by 2030. As a start, SZW has released its first triple bottom line report, setting the standard for social business. As the government starts defining G-Biz, the SZW Circular Impact Report 2022[19] could be used as a starting point.

This pandemic also made many Gandhian thoughts resurface, such as self-reliance, go local, decentralized manufacturing and rural livelihood after the reverse migration (I call them 'city-returned'). We missed 2020 and also Abdul Kalam's vision for 2020. Let's make Mahatma Gandhi's wish come true by 2030—by when the UN hopes to achieve the SDGs.

By the way, during Maatu Pongal, there is the famous Jallikattu—a traditional event happens in Tamil Nadu where people have to stop a bull released on them and ride along to remove the flag on its horns. Traditionally, it was to demonstrate a person's strength to tame the bull. So, let's ensure that both the people (farmers) and the bull are ready, before releasing it. That's what my grandfather used to do. When we were young, we always looking forward to this part of Pongal. We all helped him bathe the bull and paint its horns, and he'd make a garland of small pieces of sugarcane, palm roots, etc., to place around its neck. He would hold the bull at the entrance of the shed and we used to wait outside. He'd bring the bull out and we'd all jump to get the goodies on the garland. He would keep holding the bull until we got all the goodies. That's what the government needs to do—just be there and regulate so everyone gets their piece and is happy!

Acknowledgements

Ithank all the entrepreneurs I've met so far, who have been patient with my questions; from each and every interaction, I learnt a lot, gleaning their vast experience on many issues and solutions. Thanks to all the friends who accompanied me and translated for me during my field visits and answered all my questions.

My daughter, Nila, has already published her first storybook, which motivated me further to complete writing this book after many years of effort. Thanks also to my wife, Abirami, Nila and son, Nilan, especially since I spent most of the time during the pandemic with this book. Even though I was in the house, I wasn't with them. They reviewed, provided inputs and even typed up some parts of the book as I dictated.

Friends and other family members who helped me develop my thoughts in three stages:

Early life: My parents who believed in education and, despite facing hardships, ensured that their six children received quality education and became first-generation graduates.

Work life: Eric Musser, my long-time boss, who shaped my management thinking, which in turn helped me climb the corporate ladder rapidly. The Association for India's Development (AID) and its volunteers who awakened my conscience. I explored Gandhi more during this phase, which was further fuelled by discovering Jiddu

Acknowledgements

Krishnamurti through The Valley School's Study Centre and led me to exit the rat race at the age of forty-one.

Current life: Prof. Muhammad Yunus and Jacqueline Novogratz's Acumen that equipped me with an entirely different image of business, which I now cling on to strongly. IAN, through which I've learnt about angel investing. Prof. G. Sabarinathan at NSRCEL, IIMB, who created the first resident mentor role and allowed me to garner vast experience via supporting over 1000 entrepreneurs. Nativelead that helped me give back to my home state and apply my learning across the country.

Wikipedia, of which I'm a donor, helped me understand each and every place I visited and is a source for many of my references here.

Anushka Shetty, whose Plop Stories was incubated through NSRCEL's Women Start-up Programme, wanted my book to be the first published on her platform. She connected me with Menaka Rao who has patiently worked with me in developing this book. Kanishka Gupta for connecting me with Scharada Dubey who helped put this book together with help from Godavar. Radhika Marwah at Penguin, who patiently worked with me over a year, and Ralph Rebello for the edit support.

The quotes from the scenes and songs of the film *Swades* (2004), as indicated in the text, have been translated, with relevant credits as follows:

Swades: We, the People (2004), directed by Ashutosh Gowariker
    Story: M.G. Satya, Ashutosh Gowariker
    Screenplay: Ashutosh Gowariker, Sameer Sharma, Lalit Marathe, Amin Hajee, Charlotte Whitby-Coles, Yashodeep Nigudkar, Ayan Mukherjee
    Dialogues: K.P. Saxena
    Lyrics: Javed Akhtar

Notes

Introduction

1 Economic Survey 2022–23, Government of India, Ministry of Finance, Department of Economic Affairs, https://www.indiabudget.gov.in/economicsurvey/doc/echapter.pdf.

2 The World Bank in India, The World Bank, https://www.worldbank.org/en/country/india/overview.

3 Express Web Desk, 'Global Hunger Index 2020: India Ranks 94 out of 107 Countries, under "Serious" Category', The *Indian Express,* 19 October 2020, https://indianexpress.com/article/india/global-health-index-2020-india-6757899/.

4 Dr Prashant Kumar Choudhary, 'Income Inequality in India', The Geopolitics, 12 July 2022, https://thegeopolitics.com/income-inequality-in-india/#:~:text=According%20to%20WID%20and%20PLFS,PLFS%20reports%2C%20according%20to%20WID.

5 '10 Million Lost Jobs in COVID 2nd Wave, 97% Households' Income Declined: CMIE', BusinessToday.In, 1 June 2021, https://www.businesstoday.in/latest/economy-politics/story/income-of-97-households-declined-since-covid-19-pandemic-began-cmie-298381-2021-06-01.

6 'One Year since a Complete Lockdown Was Announced, We Look Back on How India Fought COVID', the *Economic Times,* 24 March 2021, https://economictimes.indiatimes.com/news/india/one-year-since-a-complete-lockdown-was-announced-we-look-back-on-how-india-fought-covid/first-lockdown-announced/slideshow/81662838.cms.

7 Startup India, https://www.startupindia.gov.in/.
8 'List of countries by GDP (nominal)', Wikipedia, https://en.wikipedia.org/wiki/List_of_countries_by_GDP_(nominal).
9 Katherine White, David J. Hardisty and Rishad Habib, 'The Elusive Green Consumer', *Harvard Business Review*, July–August 2019, https://hbr.org/2019/07/the-elusive-green-consumer.
10 'Richest 1% Bag Nearly Twice as Much Wealth as the Rest of the World Put Together over the past Two Years', Oxfam International, 16 January 2023, https://www.oxfam.org/en/press-releases/richest-1-bag-nearly-twice-much-wealth-rest-world-put-together-over-past-two-years.

Chapter 1: Beginning the Darshan

1 'Economy of India under the British Raj', Wikipedia, https://en.wikipedia.org/wiki/Economy_of_India_under_the_British_Raj.
2 Nitin Singh and Nikhil Venkatesa, '5 Ways Imperial Britain Crippled Indian Handlooms', SGBG Atelier, https://www.sgbgatelier.com/world/2019/11/21/5-ways-imperial-britain-crippled-indian-handlooms.
3 Rajni Bakshi, Full text of *Bapu Kuti*, Internet Archive, https://archive.org/stream/BAPUKUTIRAJANIBAKSHI/BAPU%20KUTI%20-%20RAJANI%20BAKSHI_djvu.txt.
4 'Ramasamy Elango is awarded THE WEEK "Man of the Year" Award, 2013', *Business Standard*, 30 April 2014, https://www.business-standard.com/article/news-ani/ramasamy-elango-is-awarded-the-week-man-of-the-year-award-2013-114043000886_1.html.
5 'Vasco da Gama', Wikipedia, https://en.wikipedia.org/wiki/Vasco_da_Gama#:~:text=On%208%20July%201497%20Vasco,the%20length%20of%20the%20equator.

Chapter 2: What We Grow: Clues to a Better Tomorrow

1 Bloomberg, 'How an American With a Knack for Math Saved India From Famine', The Packer, 20 May 2015, https://www.

thepacker.com/news/sustainability/how-american-knack-math-saved-india-famine.

2   Annual Report 2020–21, Department of Agriculture, Cooperation & Farmers' Welfare, Ministry of Agriculture & Farmers' Welfare, Government of India, https://agricoop.nic.in/Documents/annual-report-2020-21.pdf.

3   Harish Damodaran, 'The Cost+50% Swaminathan Formula Mirage', The Indian Express, 22 June 2017, https://indianexpress. com/article/india/the-cost-plug-50-percent-swaminathan-formula-mirage-agriculture-sector-minimum-support-price-4715922/.

4   TNN, '1 Crore Migrants, Including Those on Foot, Returned Home during Lockdown: Govt', The Times of India, 9 October 2020, https://timesofindia.indiatimes.com/india/1cr-migrants-including-those-on-foot-returned-home-govt/articleshow/78266556.cms.

5   Madhvi Sally, 'Amul Turnover Grows 17% To Rs 38,550 Crore in 2019-20', the Economic Times, 2 April 2020, https:// economictimes.indiatimes.com/industry/cons-products/food/amul-turnover-grows-17-to-rs-38550-crore-in-2019-20/articleshow/74942395.cms?from=mdr.

6   'Farm Bill Spending', USDA Economic Research Service, https:// www.ers.usda.gov/topics/farm-economy/farm-commodity-policy/farm-bill-spending/.

Chapter 3: Mainstreaming the Marginalized

1   'Honouring and Empowering the Adivasis of India', Press Information Bureau, 2 December 2022, https://pib.gov.in/FeaturesDeatils.aspx?NoteId=151222&ModuleId%20=%202.

2   'Tribal Museum', SCSTRTI, https://www.scstrti.in/index.php/89-activities/120-museum.

3   Chuktia Bhunjia, SCSTRTI, https://tribal.nic.in/repository/View Doc.aspx?RepositoryNo=TRI28-08-2017115101&file=Docs/TRI28-08-2017115101.pdf.

4   'PVTGs of Odisha', SCSTRTI, https://www.scstrti.in/index.php/communities/pvtg.

5   'Amish', https://en.wikipedia.org/wiki/Amish.

6   'Shellac', https://en.wikipedia.org/wiki/Shellac.

7 Trainers Manual for Entrepreneurship Training—2012, I-USE, Udyogini, https://collaboration.worldbank.org/content/usergenerated/asi/cloud/attachments/sites/collaboration-for-development/en/groups/bees-network/documents/_jcr_content/content/primary/blog/i-use_training_manua-Do1m/I-USE-Training-Manual-Udyogini.pdf.
8 https://udyogini.org/ntfp-lac/.

Chapter 4: Enterprise in Every Corner

1 Onmanorama Staff, 'Kerala Tops in Literacy Rate Followed by Lakshadweep, Mizoram: MOE', *Onmanorama*, 14 March 2023, https://www.onmanorama.com/career-and-campus/top-news/2023/03/14/kerala-highest-literacy-rate-says-ministry-of-education-india.html.
2 'Duitara', https://en.wikipedia.org/wiki/Duitara.
3 Sauramandala, Centre for Accelerated Development, https://www.sauramandala.org/.
4 Meghalaya Basin Development Authority, Government of Meghalaya, https://mbda.gov.in/about-us.
5 Deputy Commissioner, East Garo Hills, http://eastgarohills.gov.in/deputy_commissioner.html.
6 Sheryl Sebastian, 'What Led to the Decline of the Matrilineal Society in Kerala?', Feminism in India, 1 September 2016, https://feminisminindia.com/2016/09/01/decline-matrilineal-society-kerala/.
7 '5: Achieve Gender Equality and Empower All Women and Girls', United Nations, Department of Economic and Social Affairs, Sustainable Development, https://sdgs.un.org/goals/goal5.
8 Adriana John, '10 Surviving Matrilineal Societies of the World', Wonderslist, https://www.wonderslist.com/10-surviving-matrilineal-societies/.
9 'Jharkhand', https://en.wikipedia.org/wiki/Jharkhand.
10 Samvad, https://www.samvad.net/about.php.

Chapter 5: The Homes We Build, the Cities We Inhabit

1 Shirish Sankhe et al., 'India's Urban Awakening: Building Inclusive Cities, Sustaining Economic Growth', McKinsey & Company, 1 April 2010, https://www.mckinsey.com/featured-insights/urbanization/urban-awakening-in-india.

2 'India—Urban Population as a Share of Total Population', India Urban population, 1960–2022, knoema.com.

3 Charlotte Edmond, 'Global Migration, by the Numbers: Who Migrates, Where They Go and Why', World Economic Forum, 10 January 2020, https://www.weforum.org/agenda/2020/01/iom-global-migration-report-international-migrants-2020/.

4 'Floor area ratio', https://en.wikipedia.org/wiki/Floor_area_ratio.

5 Karthik K., 'Floor Space Index in 8 Major Cities', commonfloor.com, https://www.commonfloor.com/guide/floor-space-index-in-8-major-cities-41800.html.

6 P. Sainath, 'Over 2,000 Fewer Farmers Every Day', The Hindu, 8 June 2016, https://www.thehindu.com/opinion/columns/sainath/over-2000-fewer-farmers-every-day/article4674190.ece.

7 'BBC: Bengaluru Only Indian City in the World to Have No Water; Here Is What Can We Do', Asianet Newsable, 31 March 2018, https://newsable.asianetnews.com/karnataka/no-water-in-bangalore-bbc-report-bengaluru-to-dry-up-how-to-save-water.

8 'Trends in Solid Waste Management', What a Waste 2.0, The World Bank, https://datatopics.worldbank.org/what-a-waste/trends_in_solid_waste_management.html.

9 Silpa Kaza and Farouk Banna, 'What Does Waste Management Have to Do With Reducing Crime and Violence in Jamaica?' World Bank Blogs, 11 April 2014, https://blogs.worldbank.org/sustainablecities/what-does-waste-management-have-do-reducing-crime-and-violence-jamaica.

10 DH Contributor, 'Villagers Bear the Brunt of Bengaluru City Dwellers' Crap', Deccan Herald, 10 July 2020, https://www.deccanherald.com/city/bengaluru-infrastructure/villagers-bear-the-brunt-of-bengaluru-city-dwellers-crap-859385.html.

11 Muntazir Abbas, 'India Has 22 Cars per 1,000 Individuals: Amitabh Kant', ET Auto, 12 December 2018, https://auto.economictimes.indiatimes.com/news/passenger-vehicle/cars/india-has-22-cars-per-1000-individuals-amitabh-kant/67059021.

12 Shreyas H.S., 'Bengaluru: Namma Metro Has Failed to Resolve Traffic Woes', the Times of India, 2 January 2023, https://timesofindia.indiatimes.com/city/bengaluru/bengaluru-namma-metro-has-failed-to-resolve-traffic-woes/articleshow/96668441.cms.

13 'Bhoodan movement', https://en.wikipedia.org/wiki/Bhoodan_movement.

14 Likhitha Prasanna, 'Ricky Kej's Rhythm of Sustainability and Unity Aspires to Heal the World', the Times of India, 24 January 2023, https://timesofindia.indiatimes.com/entertainment/kannada/music/ricky-kejs-rhythm-of-sustainability-and-unity-aspires-to-heal-the-world/articleshow/97257370.cms.

15 Phillip Inman, 'Why Does Donald Trump Want to Buy Greenland?', the Guardian, https://www.theguardian.com/us-news/2019/aug/19/why-does-donald-trump-want-to-buy-greenland.

16 'Anote Tong', https://en.wikipedia.org/wiki/Anote_Tong.

17 Colin Cram, 'How Do You Solve a Housing Crisis? Study the Example of Singapore', The Guardian, https://www.theguardian.com/housing-network/2015/apr/30/how-do-you-solve-a-housing-crisis-study-the-example-of-singapore.

18 Sharanjit Leyl, 'Singapore at 50: From Swamp to Skyscrapers', BBC News, 28 February 2015, https://www.bbc.com/news/magazine-31626174.

19 Kaushal Bhaav Skill Solutions Pvt. Ltd, The Urban Agenda Platform, https://www.urbanagendaplatform.org/best-practice/kaushal-bhaav-skill-solutions-pvt-ltd.

20 https://earthshipbiotecture.com/learn/.

21 'Namma Metro', https://en.wikipedia.org/wiki/Namma_Metro#Finances.

22 'MNREGA Helped Stop Migration from Rural Areas in Dharwad', The Hindu, 14 March 2022, https://www.thehindu.

com/news/national/karnataka/mnrega-helped-stop-migration-from-rural-areas-in-dharwad/article65224914.ece.

Chapter 6: Working Models of Positive Change

1 https://www.sattva.co.in/.
2 Circular Impact 2020, July 2020, https://saahaszerowaste.com/wp-content/uploads/2023/01/Final-SZW-Impact-Report-2020-1.pdf.
3 https://www.recharkha.org/.
4 Saahas Zero Waste, 'Saahas Zero Waste on Discovery Channel India's Planet Healers—Episode 3', *YouTube* video, 6:25, 2 April 2019, https://www.youtube.com/watch?v=G6280Le-A3o.
5 'Carbonlites Climate-Conscious Bio CNG', Carbonlites, https://www.carbonlites.com/carbonlites-climate-conscious-bio-cng.html#section1.
6 'Greenhouse Gas Emissions: Natural vs. Manmade', Arcadia, https://www.arcadia.com/energy-101/resource/greenhouse-gas-emissions-natural-vs-manmade.
7 'Solid Waste Management', UN Environment Programme, https://www.unep.org/explore-topics/resource-efficiency/what-we-do/cities/solid-waste-management.
8 Samar Lahiry, 'India's Challenges in Waste Management', *DownToEarth*, 9 January 2017, https://www.downtoearth.org.in/blog/waste/india-s-challenges-in-waste-management-56753.
9 'Main Sources of Carbon Dioxide Emissions', What's Your Impact, https://whatsyourimpact.org/greenhouse-gases/carbon-dioxide-emissions.
10 Climate Solver 2017 Awardee, 'GHG Reduction: Carbonlites: Bottled Bio-CNG (By End to End Organic Waste Management)', WWFIN, https://wwfin.awsassets.panda.org/downloads/ghg_reduction_climate_solver_awardees_2017.pdf.
11 'NEWater', https://en.wikipedia.org/wiki/NEWater.
12 Sanika Athavale, 'Bengaluru May See Acute Water Shortage by 2039, Says Bangalore Water Supply and Sewerage Board', The *Times of India*, 9 June 2022, https://timesofindia.indiatimes.com/city/bengaluru/bengaluru-may-see-acute-water-shortage-by-2039-says-bwssb/articleshow/92094137.cms.

13 S. Lalitha, 'Cauvery Stage 5 Project Put on Fast Track', The *New Indian Express*, 3 May 2021, https://www.newindianexpress. com/cities/bengaluru/2021/may/03/cauvery-stage-5-project-put-on-fast-track-2297683.html.

14 https://anandwan.in/anandvan.html.

15 Chandra R. Srikanth, 'Only 1% of Private Wealth in India Is Invested in Startups, Says Infosys Co-founder Kris Gopalakrishnan', ETNowNews, 19 August 2020, https:// www.timesnownews.com/business-economy/companies/article/ only-1-of-private-wealth-in-india-is-invested-in-startups-says-infosys-co-founder-kris-gopalakrishnan/639622.

16 BW Online Bureau, 'Tamil Nadu Based Nativespecial Raises Funding from Ian and Native Angels Network', BW Disrupt, 19 January 2017, https://bwdisrupt.businessworld.in/article/ Tamil-Nadu-Based-NativeSpecial-Raises-Funding-from-IAN-and-Native-Angels-Network/19-01-2017-111728/.

17 'Nativelead Achieves a New Milestone!', Press Release, 3 January 2022, https://nativelead.org/press_release.php.

Chapter 7: Healthier Choices, Happier Outcomes

1 'Vitamin C', https://en.wikipedia.org/wiki/Vitamin_C.

2 'Sangam landscape', https://en.wikipedia.org/wiki/Sangam_landscape.

3 Katherine White, David J. Hardisty and Rishad Habib, 'The Elusive Green Consumer', *Harvard Business Review*, July–August 2019, https://hbr.org/2019/07/the-elusive-green-consumer.

4 'Glow & Lovely', https://en.wikipedia.org/wiki/Glow_%26_Lovely.

5 Consumer Guidance Society of India, http://www.cgsiindia.org/ wp-content/uploads/1668/38/CGSI-Constitution.pdf.

6 Kunal Bhagat, Monisha Nakra, S. Archana and P.D. Jose, 'Mother Earth: Great Design, Great Values', https://www. industree.org.in/wp-content/uploads/2016/08/MOTHER-EARTH-%E2%80%93-A-HUMBLE-BEGINNING.pdf.

7 Nagaraja Prakasam, 'The Best Way Towards Talent Management', *Deccan Herald*, 13 December 2011, https://www.deccanherald. com/content/211479/way-towards-talent-management.html.

8 'CDC SOFT ADR : Nagaraja Prakasam Promoted To Additional Role of Managing Director of Sales for South and Southeast Asia', MarketScreener, 25 May 2010, https://www. marketscreener.com/quote/stock/CDC-SOFTWARE-CORP-ADR-5496447/news/CDC-SOFT-ADR-Nagaraja-Prakasam-Promoted-To-Additional-Role-of-Managing-Director-of-Sales-for-South-13382459/.

9 https://www.jkrishnamurti.in/.

10 https://akshayakalpa.org/our-story/.

11 'List of Countries by English-Speaking Population', https:// en.wikipedia.org/wiki/List_of_countries_by_English-speaking_ population.

12 https://resedalife.com/hygiene/.

13 Harish Upadhya, 'Bengaluru's Varthur Lake Now Spews 10-Feet-High Froth', NDTV, 16 August 2017, https://www. ndtv.com/india-news/bengalurus-varthur-lake-now-spews-10-feet-high-froth-1738397.

14 https://www.arakucoffee.in/our_story.

Chapter 8: Food, Commodities, Pricing—Finding the Way Forward

1 P. Sainath, 'Over 2,000 Fewer Farmers Every Day', *The Hindu*, 8 June 2016, https://www.thehindu.com/opinion/columns/sainath/over-2000-fewer-farmers-every-day/article4674190.ece.

2 'About Cold Chain', Ministry of Food Processing Industries, https://www.mofpi.gov.in/Schemes/about-cold-chain.

3 '*Gloriosa superba*', https://en.wikipedia.org/wiki/Gloriosa_superba.

4 '30 Years of CCD', CCD, https://ccd.org.in/our-journey.

5 'Happy Hens Farm: Eggsactly What the World Needed!', The Business Press, 21 July 2021, https://thebusinesspress.medium. com/happy-hens-farm-eggsactly-what-the-world-needed-96a128effa6e.

6 Felicity Lawrence, 'If Consumers Knew How Farmed Chickens Were Raised, They Might Never Eat Their Meat Again', The *Guardian*, 24 April 2016, https://www.theguardian.com/environment/2016/apr/24/real-cost-of-roast-chicken-animal-welfare-farms.

7 Happy Farmers, Happy Hens, https://thehappyhensfarm.com/services/about-farm/.
8 Our Standards, Certified Humane, https://certifiedhumane.org/our-standards/.

Chapter 9: The Warp and Weft of What We Wear

1 Abhinav Singh, 'India's Share in Global Exports of Textile Shrinks Due to High Cost, Lack of FTAs', The Week, 20 July 2021, https://www.theweek.in/news/biz-tech/2021/07/20/indias-share-in-global-exports-of-textile-shrinks-due-to-high-cost-lack-of-ftas.html.
2 Praachi Raniwala, '3 Experts on What the Indian Handloom Industry Needs Right Now', Vogue, 7 August 2020, https://www.vogue.in/fashion/content/3-experts-on-what-the-indian-handloom-industry-needs-right-now.
3 Fourth All India Handloom Census, 2019–20, PARI, https://ruralindiaonline.org/en/library/resource/fourth-all-india-handloom-census-2019-2020/.
4 National minimum individual wage of Rs 4576/month.
5 Handloom Weavers, Ministry of Textiles, 13 December 2019, https://pib.gov.in/PressReleasePage.aspx?PRID=1596372.
6 Divya A., 'What Does the Dissolution of the All India Handloom Board Mean for the Industry?', the Indian Express, 29 April 2023, https://indianexpress.com/article/lifestyle/art-and-culture/what-does-the-dissolution-of-the-all-india-handloom-board-mean-for-the-industry-ministry-of-textiles-6545819/.
7 S. Balakrishnan, 'What Made Gandhiji Wear Only Loincloth or Dhoti', Press Information Bureau, Government of India, Special Service and Features, 16-September-2016, https://pib.gov.in/newsite/printrelease.aspx?relid=149833.
8 Malathy Sriram, 'Ramraj Cotton, Wrapped in Comfort and Culture', BusinessLine on Campus, 11 June 2021, https://bloncampus.thehindubusinessline.com/columns/brand-basics/ramraj-cotton-wrapped-in-comfort-and-culture/article64635169.ece.

9 'Tamil Nadu Assembly Passes Bill to End Restriction on Dhoti', The *Times of India*, 12 August 2014, https://timesofindia. indiatimes.com/india/tamil-nadu-assembly-passes-bill-to-end-restriction-on-dhoti/articleshow/40115975.cms.

10 B. Syama Sundari, 'Handlooms Are Dying—and It's Because of Our Failure to Protect Them', The Wire, 21 March 2017, https:// thewire.in/culture/handlooms-are-dying-and-its-because-of-our-failure-to-protect-them.

Chapter 10: Practices for Posterity—Clothing and Home Accessories

1 Jahnavi Reddy, 'How Rising Costs and Stagnant Wages Have Hit Mangalagiri's Handloom Weavers', The News Minute, 18 February 2021, https://www.thenewsminute.com/article/ how-rising-costs-and-stagnant-wages-have-hit-mangalagiri-s-handloom-weavers-143711.

2 Number of Handloom Cooperatives, Press Information Bureau, Government of India, Ministry of Textiles, 6 March 2013, https:// pib.gov.in/newsite/PrintRelease.aspx?relid=93095#.

3 https://safaikarmachariandolan.org/people.

4 GoCoop, 'GoCoop Unlocked', *YouTube* video, 2:58, 8 February 2017, https://www.youtube.com/watch?v=GKy7aI8-b3U.

5 S. Ramakrishna Velamuri, G Sabarinathan and Suhruta Kulkarni, 'GoCoop—Social Marketplace', Harvard Business Publishing Education, 1 June 2017, https://hbsp.harvard.edu/product/ IMB639-PDF-ENG.

6 Shonali Advani, 'GoCoop Launches ILOVEHANDLOOMS Campaign', the *Economic Times*, 3 September 2015, https:// economictimes.indiatimes.com/industry/cons-products/ garments-/-textiles/gocoop-launches-ilovehandlooms-campaign/ articleshow/48787956.cms.

7 '#ILoveHandlooms—Do You?—Flaunt It!', https://naga.farm/ ilovehandlooms/.

8 'Jaipur Rugs Wins German Design Award 2016 in Material and Surfaces Category,' Jaipur Rugs Foundation, 14 December 2015, https://www.jaipurrugs.org/awards/jaipur-rugs-wins-german-design-award-2016-in-material-and-surfaces-category/.

9 Ayman Contractor, 'The Winning Designs from EDIDA 2017', *Elle Decor*, 29 November 2017, https://elledecor.in/article/the-winning-designs-from-edida-2017/.

10 Cultural Intellectual Property Rights Initiative®, https://www.culturalintellectualproperty.com/mission.

Chapter 11: Types of Start-ups and Social Responsibility

1 Eric Pfanner, 'Softbank's Alibaba Alchemy: How to Turn $20 Million into $50 Billion', The *Wall Street Journal*, 19 September 2014, https://www.wsj.com/articles/BL-DGB-37805.

2 'Gross Domestic Product', https://en.wikipedia.org/wiki/Gross_domestic_product.

3 India, The World Bank, https://data.worldbank.org/country/india.

4 China, The World Bank, https://data.worldbank.org/country/china.

5 Eric Bellman and Raymond Zhong, 'How Long Will It Take for India to Surpass China?—The Numbers', The *Wall Street Journal*, 13 March 2015, https://www.wsj.com/articles/BL-263B-3919.

6 Koustav Das, 'India's per Capita Income Doubles, but Doesn't Mean You Are Richer', *India Today*, 6 March 2023, https://www.indiatoday.in/business/story/india-per-capita-income-doubles-what-does-it-mean-for-population-2343191-2023-03-06.

7 GDP per capita (current US$)—Bangladesh, The World Bank, https://data.worldbank.org/indicator/NY.GDP.PCAP.CD?locations=BD.

8 GDP per capita (current US$)—China, The World Bank, https://data.worldbank.org/indicator/NY.GDP.PCAP.CD?locations=cn.

9 Children in India, https://www.unicef.org/india/children-in-india.

10 'Just 24% of Indian Households Have Internet Facility to Access e-Education: UNICEF', The *Indian Express*, 28 August 2020, https://indianexpress.com/article/education/just-24-pc-of-indian-households-have-internet-facility-to-access-e-education-unicef-6573199/.

11 'Covid-19: Are Children Able to Continue Learning during School Closures?' UNICEF, https://data.unicef.org/wp-content/uploads/2020/08/COVID-19-Remote-Learning-Factsheet_English_2020.pdf.

12 'Just 24% of Indian Households Have Internet Facility to Access e-Education: UNICEF', The *Indian Express*, 28 August 2020, https://indianexpress.com/article/education/just-24-pc-of-indian-households-have-internet-facility-to-access-e-education-unicef-6573199/.

13 Gross Domestic Product 2021, World Development Indicators Database, World Bank, 15 January 2023, https://databankfiles.worldbank.org/public/ddpext_download/GDP.pdf.

14 Muntazir Abbas, 'India Has 22 Cars per 1,000 Individuals: Amitabh Kant', ET Auto, 12 December 2018, https://auto.economictimes.indiatimes.com/news/passenger-vehicle/cars/india-has-22-cars-per-1000-individuals-amitabh-kant/67059021.

15 Peerzada Abrar, 'India gets over $60 bn in PE-VC investments for third year straight: Report', *Business Standard*, 18 April 2023, https://www.business-standard.com/companies/news/indian-pe-vc-investments-surpass-60-billion-amid-global-headwinds-123041800882_1.html.

16 Eximius—IIM Bangalore, 'The Bermuda Triangle: Rebooting from Failures | Eximius 2020 (IIM Bangalore)' *YouTube* video, 1:50:18, 25 July 2021, https://www.youtube.com/watch?v=GkPWmV3IHBo.

17 'C.K. Prahalad', https://en.wikipedia.org/wiki/C._K._Prahalad.

18 GDP per capita (current US$)—India, The World Bank, https://data.worldbank.org/indicator/NY.GDP.PCAP.CD?locations=IN.

19 P. Sainath, 'Rural India: A Living Journal, a Breathing Archive', PARI, https://ruralindiaonline.org/en/pages/about/.

20 'Subramania Bharati', https://en.wikipedia.org/wiki/Subramania_Bharati.

21 'List of Countries by English-Speaking Population', https://en.wikipedia.org/wiki/List_of_countries_by_English-speaking_population

22 Anshul Dhamija, 'How Nagaraja Prakasam Is Engineering Social Change', *Forbes India*, 4 November 2016, https://www.forbesindia.com/article/startups/how-nagaraja-prakasam-is-engineering-social-change/44625/1.

23 'Next Generation Leaders', *Time*, https://time.com/collection/next-generation-leaders/#2016.

24 J. Sam Daniel Stalin, 'Umesh Sachdev Is Only Indian On Time's List Of "10 Millennials Changing The World"', NDTV, 13 June 2016, https://www.ndtv.com/india-news/chennai-entrepreneur-umesh-sachdev-is-only-indian-on-times-list-of-10-millennials-changing-the-world-1418261.

25 https://www.forbesindia.com/magazine/1117.

26 'Umesh Sachdev of Uniphore Recognised with India Edition of MIT Technology Review's "Innovators Under 35"', Uniphore, 22 March 2016, https://www.uniphore.com/press-releases/umesh-sachdev-of-uniphore-recognised-with-india-edition-of-mit-technology-reviews-innovators-under-35/.

27 Debojyoti Ghosh, 'Uniphore: Gained in Translation', *Fortune India*, 4 February 2020, https://www.fortuneindia.com/venture/uniphore-gained-in-translation/104095.

28 Saranya Chakrapani, 'Tamil Nadu Govt, IIT-Madras Launch IVRs to Collect Covid-19 Data from Non-Smartphone Users', The *Times of India*, 10 April 2020, https://timesofindia.indiatimes.com/city/chennai/tamil-nadu-govt-iit-madras-launch-ivrs-to-collect-covid-19-data-from-non-smartphone-users/articleshow/75067052.cms.

29 'Uniphore Announces $400 Million Series E Funding Round to Support Explosive Growth and Global Demand for Automating Conversations across the Enterprise; Valuation Climbs to $2.5 Billion', Uniphore, 16 February 2022, https://www.uniphore.com/press-releases/uniphore-raises-400-million-to-support-explosive-growth-and-global-demand-for-automating-conversations-across-the-enterprise/.

30 https://www.ashoka.org/en-us/about-ashoka.

31 Suparna Dutt D'Cunha, 'India's Most Remote Villages Are Getting Better Healthcare With This Cloud-Based Solution', *Forbes*, 21 November 2016, https://www.forbes.

com/sites/suparnadutt/2016/11/21/indias-most-remote-villages-are-getting-better-healthcare-with-this-cloud-based-solution/?sh=3489f30c593b.

32 https://ladydoakcollege.edu.in/Iqac_Meet.html.

33 Neurosynaptic Communications—Telemedicine Solutions India.

34 Anshul Dhamija, 'How Nagaraja Prakasam Is Engineering Social Change', *Forbes India*.

35 'WHO Compendium of Innovative Health Technologies for Low-Resource Settings, 2016- 2017', World Health Organization, 22 January 2018, https://www.who.int/publications/i/item/9789241514699

36 Express Web Desk, 'India Has a Doctor for Every 10,189 People, Finds WHO Survey', The *Indian Express,* 22 July 2019, https://indianexpress.com/article/india/who-health-index-doctor-patient-ratio-5842648/.

37 'General Electric', https://en.wikipedia.org/wiki/General_Electric.

38 'Startup Funding in India Drops 33% to $24 Billion in 2022: Report', the *Economic Times*, 11 January 2023, https://economictimes.indiatimes.com/tech/funding/startup-funding-in-india-drops-33-to-24-billion-in-2022-report/articleshow/96911190.cms

39 Muntazir Abbas, 'India Has 22 Cars per 1,000 Individuals: Amitabh Kant', ET Auto, 12 December 2018.

Chapter 12: Inclusion in Practice

1 'Poorest Areas Civil Society Program', https://en.wikipedia.org/wiki/Poorest_Areas_Civil_Society_Program.

Chapter 13: Equity Models and Their Limitations

1 Prableen Bajpai, 'The 5 Largest Economies In The World And Their Growth In 2020', Nasdaq, 22 January 2020, https://www.nasdaq.com/articles/the-5-largest-economies-in-the-world-and-their-growth-in-2020-2020-01-22.

2 'NASDAQ Composite—45 Year Historical Chart', https://www.macrotrends.net/1320/nasdaq-historical-chart.

3 'Irrational exuberance', https://en.wikipedia.org/wiki/Irrational_
    exuberance.
4 'How Did the Great Recession Affect Structural Unemployment?',
    Investopedia, 31 October 2021, https://www.investopedia.com/
    ask/answers/050715/how-did-great-recession-affect-structural-
    unemployment.asp.
5 'Too big to fail', https://en.wikipedia.org/wiki/Too_big_to_fail.
6 Occupy Wall Street, https://en.wikipedia.org/wiki/Occupy_
    Wall_Street.
7 The Global Wealth Report 2022, Credit Suisse, https://www.
    credit-suisse.com/about-us/en/reports-research/global-wealth-
    report.html.
8 'The State of Food Security and Nutrition in the World 2021',
    Food and Agriculture Organization of the United Nations,
    https://www.fao.org/state-of-food-security-nutrition/2021/en/.
9 'Creating a Vibrant Entrepreneurial Ecosystem in India:
    Report of the Committee on Angel Investment and Early Stage
    Venture Capital', Ideas, https://ideas.repec.org/p/ess/wpaper/
    id5118.html.
10 Sarosh Amaria, 'MSMEs: The Growth Engine of India', The
    Times of India, 24 October 2022, https://timesofindia.indiatimes.
    com/blogs/voices/msmes-the-growth-engine-of-india/.
11 https://givingpledge.org/.
12 'MSME and National Innovation Council Launch the India
    Inclusive Innovation Fund', Press Information Bureau,
    Government of India, Ministry of Micro, Small & Medium
    Enterprises, 27 January 2014, https://pib.gov.in/newsite/
    PrintRelease.aspx?relid=102774.
13 'Govt Commits Rs. 7,385 crore under Fund of Funds for Startup
    India Investment for 88 Alternative Investment Funds (AIFs);
    720 Startups Supported by AIFs', Azadi ka Amrit Mahotsav,
    Ministry of Commerce & Industry, 26 September 2022, https://
    pib.gov.in/PressReleasePage.aspx?PRID=1862374.
14 'SEBI Clears Framework for Social Stock Exchange', The Times
    of India, 28 September 2021, https://timesofindia.indiatimes.
    com/business/india-business/sebi-clears-framework-for-social-
    stock-exchange/articleshow/86588194.cms.

15 Harichandan Arakali, 'Needed: Entrepreneurial Models That Work for "Bharat"', *Forbes India*, 15 February 2016, https://www.forbesindia.com/article/startup-india-2016/needed-entrepreneurial-models-that-work-for-bharat/42327/1.

Chapter 14: Models of Conscious Capitalism

1 'Capitalism', Wikipedia, https://en.wikipedia.org/wiki/Capitalism.
2 Ibid.
3 'Conscious Capitalism Philosophy', Conscious Capitalism, https://www.consciouscapitalism.org/philosophy.
4 Larry Elliott, 'Inequality Gap Widens as 42 People Hold Same Wealth as 3.7BN Poorest', The *Guardian*, 22 January 2018, https://www.theguardian.com/inequality/2018/jan/22/inequality-gap-widens-as-42-people-hold-same-wealth-as-37bn-poorest
5 To learn more about EPIC, you can read the EPIC report at https://assets.ey.com/content/dam/ey-sites/ey-com/en_gl/topics/long-term-value/ey-epic-report.pdf.
6 Ten guidelines are proposed here: https://www.forbes.com/sites/nigelwilson/2019/03/05/10-guidelines-for-inclusive-capitalism-part-2/?sh=78c7f51164b9.
7 'How's Life? 2020', OECD, 9 March 2020, https://www.oecd.org/wise/how-s-life-23089679.htm.
8 'About Huber Social', Huber Social, https://hubersocial.com.au/mission.

Chapter 15: Future Safe

1 'Social Enterprise, Mutual, Cooperative and Collective Ownership Models: A Practical Guide', Local Government Group, https://www.local.gov.uk/sites/default/files/documents/practical-guidance-counci-a3f.pdf.
2 Securities and Exchange Board of India (Alternative Investment Funds) Regulations, 2012.
3 http://www.brac.net/downloads/BRAC-Annual-Report-2020e.pdf.

4 'Creating a World Without Poverty', Yunus Centre, 30 May 2009, https://www.muhammadyunus.org/post/252/creating-a-world-without-poverty.
5 'Grameen Bank', https://en.wikipedia.org/wiki/Grameen_Bank.
6 'IIM Bangalore Inaugurates Israel Centre to Promote Academic Collaborations, Research', The *Indian Express*, 6 November 2017, https://indianexpress.com/article/education/iim-bangalore-inaugurates-israel-centre-to-promote-academic-collaborations-research-4924681/.
7 https://www.yunussb.com.
8 https://ivn.org.il/.

Chapter 16: The Way Ahead

1 https://golab.bsg.ox.ac.uk/.
2 'Indicators Aotearoa New Zealand—Ngā Tūtohu Aotearoa', Stats NZ, 9 July 2019, https://www.stats.govt.nz/indicators-and-snapshots/indicators-aotearoa-new-zealand-nga-tutohu-aotearoa/.
3 'Urban India 2011: Evidence', Indian Institute for Human Settlements, Third Edition: 21 January 2012, https://iihs.co.in/wp-content/uploads/2013/12/IUC-Book.pdf.
4 Phillip Connor, 'India Is a Top Source and Destination for World's Migrants', Pew Research Center, 3 March 2017, https://www.pewresearch.org/short-reads/2017/03/03/india-is-a-top-source-and-destination-for-worlds-migrants/.
5 Tarang Singh, 'Achieving the SDGs through Legislation in Sikkim', Alternative Perspectives, 24 April 2017, http://www.perspectives.devalt.org/2017/04/01/achieving-the-sdgs-through-legislation-in-sikkim/.
6 'The Well-being of Future Generations', Llywodraeth Cymru—Welsh Government, https://www.gov.wales/well-being-of-future-generations-wales.
7 Nagaraja Prakasam, 'Define Social Businesses to Reduce Trust Deficit between People and Corporates', *Forbes India*, 22 January 2021, https://www.forbesindia.com/blog/economy-policy/define-social-businesses-to-reduce-trust-deficit-between-people-and-corporates/.

8 Naini Thaker and Anubhuti Matta, 'WhatsApp's Privacy Update: To Flee or Not to Flee', *Forbes India*, 15 January 2021, https://www.forbesindia.com/article/take-one-big-story-of-the-day/whatsapps-privacy-update-to-flee-or-not-to-flee/65679/1.

9 'India's CSR Story', India Data Insights, 7 August 2020, https://indiadatainsights.com/indias-csr-story/.

10 Nagaraja Prakasam, 'Social Businesses Must Receive Risk Capital from the Government and CSR', *Forbes India*, 16 January 2017, https://www.forbesindia.com/article/social-impact-special/social-businesses-must-receive-risk-capital-from-the-government-and-csr/45403/1.

11 https://www.danone.com/about-danone/sustainable-value-creation/danone-societe-a-mission.html#Framework.

12 'Entreprise à Mission', https://en.wikipedia.org/wiki/Entreprise_%C3%A0_Mission.

13 'Unilever Sets Out Plans to Help Build a More Equitable and Inclusive Society', Unilever, 21 January 2021, https://www.unileverusa.com/news/press-releases/2021/unilever-sets-out-plans-to-help-build-a-more-equitable-and-inclusive-society/.

14 '2020 Social and Environmental Assessment Report', Ben & Jerry's, https://www.benjerry.com/about-us/sear-reports/2020-sear-report.

15 'About WFTO', World Fair Trade Organization, https://wfto.com/about-wfto.

16 Harichandan Arakali, 'Needed: Entrepreneurial Models That Work for "Bharat"', *Forbes India*, 15 February 2016, https://www.forbesindia.com/article/startup-india-2016/needed-entrepreneurial-models-that-work-for-bharat/42327/1.

17 'NSE Gets Final Nod from SEBI to Launch Social Stock Exchange', The *New Indian Express*, 23 February 2023, https://www.newindianexpress.com/business/2023/feb/23/nse-gets-final-nod-from-sebi-to-launch-social-stock-exchange-2550189.html.

18 'Robert Reich', https://en.wikipedia.org/wiki/Robert_Reich.

19 'Circular Impact Report 2022', Saahas Zero Waste, https://saahaszerowaste.com/wp-content/uploads/2022/11/Saahas-Impact-Report-2022.pdf.